JOHN LOCKE

Questions concerning the Law of Nature

JOHN LOCKE 1672, by John Greenhill.
Courtesy of the National Portrait Gallery, London.

The greatest part cannot know, and therefore they must believe.
—John Locke, *The Reasonableness of Christianity*

JOHN LOCKE

Questions concerning the Law of Nature

with an Introduction, Text, and
Translation by Robert Horwitz,
Jenny Strauss Clay, and Diskin Clay

Cornell University Press

Ithaca and London

Publication of this book is supported in part
by subventions from Kenyon College
and the Earhart Foundation.

First published 1990 by Cornell University Press.

International Standard Book Number 0-8014-2348-1
Library of Congress Catalog Card Number 89-46178
Printed in the United States of America
*Librarians: Library of Congress cataloging information
appears on the last page of the book.*

♾ The paper used in this publication meets the minimum
requirements of the American National Standard for Permanence
of Paper for Printed Library Materials Z39.48—1984.

For Mavis

Contents

Acknowledgments

John Locke: Questions concerning the Law of Nature has been a work of collaboration. It has three authors and many other contributors. Its beginning and driving force was Robert Horwitz, and were he alive to see this presentation of Locke's first truly philosophical work in print, these acknowledgments would be fuller and more generous than we can make them now. In the fourteen years he devoted to this work, he gathered many debts even as he inspired his students and colleagues with an interest in his project. The first of his debts is surely to his students at Kenyon College, who contributed to his understanding of Locke's *Questions* (which were themselves addressed to Locke's students at Christ Church, Oxford) in a number of seminars Horwitz offered on our text and translation until his death in May of 1987. His students and colleagues will sorely miss the publication of the commentary he meant to be the companion volume to our presentation of the text of Locke's *Questions*.

Our debt to institutions is also great. We must name first the Bodleian Library and its Duke Humphreys and Locke rooms; then the National Endowment for the Humanities; Kenyon College; the Earhart Foundation of Ann Arbor, Michigan; and Cornell University Press, whose director, John G. Ackerman, provided us with two very helpful reader's reports and just the support we needed as we were looking for a publisher.

To name the individuals who helped in the various stages of the preparation of this book is to risk passing over in ungenerous silence some of Professor Horwitz's many friends and colleagues. We can only hope that our ignorance of the full extent of his debts will be

understood by those who have gone unmentioned. We thank Anne Hartle, Richard Kennington, Philip N. Marcus, Will Morrisey, Thomas Pangle, Louise Rosenthal, Charles Rubin, Henry Shankula, the late Robert Shackleton, the late Mrs. Hope Weir, and most especially Christopher Dadian, who kept this book of three parts together, legible, and correct for many years and whose commitment to it was a constant source of encouragement.

DISKIN CLAY

Baltimore, Maryland

JENNY STRAUSS CLAY

Durham, North Carolina

JOHN LOCKE

Questions concerning the Law of Nature

Introduction

ROBERT HORWITZ

1. Locke and "The Thinkeing Men at Oxford"

Enemies and admirers alike among John Locke's contemporaries, along with countless interpreters of his work during the past three centuries, have persistently expressed concern that nowhere in his published writings does he deal systematically with the issue of natural law. Locke's apparent neglect of a subject of such transcendent importance has been widely regarded as virtually incomprehensible, given the critical role that natural law plays in his overall work. His interpreters have seldom failed to observe that some kind of doctrine of natural law or natural right figures prominently in many of his major writings, as, for example, the *Two Treatises of Government* (1690), especially the second treatise, "An Essay concerning the True Original, Extent, and End of Civil Government." In the second treatise one finds extensive sections in which Locke discusses such matters as "the state of nature" within which humankind is said to be guided in principle by "the law of nature." Further, human beings are said to possess certain unalienable natural rights.[1] Finally, doctrines of natural law or natural right are adduced by Locke in his discussion of the origins, the limits, and various other aspects of civil government. Similar considerations could readily be advanced from such other major works of Locke's as *An Essay concerning Human Understanding* (1690).

[Note: Passages added in square brackets identify my editorial additions. DC.]
[1]John Locke, *Two Treatises of Government*, ed. Peter Laslett (New York: Cambridge University Press, 1960), see second treatise, esp. secs. 6 and 12.

1

Locke's various allusions to natural law are "scattered up and down" (a term he was inclined to use to describe the characteristic style of some other writers). Nevertheless, his passing reflections on natural law produced acrimonious disputes during his lifetime and gave rise to seemingly endless controversy among scholars during the centuries following his death. To judge from the reception accorded Locke's *Essay* in the 1690s, these exchanges would have been all the more vitriolic had not Locke, who was wont to describe himself as "no friend to controversy," published most of his works anonymously.[2] Among his very few major works whose authorship

[2]Locke took great pains to conceal authorship of many of his most important—and potentially most controversial—works from the time they were written and published until a few weeks before his death. His remarkable prescience in anticipating the approach of death may be explained to an extent by the fact that he was a very skillful physician, something not now widely appreciated. Realizing, as he did, that death was very close at hand, he responded to a letter from Dr. John Hudson, "Bodley's Librarian at Oxford, [who] asked Locke if he would be willing to give copies of his works to the Bodleian Library. . . . Locke consented; he instructed the Churchills [his chief publishers] to send Dr. Hudson a copy each of the *Essay*, of *Some Thoughts concerning Education* and of his pamphlets about interest and money. In writing to thank him, Dr. Hudson said that he would not presume to inquire if these were *all* the books Locke intended for the Bodleian. He would have been foolish to have so presumed. Even in the catalogue of his own library . . . Locke classified neither the *Two Treatises on* [sic] *Government* nor the *Letters concerning Toleration* . . . under 'Locke.' But he did not deny Dr. Hudson what Dr. Hudson so plainly expected. He waited till . . . death was imminent, and then in a codicil to his will he bequeathed to the Bodleian Library copies of 'all the books whereof I am the author which have been published without my name.'" The hitherto unacknowledged volumes included virtually everything important that he had published on religion and politics, including some tracts he had suggested might be published posthumously, e.g., a *Discourse of Miracles* (Maurice Cranston, *John Locke: A Biography* [London: Longmans, Green, 1957], pp. 459–60; emphasis supplied).

Throughout his life, Locke persistently characterized himself as "no friend to controversy." Indeed, Locke wrote to his literary executor Peter King, in what was to be the final letter of his life: "I could never consent to print it [the hitherto unpublished manuscript of *Seeing All Things in God*] . . . both because I am no friend to controversy and also because it is an opinion that spreads not and is like to die of itself or at least do no great harm" (Cranston, *John Locke*, p. 478). One may be forgiven for wondering how a man who was "no friend to controversy" permitted himself to become engaged in an extraordinarily prolonged and acrid controversy with Edward Stillingfleet, the bishop of Worcester, in the closing years of the seventeenth century. In response to Stillingfleet's fierce attack on the *Essay*, Locke wrote (and subsequently published) a longish "letter" that in printed form runs to ninety-four pages in the collected *Works* of 1823. In response to the bishop's rejoinder, Locke wrote an eighty-five-page reply in May 1698. Finally, also in May 1698, his reply to the bishop's

he openly acknowledged was *An Essay concerning Human Understanding,* that monumental investigation through which he was to earn universal fame. In it, he touches frequently but inconclusively on the subject of natural law. Despite his caution, Locke found himself engulfed in a storm of controversy on this delicate and dangerous issue shortly after publication of the *Essay.* By identifying basic aspects of this seventeenth-century argument, we may be directed toward important dimensions of Locke's understanding of natural law, the subject with which this volume is chiefly concerned. First, however, it may prove useful if I were quickly to sketch the intellectual-theological context within which Locke confronted the critics of his reflections on natural law as they appear in the *Essay.*

When Locke published the first edition of the *Essay,* his name did not appear on the title page, though he acknowledged authorship in the Epistle Dedicatory.[3] The *Essay* had been carefully shaped and polished for some two decades, and its publication had been long and avidly awaited. It created an immediate stir. As Peter H. Nidditch, editor of the definitive twentieth-century edition of this work,

---

"second letter" ran to more than three hundred pages. Altogether, nearly five hundred printed pages were expended in response to the bishop's criticisms. These had been largely directed to the question of the orthodoxy of Locke's religious opinions, especially on such matters as the Trinity, the nature of the soul, and the like.

It would have required in fact very few pages for Locke effectively to have demolished the bishop's arguments. There was no contest between the philosopher and the theologian, however renowned the latter may have been. Why then did Locke devote such efforts to this argument? A clue to his intention in sustaining the controversy may be found in the final paragraph of the "second," or final reply: "Before I conclude," he wrote to the bishop, "it is fit I take notice of the obligation I have to you, for the pains you have been at about my Essay, which I conclude could not have been any way so effectually recommended to the world, as by your manner of writing against it. And since your lordship's sharp sight, so carefully employed for its correction, has, as I humbly conceive, found no faults in it . . . I hope I may presume it will pass the better in the world, [in] the judgment of all considering men"! (*The Works of John Locke* [London, 1823], 3:498).

[3] An illuminating dimension of Locke's political sagacity is revealed by the fact that he dedicated the *Essay* to Thomas Herbert, earl of Pembroke. On this point, Thomas Macaulay, having sketched Pembroke's distinguished career in statesmanship, observed that although he was a Tory, it was not "of a narrow and illiberal kind," a fact "sufficiently proved by the fact that immediately after the Revolution, the Essay on Human Understanding was dedicated to him by John Locke, in token of gratitude for kind offices done in evil times" (Thomas Macaulay, *History of England* [New York: Harper and Brothers, 1856], 3:497).

observes, "the doctrines of the *Essay* quickly encountered unsympathetic critics,"[4] but Locke also had staunch defenders among his contemporaries. One of them, Samuel Bold, reported that "This excellent Treatise having been published several Years . . . *a mighty Out cry was at last, all of the sudden, raised against it here at Home. . . .* Some have spoken handsomely of the Author, others have treated that Incomparable Gentleman with a rudeness peculiar to some, who make a Profession of the Christian Religion, and seem to pride themselves in being of the Clergy of the Church of *England.*"[5] The clamorous bishop of Worcester had charged that Locke's "new way of ideas" undermined the principles of Christianity. Nor was the bishop alone in this view. In Oxford "a resolution was moved at a meeting of Heads of colleges to suppress the *Essay concerning Human Understanding.*" In 1703 the recorder of Oxford wrote Locke's old friend James Tyrrell: "I have enquired into the proceedings of the Heads of Houses concerning Mr. Locke's books, and am informed that at a meeting toward the end of November last they agreed to prohibit all scholars to read any of these books . . . !"[6] A twentieth-century commentator on these matters, Richard Ashcraft, concludes that "the general consensus of opinion among those who have read the *Essay concerning Human Understanding* in the last two centuries would probably agree with the bishop as to the subversive character of Locke's exploration of the foundations of religious belief."[7]

In the course of preparing successive editions of the *Essay,* Locke responded occasionally to the encouragement and criticisms of his friends. Among these avowedly friendly critics was one of Locke's friends of longest standing, James Tyrrell. Tyrrell was the son of Sir Timothy Tyrrell, baronet of Oakley (near Oxford) and grandson of the famous divine Archbishop Ussher. Tyrrell authored several

---

[4]*John Locke: An Essay concerning Human Understanding*, ed. Peter H. Nidditch (Oxford: Clarendon Press, 1975), p. xix.

[5]Samuel Bold, *Some Considerations on the Principal Objections and Arguments . . . against Mr. Locke's Essay of Humane Understanding* (London: A. and J. Churchill, 1699), pp. 1–2; emphasis original.

[6]Cranston, *John Locke*, p. 466.

[7]In John W. Yolton, ed., *John Locke: Problems and Perspectives* (Cambridge: Cambridge University Press, 1969), p. 194.

works of note, including *Patriarcha non Monarcha* (1681), *Bibliotheca Politica* (1691), and *A Breif Disquisition of the Law of Nature* (1692).[8]

On 30 June 1690, less than a year after the publication of *An Essay concerning Human Understanding*, Tyrrell wrote to Locke from Oakley to observe that "I have began again to read over your excellent Essay; with great satisfaction; and discourseing with some thinkeing men at Oxford, not long since; I found them dissatisfyed with what you have sayed concerning the Law of nature."[9] Continuing, Tyrrell cautioned Locke that these "thinkeing men" suspected that he had

> resolved all vertue and vice, and the Law by which it is establisht, out of a commonwealth, and *abstracted from divine Revelation;* into the praise, or dispraise that men *give to certaine actions in several clubs or societyes,* by which hypothesis. if Drunkennesse, and sodomy, and cruelty to Enemyes (for example) (which are not vices directly contrary to the peace of civil society) should be in any Countrey . . . thought praise worthy; and that those that could drinke most; or enjoy most boys and be most cruel (not only) should be counted the gallantest, and most vertuous, but allso be so indeed.[10]

A heavy charge this, but one may readily understand the overwhelming concern of these Oxford divines. The foundations of morality in their view rested on divine revelation, as found in Sacred Scripture. If one were to abstract from Christian revelation, then on what objective and eternally sound basis could morality be understood to rest? These sober, serious, orthodox Christian thinkers readily rejected as inadequate the obvious response that every commonwealth must necessarily enact legislation designed to prohibit infractions of the public peace: murder, theft, counterfeiting, and the like. Such legislation might tentatively serve to preserve "the peace of civil society," but, important as that surely is, it was seen by them as providing an insufficient foundation for a sound and genuine polity. They of course understood a genuine commonwealth in terms of a *moral* order, one perforce primarily concerned with the

---

[8]Cranston, *John Locke*, p. 38.

[9]*The Correspondence of John Locke*, vol. 4, ed. E. S. de Beer (Oxford: Clarendon Press, 1979), p. 101.

[10]Ibid.; emphasis supplied.

development of Christian character and virtues. Their reading of Locke's *Essay* rightly led them to question whether he shared those views, and, if not, then what, if any, were the alternative, universal moral standards on which justice might rest within the commonwealth.

Having duly considered Locke's views in the *Essay*, Tyrrell's Oxford friends ominously commented that his account of the source of morality and law and his conclusions thereon "come very near to what is so much cryed out upon in Mr: Hobs: when he asserts [also] that in the state of nature . . . there is no moral good or evil."[11] Hardly an insignificant indictment, especially when directed against a figure of such prominence as John Locke, a respected Christian communicant, a philosopher of growing international repute, and a political advisor whose counsel was sought in the highest quarters, including, some say, by the king of England.[12] Such a man was properly concerned about his reputation, while his critics were no less legitimately concerned with the foundations of his morality, as explicated in his writings.

Agreeing in considerable measure with these seventeenth-century critics, his twentieth-century biographer Maurice Cranston opines that there are instances in which Locke's doctrines do seem similar to those of Hobbes, but, he adds, "at no time in his life would

[11]Ibid., p. 102. A telling example of this point "that is so much cryed out upon in Mr: Hobs" regarding the source of morality and law is to be found in John Bramhall's *Defence of True Liberty*. Bramhall argues that "the will of God, and the Eternall Law which is in God himself, is properly the rule and measure of Justice. As all goodness whether Naturall or Morall, is a participation of divine goodness, and all Rectitude is but a participation of divine rectitude, so all Lawes are but participations of the eternall Law, from whence they derive their power. . . . See then how grossely T[homas]. H[obbes]. doth understand that old and true principle, that *the Will of God is the rule of Justice, as if by willing things in themselves unjust, he did render them just, by reason of his absolute dominion and irresistable power. . . . This were to make the eternall Law a Lesbian rule."* John Bramhall, *A Defence of True Liberty* (London, 1655), pp. 85–86.

[12]Locke served as a confidant and advisor for many years to the leader of the Whigs, the earl of Shaftsbury, subsequently to Lord Pembroke, who held a series of high offices, and finally to the solicitor-general, John Somers, who was elevated to the peerage as Lord Somers. During the winter of 1697–1698, Locke received an urgent summons from King William to wait upon his majesty at Kensington (Cranston, *John Locke*, p. 433). Cranston speculates that the king had sought to persuade Locke to accept "a diplomatic post, . . . probably it was that of Embassy Secretary in Paris" (p. 435).

Locke *admit* his debt to Hobbes. He even came to pretend he had
never read Hobbes properly."[13] Rather more precisely, Locke took
extravagant pains to maintain that he had read Hobbes not at all,
and that his own name should be completely disassociated from that
of "the monster of Malmesbury." Evidence for this suggestion may
be found in Locke's responses to Edward Stillingfleet, who vig-
orously attacked both *The Reasonableness of Christianity* and the *Essay*,
as we have seen. In response to the bishop's charge that Locke was
guilty of paraphrasing and following Hobbes, Locke retorted:
"I . . . did not know those words [the bishop's] quoted out of the
Leviathan, were there, or any thing like them. Nor do I know yet,
any farther than as I believe them to be there, from his quotation."[14]
Or, again, in response to the bishop's charge that Locke was following Hobbes and Spinoza with regard to the nature of the soul, Locke
replied: "I am not so well read in Hobbes or Spinosa, as to be able to
say what were their opinions in this matter. But possibly there be
those, who will think your lordship's authority of more use to them
in the case than those justly decried names."[15]

Peter Laslett baldly suggests that "Locke may be prevaricating
here,"[16] and another twentieth-century commentator, Maurice
Cranston, puts forward a related hypothesis, viz., that Locke's caution with respect to Hobbes may "have been due to the fact that the
word 'Hobbist' came to be a pejorative one in all but a very few
quarters, and Locke was forever anxious to avoid a bad name."[17] A
similar point is made by Dr. E. S. de Beer, editor of *The Correspondence of John Locke*. He reports that by "1680 *Leviathan* was completely discredited; . . . the book was an atheistic vindication of
Cromwell."[18] Yet another eminent authority on Locke, Dr. Wolf-

---

[13]Ibid., p. 62; emphasis supplied.
[14]*Works* (1801), 3:420.
[15]John Locke, *Second Reply to the Bishop of Worcester*, in ibid., p. 477.
[16]Locke, *Two Treatises*, ed. Laslett, p. 86, n. 19.
[17]Cranston, *John Locke*, pp. 62–63.
[18]Yolton, *John Locke*, p. 40. De Beer's view finds support in a work published in
1676 by the earl of Clarendon, who considered it an important service to the king to
"answer Mr. Hobbes's *Leviathan*, and to confute the doctrine therein contain'd, so
pernicious to the Sovereign Power of Kings, and destructive to the affection and
allegiance of Subjects." The earl goes on to observe: "I would make no scruple to
declare, that I never read any Book that contains in it so much Sedition, Treason, and

gang von Leyden, goes further when he suggests that "in cases where [Locke] agreed with Hobbes and borrowed his views . . . he could not have easily acknowledged his debt for fear of being decried as a Hobbist."[19]

Impiety as this *Leviathan*; and therefore that it is very unfit to be read, taught, or sold, as dissolving all the ligaments of Government, and undermining all principles of Religion" (Edward Hyde Clarendon, *A Brief View and Survey of the dangerous and pernicious Errors to Church and State in Mr. Hobbes's Book, entitled Leviathan* [London, 1676], quotations from the Epistle Dedicatory and p. 319.

[19]*John Locke: Essays on the Law of Nature*, ed. W. von Leyden (Oxford: Clarendon Press, 1954), pp. 37–38. Without attempting to assess these charges of some sort of "hidden Hobbism" in Locke's work, one must at least take note of the gravity and the problems to which they point. One may readily identify three distinct positions on the issue. First, there are those many interpreters, such as those quoted above, who emphasize that Locke was in part a Hobbist, but one who went to exquisite pains to conceal any trace of Hobbist influence in his writings. These interpreters oftentimes observe that Locke refused to mention Hobbes's "justly decried name" and mentioned it only when challenged to by such opponents as the bishop of Worcester and others who accused him of following Hobbes, particularly in the *Essay*. Such critics generally leave it at this. They deny that Locke practiced any *other* arts of concealment in his writings. Furthermore, unlike Locke's seventeenth-century "thinkeing men at Oxford," they flatly reject suggestions of religious heterodoxy in Locke's thought. At the most, some of them express surprise at Locke's "carelessness," i.e., the incredible number of contradictions, major and minor, as they see them, in his writing, along with misquotations from the Bible, Hooker, and other authorities whom Locke professes to follow. For reasons that I find difficult to fathom, Laslett fails almost completely to explore these phenomena, although he grants that they were part and parcel of Locke's successful attempts to conceal his authorship of the *Two Treatises*. He summarizes and dismisses the evidence gathered regarding Locke's style of writing by characterizing it as "abnormal, obsessive." He thereby provides us with a pseudo-psychological rationalization of the author's allegedly neurotic behavior, rather than with a genuine political or theological explanation, both of which were warranted by Locke's situation during a time of political terror in England and the awful price paid for "heresy." A sound political-theological explanation would not be exhausted by these comments, as we have attempted to explain in part above.

In the present volume we have found it unnecessary to take sides on such issues as Locke's alleged "Hobbism," his religious orthodoxy, and the like. Rather, we have attempted to provide a straightforward presentation of Locke's text, one that makes no attempt to provide a priori speculations about his meaning. We have attempted to present Locke strictly on his own terms.

The translation seeks to present as literally as possible Locke's usage and meaning without any presuppositions about the character or intention of the overall argument. We therefore urge our readers to concentrate their attention solely on the difficult task of understanding Locke's reflections on the law of nature in precisely the form in which Locke has left them to us. One may be assured that this is no small task. It should not be complicated by extraneous considerations such as the search for hidden elements of "Hobbism," or other such arcane speculations.

What can be unambiguously asserted is that Thomas Hobbes had in fact earned a very bad reputation during the latter half of the seventeenth century and was under attack from many quarters.[20] Common sense dictated that Locke, or any other prudent writer of the period, would exercise caution in taking cognizance of Hobbes's work. When he was directly accused of "Hobbism" by the bishop of Worcester, he perforce had to speak of "the monster of Malmesbury," whom he was always careful to denounce as that "justly decried Hobbes"[21] or in other pejorative terms.

"Decried," to be sure, but the attack against Hobbes and "Hobbism" in Locke's day did not stop with mere calumny. Locke may well have been present on the afternoon of 21 July 1683 when the last major public book burning took place at Oxford. That dire action had been deemed necessary by the university's vice chancellor following identification by the professor of divinity of "certaine propositions taken out of severall rebellious and seditious authours." It was duly proposed, and unanimously agreed, that they, the books, be condemned to be burned, "after which the Convocation was dissolved, and the vice-chancellor, bishop, Drs. and Mrs. in their formalities, went into the School quadrangle, where a bonfier being prepared in the middle thereof, were severall books, out of which those damnable tenets and propositions were extracted, committed to the flames by Gigur, the Universitie bedell. . . . The scholars of all degrees and qualities in the meane time surrounding the fier, gave *severall hums* whilst they were burning." Among the heretical books burned that afternoon were "Thomas Hobs' *Leviathan* and *De Cive, The Shaftsburian Association*," and works by ten other authors.[22]

[20]See Samuel I. Mintz, *The Hunting of Leviathan* (Cambridge: Cambridge University Press, 1962), for a "Checklist of Anti-Hobbes Literature and Allusion in England, 1650–1700," pp. 157–60. This bibliography lists more than one hundred titles, many of them intriguing, such as Robert Parsons's *True Effigies of the Monster of Malmesbury*. One may wonder how many items besides those listed also appeared—sermons preached against Hobbes during this period, as well as critical pamphlets and manuscripts that were never published or have been forever lost to sight.

[21]Cranston, *John Locke*, p. 62.

[22]Anthony Wood, *The Life and Times of Anthony Wood*, ed. Andrew Clark (Oxford: Oxford Historical Society, 1891–1892), 3:62–63, emphasis supplied. Peter Laslett adds some interesting suggestions to Wood's account. According to him, the decree ordering the book burning "was displayed to the halls and libraries of the colleges, and it anathematized doctrine after doctrine already written into [Locke's as yet

In view of evidence such as this, one cannot doubt but that the
"thinkeing men" of Oxford quoted earlier were intimately ac-
quainted with Hobbes's heterodox views on natural law and were
determined to expose and to anathematize such allegedly pernicious doctrines wherever they seemed to show themselves. To
summarize, whatever Locke's views may have been on natural law,
one may readily appreciate that he could hardly have been compla-
cent about having his views and his writings condemned as "very
near what is so much cryed out upon in Mr: Hobs."[23]

If we are properly to understand the extended and complex
controversy among Locke, Tyrrell, and the "thinkeing men at Oxford," together with his other critics, we should at this point discuss
certain aspects of the Christian doctrine of natural law around
which the dispute turned. Such a discussion is also requisite if we are
fully to understand the considerable difference in perspective between the authors of the present volume and the opinion on these
matters among most other twentieth-century commentators, especially the position set forth by Dr. von Leyden in his *John Locke:
Essays on the Law of Nature,* some aspects of which will subsequently
be treated in detail in this Introduction.

Before entering this discussion, however, it is essential to express
a critical caveat. Perforce I must write here in rather general terms
of the "Christian natural law tradition." I am assuredly not unaware
of the simplistic implications inherent in speaking in this fashion of
this great and complex tradition taken as a whole. Many readers will
be well aware that such Christian natural law thinkers as Aquinas,

---

incomplete and unpublished] *Two Treatises.* Amongst the authors . . . condemned to
the fire were some of . . . the books which then stood on the shelves of Locke's
chamber at Christ Church. . . . Within a few weeks he . . . left Oxford. . . . Locke never
went to Oxford again in his life" (Locke, *Two Treatises,* ed. Laslett, pp. 36–37).

Those readers curious about the significance of the "severall hums" arising from
the throats of the assembled scholars will find Macaulay instructive. He explains and
illustrates the practice of our seventeenth-century "ancestors," as he terms them, in a
number of passages in his famous *History.* Writing of Bishop Burnet's inspired
preaching at the coronation of William and Mary, Macaulay observes that it "drew
forth the loudest hums of the Commons" (3:108). Or again, in describing the reaction
to an address by King William to Parliament, he tells us that "the speech was received
with a low but very significant hum of assent" (4:576).

[23]*Correspondence* 4:102.

Hooker, Culverwel,[24] and others whom I quote were not in agreement on many important aspects of that tradition. The differences among and within the ranks of Catholic and Protestant interpreters of the tradition are important and substantial in some respects. For present purposes, however, that is, to understand Locke's overall position on natural law and to contrast it with the tradition as a whole, we need not enter into the complicated task of precisely delineating these differences. Locke himself, as we shall see, deals with this great and diverse tradition in a comparable fashion. The critical issue posed by Locke's reflections on natural law is whether he writes from within or from without this tradition broadly understood. Our concern with the Christian natural law tradition stems from our effort to understand Locke's *Questions,* not the nuances of the tradition itself.

Turning now to the substance of the Christian natural law tradition, one finds at its core an explicit understanding of the nature and genesis of law. We begin with the exposition of Richard Hooker, who, in an arresting passage in his *Ecclesiastical Polity* (1594), tells us that "of Law there can be no less acknowledged, than that her seat is the bosom of God, her voice the harmony of the world: all things in heaven and earth do her homage, the very least as feeling her care, and the greatest as not exempted from her power: but Angels and men and creatures of what condition soever, though each in different sort and manner, yet all with uniform consent, admiring her as the mother of their peace and joy."[25]

The seat of law "is the bosom of God." It is God who created the cosmos from nothing, who shaped everything within it in unique forms or essences, and who governs all of his creation through law. This highest and most comprehensive manifestation of law in the

[24]It has been our practice to retain as much as possible the orthography of the seventeenth-century authors whom we have quoted. Therefore, we have spelled the name Nathanael Culverwel as it appeared on the title page of his *Elegant and Learned Discourse of the Light of Nature* of 1652. This spelling appears to have been generally accepted. However, the 1971 edition of this *Discourse* (ed. Robert A. Greene and Hugh MacCallum) published by the University of Toronto, on which we have relied extensively, introduces the spelling as Culverwell. We decided to retain the seventeenth-century spelling throughout our text.

[25]Richard Hooker, *Of the Laws of Ecclesiastical Polity,* vol. 1 of *Works,* ed. John Keble et al., 3 vols. (Oxford: Clarendon Press, 1888), p. 285.

Christian natural law tradition is called the eternal law. This, as Nathanael Culverwel suggests,

> is not really distinguished from God himself. For *Nil est ab aeterno nisi ipse Deus* [nothing exists eternally except God himself], so that 'tis much of the same nature with those decrees of his, and that Providence which was awake from everlasting. For as God from all eternity by the hand of infinite wisdom did draw the several faces and lineaments of being, which he meant to shew in time: So he did then also contrive their several frames with such limits and compasse as he meant to set them; and said to everything, *Hither shalt thou go, and no farther.*[26]

In majestic passages such as these, Culverwel, Hooker, and other Christian thinkers formulated a fundamental tenet of the Christian natural law doctrine, one that holds that the perfectly structured, precisely articulated order of the world is a manifestation of God's eternally fixed intention as expressed in the "law eternal." This comprehensive and everlasting law constitutes "an eternal Ordinance made in the depth of Gods infinite wisdom and councel for regulating and governing of the whole world."[27] "By this great and glorious Law every good action was commanded, and all evill was discountenanc'd, and forbidden from everlasting" by God.[28] "At the command of this Law all created beings took their several ranks and stations, and put themselves in such operations as were best agreeable and conformable to their beings."[29]

[26]Nathanael Culverwel, *Discourse*, p. 34. Culverwel adds that "thus God framed this great Organ of the world, he tuned it . . . that it might be fitted and prepared for the finger of God himself, and at the presence of his powerful touch might sound forth the praise of its Creatour in a most sweet and harmonious manner" (p. 26). Culverwel's formulations of the tenets of the Christian natural law doctrine are of special interest to us, for, according to von Leyden, "Culverwel was one of the Cambridge Platonists who had a direct influence on the formation of Locke's mature [natural law] doctrines" (*John Locke: Essays*, ed. von Leyden, p. 39). He presents a detailed comparison of Culverwel's and Locke's views in order to suggest that Culverwel may have been a "source of several Lockean ideas" (p. 39). He goes further with his assertion that "to all appearance *Locke borrowed from Culverwel* for insertion in his *Essays [on the Law of Nature]*" (p. 40; emphasis supplied). See also n. 1 to fol. 9 (translation) and n. 28 to fol. 25 (translation).

[27]Culverwel, *Discourse*, p. 36.

[28]Ibid.

[29]Ibid. Culverwel adds that "hence it is that those laws are most radical and fundamental that principally tend to the conservation of the vitals and essentials of a

While it is God alone who comprehends in his very being the eternal law and manifests it in his works, Thomas Aquinas adds significantly that "it is evident that all things partake somewhat of" it from "*its being imprinted on them*," and they thereby "derive their respective *inclinations*" to act properly. A rational creature therefore possesses a share of the eternal reason, whereby it has a natural inclination to its proper act and end, and this participation of the eternal law in the rational creature is called the natural law.[30] This teaching is of critical importance for understanding the Christian natural law doctrine and must be kept uppermost in mind. It is reinforced by Culverwel, who also identifies eternal law as the source of the natural law. Speaking metaphorically in his characteristic fashion, he describes the eternal law as a veritable "fountain of Law, out of which you may see the Law of *Nature* bubbling and flowing forth to the sons of men."[31] On this point he again cites Thomas, observing that "as *Aquinas* does very well tell us, the Law of *Nature* is nothing but *participatio Legis aeternae in Rationali creatura*, the copying out of the eternal Law, and the imprinting of it upon the breast of a Rational being, that eternal Law was in a manner incarnated in the Law of *Nature*."[32]

It is also the case in this understanding of natural law "that Law ... is intrinsecal and essential to a rational creature; ... for such a creature as a creature has a superiour to whose Providence and disposing it must be subject, and then as an intellectual creature 'tis capable of a moral government, so that 'tis very suitable and

---

Kingdome; and those come neerest the law of God himself, and are participations of that eternal law, which is the spring and original of all inferiour and derivative lawes" (p. 32).

[30][*Summa Theologiae* Ia 2ae 91.2.]

[31]Culverwel, *Discourse*, p. 34; emphasis original.

[32]Ibid.; emphasis original. Richard Hooker helpfully adds: "if we will give judgment of the laws under which we live; first let that law eternal be always before our eyes, as being of principal force and moment to breed in religious minds a dutiful estimation of all laws, the use and benefit whereof we see; because there can be no doubt but that laws apparently good are (as it were) copied out of the tables of that high ever-lasting law; even as the book of that law hath said concerning itself, 'By me kings reign, and' by me 'princes decree justice' [Proverbs 8:15]. Not as if men did behold that book and accordingly frame their laws; but because it worketh *in them*, because it discovereth and (as it were) *readeth itself to the world by them*, when the laws which they make are righteous" (Hooker, *Ecclesiastical Polity*, p. 278; emphasis supplied).

connatural to it to be regulated by a Law; to be guided and commanded by one that is infinitely more wise and intelligent then it self
is; and that mindes its welfare more then it self can."[33] Even "angeli-
cal beings, and glorified souls are subject to a Law," Culverwel
contends, "though with such an happy priviledge, as that *they cannot
violate and transgresse it;* whereas the very dregs of entity, the most
ignoble beings are most incapable of a Law; for you know inanimate
beings are carried on only with the vehemency and necessity of
natural inclinations"[34] in the sense that an unobstructed stone, if
dropped, will fall to the earth through what we term "the law of
gravity." The stone is not rational. It has no will of its own, nor any
appreciation of what is happening to it. Nevertheless, it responds, in
a sense, to the workings of eternal law from which it has received
fixed properties. In view of the subsequent discussion of Locke's
understanding of natural law, it is essential to emphasize that the
Christian teaching, as expounded by Culverwel and others, holds
that the natural law cannot be transgressed by either the highest
beings, viz., obedient angels, or by the lowest beings, "the very dregs
of entity." It is humans alone who, having the God-given capacity
for moral choice, may and do commit transgressions against this law.
Given our free will and our unique freedom of choice between good
and evil, it is absolutely imperative that we know the commands
of the law of nature. Otherwise, our conduct cannot be properly
guided. We would be morally adrift, utterly lacking standards for
lawful conduct.

One is therefore left to inquire how it is that we may come to know
the law of nature. Culverwel responds with yet another metaphor.
Paraphrasing Grotius, he observes that "the Law of *Nature* is a
streaming out of Light from *the Candle of the Lord,* powerfully dis-
covering such a deformity in some evil, as that an intellectual eye
must needs abhor it; and such a commanding beauty in some good,

[33]Culverwel, *Discourse,* p. 39.

[34]Ibid.; emphasis supplied. It should be noted here that Culverwel uses the phrase
"natural inclinations" in two ways. One is said to have certain natural inclinations that
are rooted in one's "participation [in] the eternal law" as a "rational creature." At the
other extreme, "the very dregs of entity," those that "are most incapable of a [ra-
tional] law" are also directed by the "vehemency and necessity of natural inclinations," in the sense suggested by me in the text.

as that a rational being must needs be enamoured with it; and so plainly shewing that God stampt and seal'd the one with his command, and branded the other with his disliking."[35] Even so, the divine illumination provided by "the Candle of the Lord" would not properly guide human beings unless it were in harmony with—and thereby served to reinforce—their *natural inclinations*. The Christian tradition holds this to be precisely the case. Quoted earlier was the observation of Thomas Aquinas that it is through our "share of the eternal reason" that we have a "natural inclination" to our "proper act and end," and, as Hooker adds, "We see, therefore, that our sovereign good is desired naturally; that God the author of that natural desire had appointed natural means whereby to fulfil it."[36] The Christian natural law doctrine reiterates that we have natural inclinations that direct us to the realization of our proper ends. We are not directed by mere inclination in the same ways as are other animals. Each of us is a rational creature, and our reason tells us that the things to which we have a natural inclination are good. Our first inclination is to the good which we have in common with all substances: every substance seeks to preserve itself. Our second inclination is in accordance with the nature we share with other animals: sexual intercourse and the development of offspring are among the goods to which we are thus inclined. Finally, we are inclined to good inasmuch as rationality is natural to us. Thus we have a natural inclination to know the truth about God and to live in society. These last two points are reinforced by Hooker's contention that, inasmuch "as we are not by ourselves sufficient to furnish ourselves with competent store of things needful for such a life as our nature doth desire, a life fit for the dignity of man; therefore to supply those defects and imperfections which are in us living single and solely by ourselves, we are naturally induced to seek communion and fellowship with others. . . . This was the cause of men's uniting themselves at the first in politic Societies, which societies could not be without Government, nor Government without a distinct kind of Law."[37] There are "two foundations . . . which bear up public societies; the

---

[35] Ibid., p. 45; emphasis in the original.
[36] Hooker, *Ecclesiastical Polity*, p. 264.
[37] Ibid., p. 239; emphasis supplied.

one, *a natural inclination, whereby all men desire sociable life and fellow-ship;* the other, an order expressly or secretly agreed upon touching the manner of their union in living together."[38] The basic characteristic of human nature, one that makes political society essential, is that "natural inclination whereby all men desire sociable life and fellowship." Viewed from this perspective, "politic Societies" cannot properly be understood in the formulation of Hobbes, that is to say, as mere conveniences or conventional arrangements designed primarily to ensure bodily security or material abundance. On the contrary, they are requisite for that complete and lofty moral development of which humans, unlike mere brutes, are capable. They are a sine qua non for the achievement of a life through which "the dignity of man" can be realized, a life that enables members of the community to develop their uniquely human and spiritual virtues to the fullest.

Essential as political societies are for earthly human development, the Christian view holds that only through a far higher association may we realize our ultimate natural inclination, the inclination to know the truth about God and to be united with God. "No good is infinite but only God; therefore he is our felicity and bliss. Moreover, desire tendeth unto union with that it desireth. If then in Him we be blessed, it is by force of participation and conjunction with Him."[39] This is the supernatural end that transcends life on earth and the final happiness that "all men" should seek. "Therefore this desire in man is natural."[40]

Our quest for realization of our natural inclinations is guided, as Culverwel and others propound the matter, through illumination provided by "the Candle of the Lord," or reason. But this necessary though insufficient guidance requires fortification by yet another powerful God-given force, conscience. Thomas Aquinas, as explicated by Culverwel, explains the functioning of conscience by linking its workings with a manifestation of the eternal law. Quoting Thomas directly, Culverwel observes, "Laws framed by man are either just or unjust. If they are just, they have the power of binding

[38]Ibid. The relationship of Hooker's discussion of the basis of "politic Societies" to Classical thought should be considered.
[39]Ibid., p. 256.
[40]Ibid.

in conscience, from the eternal law whence they are derived, according to Prov. viii. 15: *By Me kings reign, and lawgivers decree just things*."[41] Robert Sanderson, bishop of Lincoln, writing in a similar vein some four hundred years later (in a work Locke is thought to have studied), writes that "conscience is a faculty, . . . by which, the mind of Man doth by the discourse of reason apply that light with which he is induced to his particular moral Actions."[42] For his part, Calvin observed that conscience, which distinguishes between good and evil, responds to the judgment of God. This is said to signify an immortal spirit. To summarize: according to the Christian natural law teaching, conscience is held to reinforce by its divine guidance the natural law, which in turn reflects the structure of the eternal law as manifested through humanity's natural inclinations.

Given God's infinite concern for humanity and His grace in having provided these natural inclinations and other powerful directives toward moral conduct, including the light of reason, one may wonder how it is that we, as divinely created and directed, could ever wander from the "straight and narrow path." We must remind ourselves that in the Christian view, humankind as a whole suffers the wages of original sin. Adam and Eve's disobedience to God's injunction led to "the Fall" and thereby, as many theologians emphasize, struck flaws into our nature, including our natural reason. It follows that although we remain subject to God's will and guidance, we are incredibly frail. Sacred Scripture portrays our brief sojourn on this earth as plagued by disobedience to God and characterized by sin. God has created us with that freedom of will that distinguishes us from lower orders of creation. At the same time, he has sought to safeguard us by providing the most direct and surest guide toward moral conduct.[43] This God-given guidance is Holy Scripture itself, the divine law, as it is generally termed in Christian doctrine. Of it, Hooker says:

> any man, what place or calling soever he hold in the Church of God, may have thereby the light of his natural understanding so perfected,

---

[41] Aquinas, *Summa Theologiae* Ia 2ae 96.4. p. 96; emphasis original.

[42] Robert Sanderson, *Several Cases of Conscience Discussed.* . . . (London: Tho. Leach, 1660), p. 3.

[43] Hooker, *Ecclesiastical Polity*, p. 271.

that the one being relieved by the other, there can want no part of needful instruction unto any good work which God himself requireth, be it natural or supernatural, belonging simply unto men as men, or unto men as they are united in whatsoever kind of society. It sufficeth therefore *that Nature and Scripture do serve in such full sort, that they both jointly and not severally either of them be so complete, that unto everlasting felicity we need not the knowledge of any thing more than these two may easily furnish our minds with on all sides.*[44]

Through his infinite grace, God has provided us with every part of "needful instruction" by which each may lead a life of righteousness and do "any good work which God himself requireth." Nevertheless, it is obvious that many of us, probably the greater part of humankind, "either altogether fail or fall short" in carrying out the duties of this life. Even more shocking: one's knowledge of the world suggests that evildoers prosper and enjoy prosperity in life on earth, while the righteous often suffer.[45] Bishop Richard Cumberland expresses this seemingly eternal paradox succinctly in a passage reminiscent of the famous "unjust speeches" of Glaucon and Adeimantus in Book II of Plato's *Republic:* "divers Evils or Afflictions too often happen to those who are truly good, pious and virtuous; and also that all those outward good things, that constitute this external Felicity, do often attend those that are Wicked, unjust and violent."[46]

---

[44]Hooker writes further that "there can be no goodness desired which proceedeth not from God himself . . . all things in the world are said in some sort to seek the highest, and to covet more or less the participation of God himself" (ibid., p. 215; emphasis added). J. W. Allen makes a pertinent comment on this aspect of Hooker's argument: "The Law of Reason, says Hooker, 'is the law whereby man in all his actions is directed to the *imitation of God.*' " He suggests that "all action whatever must necessarily refer to an end; and that end is necessarily conceived as a 'good' to be obtained or to be preserved. . . . The world is governed by a will to goodness or a will to more perfect life. . . . Sin consists essentially in the willful preference of a lesser to a greater good. 'The object of Will is that good which Reason doth lead us to seek.' Reason is the director of man's will, by discerning that which is good. 'For the laws of right doing are the dictates of right reason' " (J. W. Allen, *A History of Political Thought in the Sixteenth Century* [London: Methuen, 1928], pp. 186–87; emphasis supplied.)

[45]Hooker, *Ecclesiastical Polity*, p. 271.

[46]James Tyrrell: *A Breif Disquisition of the Law of Nature. According to the principles and Method laid down in the Reverend Dr. Cumberland's (now Bishop of Petersboroughs) Latin Treatise on that subject. As also His confutations of Mr. Hobb's Principles put into another Method. With the Right Reverend Author's Approbation* (London, 1692), p. 132.

This appalling situation has forced people throughout the ages to ask whether *God* condones the manifest injustices as described, for example, in Cumberland's work. Because God cannot, Cumberland continues, "we may thence with the highest Reason" rightly conclude "that God will recompense those Losses and Afflictions with a far larger share of Happiness to be enjoyed by the Good and Vertuous, in a Life after this; since otherwise the Wisdom and Providence of God, would prove Insufficient for the Ends it designed." Cumberland's reassurance on this score is underscored by his further observation that the "Laws of Nature would signify but little . . . without a due Administration of Rewards and Punishments, which since they so often fail in this Life, ought to be made up in that to come." God, as "a Just and True Legislator," provides these eternal rewards and punishments as the ultimate "Sanction" for his laws. He provides "the greatest assurance we have of that grand Motive to Religion and Virtue, *the immortality of the Soul*," for it is the immortal soul that will be "either eternally happy or miserable" in another life, "when this life is ended."[47]

To sum up, I have thought it helpful to provide a sketch of certain fundamental tenets of the traditional Christian doctrine of natural law, since in my view it is within this general framework that Locke's reflections on the law of nature appear to have been composed and are generally interpreted. I suggested that in the initial discussion of the controversy between Locke and the "thinkeing men at Oxford" and other contemporary critics, although Locke took pains not to endorse their understanding of his views on natural law, he replied to them and to his other critics in a fashion designed, as it appears, to confound them—without clarifying adequately the issues with which they were concerned, for instance, the relationship of divine law to natural law, the status of supernatural revelation, the immortality of the soul, the foundations of morality and the assurance of rewards and punishments in another life, together with whatever bearing issues such as these might have had on other dimensions of his understanding of natural law. By leaving such fundamental issues unresolved during his lifetime, he intentionally, in my opinion, left the way open for diametrically opposed understandings of his understanding of natural law.

[47]Ibid., pp. 132–33.

This ambiguity, if such it be, may have contributed to the protracted dispute between Locke and Tyrrell and the "thinkeing men at Oxford." Locke, as we have seen, had been charged by them with having abstracted natural law from divine revelation in establishing standards of morality. He had been further assailed on the grounds that the source of morality and law and his conclusions thereon "come very near what is so much cryed out upon in Mr: Hobs," on a number of counts.

Bearing these charges in mind, one may better appreciate the increasing apprehension on the part of his longtime friend James Tyrrell when he concluded a longish letter to Locke by begging him to "tell me what I shall say to those that make this objection" to your views.[48] Unfortunately, Tyrrell did not preserve Locke's reply to this appeal,[49] but one infers from the conclusion of his next, and evidently more imperious, letter of 27 July 1690 that Locke had become perturbed, even angered, by his persistence. In his second letter Tyrrell struck a posture of righteous indignation: "if you doe not like that I should tell you what objections the world make against what you write," Mr. Locke, "I shall for the future be more reserved."[50] Having said that, the congenitally unreserved Tyrrell imprudently pushed Locke yet harder on the sensitive issue of natural law, while continuing to disavow any personal doubts regarding the orthodoxy of his friend's views: "I am sorry any thing I sayed in my last [letter] should make you beleive the conclusions which some had drawne from that passage in your booke should proceed from my self, for I did intend no more then to give you an account not of my owne but other mens censures: and therefore desired your meaneing of that place; that I may know how to answere them, or any others upon occasion."[51]

One may infer that in his response to Tyrrell's first letter Locke had attempted to help him counter the deadly charge of "Hobbism" by directing attention to the famous passage on "Divine Law" in the

---

[48]*Correspondence* 4:102.

[49]It is a great loss that Tyrrell, unlike many of Locke's other correspondents, did not retain the many letters written to him by his extraordinary friend over a period of some forty years.

[50]*Correspondence* 4:109.

[51]Ibid., p. 107.

Essay where the divine law is defined as "that Law which God has set to the actions of Men, whether promulgated to them by the light of Nature, or the voice of Revelation. That God has given a Rule whereby Men should govern themselves, I think there is no body so brutish as to deny . . . and he has Power to enforce it by Rewards and Punishments, of infinite weight and duration, in another Life: for no body can take us out of his hands."[52] Nevertheless, Tyrrell had been directed by his Oxford friends to inquire specifically of Locke whether the references to God and his law might refer to something "*other* then the divine, or reveald, Law given by Moses, and Reinforced by Jesus Christ with higher, rewards and greater punishments in the world to come, then were expressely promised . . . either by the Law of nature or that of Moses."[53]

The passage quoted from the *Essay* tentatively suggests that Locke maintains that God is the source of both natural law and divine law. In the Christian natural law tradition, natural law is regarded as divine in the sense that it is the participation by a rational creature in the eternal law. God is the source and sanction of natural law. The specific term "Divine Law" refers to the Bible, both the Old Law and the New Law, in prevailing Christian usage.

There are, in any event, numerous questions raised by the notion that the New Testament is a "law." It contains no code of conduct, no positive law, in the sense in which the precepts of the Mosaic law constitute a legal code. Christians are bound by the Ten Commandments but not by other precepts of the law of Moses. It is surely beyond the scope of this Introduction to deal with the complex question of the relationship between Christian natural law and politics. For Tyrrell's Oxford friends the "divine, or revealed, Law given by Moses" is reinforced by the promise of eternal rewards and punishments.

The passage from the *Essay* notwithstanding, his Oxford critics remained unconvinced that Locke's views on natural law and divine law were in accord with the prevailing Christian orthodoxy. This is the point on which I would insist: Locke's contemporaries, immersed as they were in every aspect of the Christian natural law

[52]Locke, *Essay*, ed. Nidditch, bk. 2, chap. 28, sec. 8, p. 352; emphasis original.
[53]*Correspondence* 4:107; emphasis supplied.

teaching, perceived an important and critical ambiguity in Locke's position on these matters. In particular, they demanded that Locke make clear his views on the relationship between natural law and revelation, as well as his understanding of the relationship of divine law to the law of the Bible.

One infers from Tyrrell's inquiry that these tenacious opponents were determined to force Locke to assert plainly that "Divine Law" is the Bible. These are the very things Locke refused to do, however great the compulsion. Locke's unwillingness to do so put Tyrrell on the spot. When pressed by his Oxford colleagues to designate precisely where Locke identified divine law with Christian revelation, he was understandably stumped. He complained to Locke: "I must confesse I could not tell positively what replye to make; because you doe not expressely tell us, where to find, this [Divine] Law, unlesse in the SS [Sacred Scripture]. And since it is likewise much doubted by some whether the Rewards and punishments you mention can be demonstrated as established by your divine Law . . . I must freely tell you that you your self have bin in great part the occasion of this mistake; since you there take no notice at all of Gods reveald will, or Law, given in the SS."[54]

One might respond that Locke does indeed identify divine law as the Bible in the passage from the *Essay* given above. But, as we see from one of his replies to Tyrrell (on the identification of natural law as divine), Locke is unwilling to identify the Bible simply as the revealed word of God. Responding to a suggestion from Tyrrell to clarify a particular passage by equating divine law with the law of nature, Locke replied that to do so would be

> so far from what I meant that it had been contrary to it For I meant the Divine law indeffinetly and in general how ever made known or supposed; and if ever any men referd their actions to the law of nature as to a Divine law 'twas plain I meant that if any judgd of their actions by the law of Moses or Jesus christ as by a divine law 'twas plain I meant that also. *Nay the Alcoran of the Mahumetans and the Hanscrit of the Bramins could not be in this case Excluded . . . or any other supposd divine revelation whether true or false.*[55]

[54]Ibid., pp. 107–8; emphasis supplied.
[55]Ibid., p. 113. When speaking of the divine law, as revealed in the "Alcoran of the

Having identified, as he thought, the sources of what he regarded as Locke's critical error, Tyrrell took it upon himself to rally to his old friend's assistance. In so doing, he established himself as the progenitor of a long line of interpreters whom one may generously characterize as "Locke's helpers," an intrepid band of commentators who have sought over the centuries to extricate Locke from what appear to them to be more or less easily resolved difficulties in the great philosopher's work.

Tyrrell advised Locke that he should have "more clearly express[d] what you meant by a divine Law: since it had bin easy for you to have added, in a Parenthesis, *which others call the Law of nature,* or els to have allso expressely mentiond the reveald Law of God: as distinct from that, to have taken away all ambiguity; and so I should have advised you to have worded it, if I had had the honour of haveing it communicated to me before it had bin made publick."[56]

Locke's fatal error then, according to Tyrrell, lay in his unwillingness to make explicit the relationship between natural law and the Bible, and in his reluctance to identify the biblical God as the direct source of natural law. Rather ominously, this particular failure also happened to have been widely condemned as another of Thomas Hobbes's most damnable and dangerous heresies. Locke was thereby further subjected to the malignant charge of Hobbism. As Tyrrell stated the by now familiar issue, the problem with Hobbes's formulation of natural law was that, since it did "not proceed from God as a Lawgiver I am satisfyed it could not properly be called a Law; and the not takeing God into this Hypothesis has bin the great reason of Mr: Hobs mistake that the Laws of nature are not properly Laws nor

---

Mahumetans and the Hanscrit of the Bramins," Locke permitted himself a touch of irony by adding that "perhaps you or your freinds would have thought it more worth their censure if I had put them in and then I had laid open to I know not what interpretations" (ibid.).

The unrelentingly persistent Tyrrell addressed himself to Locke on these very themes even after receipt of Locke's devastating letter of 4 August 1690. Six months later, he again wrote to Locke and in this letter of March 1691 announced: "I am about to publish my Epitome of Dr: Cumberlands Law of nature: with his Answere to Mr: Hobss Principles." He suggested to Locke, "if you please first to peruse it I shall take it as a Favour: however it may provoke you to publish somewhat more perfect: which will be a great satisfaction" (ibid., pp. 243–44; emphasis original).

[56]Ibid., p. 108.

doe oblige mankind to their observation when out of a civil state, or commonwealth."[57]

These considerations point to yet another alleged error in the Hobbesian natural law doctrine, again one for which Locke was also harshly indicted by Tyrrell's Oxford contemporaries. This particularly fatal heresy in Hobbes's thought was described and criticized by Richard Cumberland in his critique of *Leviathan* in 1672 and was subsequently emphasized by Samuel Parker in his own critical examination of Hobbes. These interpreters of the Christian natural law doctrine, along with James Tyrrell, set forth an indispensable dogma that Hobbes is accused of having altogether ignored in his discussion of natural law. That is, as we have seen, when earthly rewards and punishments fail to provide sufficiently stringent sanctions for the law of nature, then, as Tyrrell wrote to Locke, "God will make it up in the life to come." Tyrrell emphasized that "Dr: Cumberland hath very fully proved [this] in the booke of the Laws of nature against Mr: Hobs." Furthermore, "Dr. Parker" has gone even further in establishing "the necessity of a future state . . . more fully made out in his Demonstration of the Law of nature according to Mr: Cum[berland's]: Principles."[58]

Locke responded quickly to Tyrrell's unsolicited and unwelcome suggestions. His letter, dated 4 August 1690, was copied by an amanuensis. Locke may well have wanted a record of this exchange with Tyrrell on the delicate subject of natural law, and therefore we

---

[57]Ibid. It is perhaps worth observing that in his rather popular, if not to say somewhat "popularized," presentation of natural law doctrine in his second of the *Two Treatises of Government*, Locke took considerable pains to appear to meet this particular objection to Hobbes. Very early in the treatise he emphasizes that "The *State of Nature* has a law of Nature to govern it, which obliges every one: And Reason, which is that Law, teaches all Mankind who will but consult it, that being all equal and independent, no one ought to harm another in his Life, Health, Liberty, or Possessions. For Men being all the Workmanship of one Omnipotent, and infinitely wise Maker; All the Servants of one Sovereign Master, sent into the World by his order and about his business, they are his Property, whose Workmanship they are, made to last during his, not anothers Pleasure." *Two Treatises*, ed. Laslett, chap. II, sec. 6, p. 311; emphasis original.

[58]*Correspondence* 4:108–9. Tyrrell's reference is to Dr. Richard Cumberland, whose work *De Legibus Naturae Disquisitio Philosophica* (1672) was written specifically to refute Hobbes. Dr. Samuel Parker's work referred to by Tyrrell is *A Demonstration of the Divine Authority of the Law of Nature and of the Christian Religion*. It was published in 1681.

have available what is, presumably, the full text of his letter. Locke's response is sharp and polemical. It bristles with sarcasm and heavy irony, beginning with a rather nasty opening gibe: "I see you *or* your freinds are so far from understanding me yet rightly that I shall give you the trouble of a few lines to make my meaning clearer, if possible, then it is, though I am apt to thinke that to any unprejudiced Reader, who will consider what I there ought to say, and not what he will phansy I should say besides my purpose, it is as plain as any thing can well be."[59]

Contrary to what Tyrrell and his friends had asserted, Locke argued that his disjunction between the law of nature and the "*Divine Law*" as revealed in Sacred Scripture was necessary and perfectly sound. In his view "there is a Law of Nature Knowable by the light of nature,"[60] in *contrast* to the divine law of Sacred Scripture that was revealed by God only to a tiny portion of mankind, the Jews, and "to the children of men" by Jesus. But, asks Locke, how revelations such as these "can be cald a law given to mankinde is hard to conceive, unless that men borne before the times of the Gospel were no part of mankinde, or the Gospel were reveald before it was reveald."[61]

One may readily imagine that Locke's response further inflamed the smoldering suspicions of his dogged critics. He had provided them with further reason to question the orthodoxy of his understanding of natural law through his answer to Tyrrell's question, which, as restated by him, was: "*whether the rewards and punishments you mention can be demonstrated as established by your divine law.*"[62] The foregoing discussion of Christian natural law doctrine strongly emphasizes the orthodox doctrine that rewards and punishments of the greatest magnitude, as received in another life, and as revealed by the divine law, were understood as indispensable sanctions for the natural law.

Locke adamantly refused to respond directly to Tyrrell on this and other substantive points. Rather, he attempted to divert Tyrrell's attention by castigating him for the alleged weakness of his

---

[59]*Correspondence* 4:110; emphasis supplied.
[60]Ibid.
[61]Ibid., p. 111.
[62]Ibid.; emphasis original.

faith. This subtle diversion on Locke's part served also to contrast the character and status of religious faith with that of knowledge. This major tenet of the *Essay* was an issue that Locke never tired of expounding. "Will nothing then passe with you in Religion or Morality but what you can demonstrate? If you are of so nice a stomach I am afraid If I should now Examine how much of *your* religion or Morality *you could demonstrate* how much you would have left. . . . The *probability* of rewards and punishments in another life I should thinke *might* serve for an inforcement of the Divine law if that were the businesse in hand But in the present case demonstration of future rewards and punishments was no more my businesse then whether the Squaring of the circle could be demonstrated or no."[63]

What should we make of this? *Perhaps* the ultimate sanction of "rewards and punishments in another life" *can* be demonstrated, but it could also be that in Locke's view this doctrine is in fact as indemonstrable as "the Squaring of the circle." At any rate, Locke is unambiguously asserting that this is a question that lies exclusively within the domain of faith, along with all other religious dogmas. That was surely not the position held by those who dogmatically accepted and tried to demonstrate (as did Samuel Parker) the absolute truth of the fundamental tenets of the Christian revelation and the natural law tradition that follows from it. But Locke simply dismisses these critics, contending that in writing the *Essay* "I had nothing to do with all this. . . . Twas my businesse there to shew how men came by moral Ideas or Notions," and not to demonstrate "whether they be as much as true or noe."[64]

Tyrrell was manifestly dissatisfied by Locke's responses, as were his fellow Oxonians and many other critics, especially those outraged clerics who continued to attack his views on religion and natural law as heterodox. Among his harshest critics were Thomas Beconsall of Brasenose College, who assaulted Locke in *The Grounds and Foundation of Natural Religion* (1698), and the remarkably vulgar and unrestrained John Edwards of Cambridge. In his *A Breif Vindication of the Fundamental Articles of the Christian Faith* Edwards denounced Locke as gravely mistaken in his understanding of natural

---

[63] Ibid., pp. 111–12; emphasis supplied.
[64] Ibid., p. 112.

law, and a dangerous enemy to Christian morality and religion altogether. Edwards consistently alleged that the foundations of Locke's thought were to be found in the work of "'Mr. Hobbes . . . [who] had espoused a set of notions which were destructive . . . to . . . all religious principles. But a later instance we have in one Mr. Locke, who though he infinitely comes short of the fore-named person in parts and good letters, yet hath taken the courage to tread in his old friend's steps. . . . Nor is he pleased with our old Christianity, but hath offered a new scheme to the world, the same . . . with what Mr. Hobbes propounded as the perfect and complete model of faith.'"[65] Locke, as Peter Nidditch observes, had good reason for tending "to dismiss hostile objections as careless misunderstandings or as offshoots of a critic's fanciful and incoherent presuppositions."[66]

To conclude, I would like to reiterate that James Tyrrell may well have been correct in his contention that the controversy over Locke's understanding of natural law was largely one of his own making. Going somewhat beyond Tyrrell's observations, I may again hazard the hypothesis that Locke, for what could well have been understood by him as important and sensible reasons, may intentionally have obfuscated his position regarding the character of natural law. If such were the case, his intention was effectively realized, as any reader may easily verify in the secondary literature on this subject. Quite remarkably, the seventeenth-century clash of opinion regarding Locke's understanding of natural law continues to this very day to generate sharply opposed schools of thought

[65] John Edwards, *A Breif Vindication of the Fundamental Articles of the Christian Faith* (London, 1697); Cranston, *John Locke*, p. 430. Edwards was unquestionably Locke's most vitriolic and vicious critic. He attacked not only the *Essay* and *Some Thoughts concerning Education*, works to which Locke admitted authorship, but also *The Reasonableness of Christianity*, which Locke had published anonymously. The latter work bears the brunt of Edwards's attack. No less a friend and close correspondent of Locke's than Isaac Newton briefly entered the fray. Newton attacked Locke in a curious letter in which, as he subsequently explained, "I took you for a Hobbist." *Correspondence* 4:727.

[66] Locke, *Essay*, ed. Nidditch, p. xix. Locke makes the same point quite forcefully at the conclusion of his *Second Reply to the Bishop of Worcester*, where he writes: "I know better to employ the little time my business and health afford me, than to trouble myself with the little cavillers, who may either be set on, or be forward (in hope to recommend themselves)" (*Works* 3:497).

reminiscent of those outlined in this brief examination of the exchanges between Locke and his contemporary critics. This is a matter to which we shall return.

2. An Introduction to the Manuscripts of Locke's
Questions concerning the Law of Nature

Locke's refusal during his lifetime to deal fully and systematically with the subject of natural law in his published writings may be seen as especially perplexing by those familiar with James Tyrrell's repeated remonstrations with him to publish an allegedly existing manuscript on the subject. Tyrrell insisted, "I know you have made long since a Treatise or Lectures upon the Law of nature."[67] On this point he knew whereof he spoke. Von Leyden presents plausible evidence that Tyrrell had carefully perused one of the unpublished manuscripts of Locke's "Treatise or Lectures" on natural law. Tyrrell could well have been in possession of one of the three copies of the manuscript during an extended portion of Locke's political exile in Holland from 1683 to 1689, that is, roughly the last seven years of Stuart reign. Tyrrell's insistence that Locke publish his work on natural law could scarcely have been less relenting had he known of the existence of another two copies of the manuscript, especially MS C, the "fair copy," prepared by Locke's amanuensis, Sylvanus Brownover, as late as 1681 or 1682, only a little more than a year before Locke went into political exile in Holland.

Despite this unrelenting pressure by Tyrrell, we have observed that Locke persistently refused to publish any portion of these reflections on natural law. On the contrary, he artfully concealed all copies of the manuscript within his various notebooks and other papers. He managed this so skillfully that these manuscripts remained unnoticed, or at least unreported, from the time of Locke's death in 1704, when they were willed, along with his other personal papers and manuscripts, to his cousin Peter King (1670–1734).[68]

---

[67]*Correspondence* 4:109.

[68]Peter King was a man whom Locke treated almost like a son. These expectations were realized in full only after Locke's death in 1704. King's subsequent elevation to

These unpublished manuscripts remained in the unbroken possession of King's direct descendants until 1942 when, in order to protect them against potential wartime damage, they were transferred to the Bodleian Library in Oxford. Thanks to that move, the goal that James Tyrrell had been earlier unable to achieve was reached by Dr. Wolfgang von Leyden, who published them in 1954.

During a period of several years following the acquisition of Locke's papers by the Bodleian, they were examined by von Leyden "on behalf of the Clarendon Press, Oxford."[69] He submitted a report in 1946, in which he rightly observed that "the most important of Locke's unpublished philosophical manuscripts" were, as he described them, "a set of early essays on the law of nature."[70] Three copies of the "Treatise or Lectures" to which James Tyrrell had made reference in his letter of 1690 were discovered. The earliest MS was, according to the editor's calculations, composed by Locke somewhere between 1660 and 1664. Following the editor's designation, we shall refer to this manuscript as MS A.

In neither his published nor unpublished writings, nor in his voluminous correspondence, does Locke ever discuss the existence of this manuscript, much less the considerations that led him to have two or more additional copies made of his reflections on natural law. To be sure, circumstantial evidence suggests that he may have initially prepared at least some of the material for use in *disputationes* with his advanced students in Christ Church College, probably during the academic year 1663–1664.[71] During Locke's final year at Oxford he served as the censor of moral philosophy of Christ Church College. In December 1664 he was required to conclude his term of service as censor by delivering the traditional *Oratio Censoria Funebris*, an oration marking the "death" of the censor with the expiration of his term of office. Locke's extraordinary Censorial

---

the peerage, his appointment as lord chancellor, and his other grand achievements would have come as no surprise to Locke, who had good reason to hope that his protégé would become the founder of a noble family—one that would retain the material resources and understanding required for making proper use of this splendid legacy. If these were indeed Locke's expectations, they were amply fulfilled.

[69]*John Locke: Essays*, ed. von Leyden, p. 1.

[70]Ibid., p. 4.

[71]Ibid., p. 12.

Address concerns itself with far more than the traditional subjects, such as the behavior and academic performance of the young baccalaureates. Among other things, in the course of his oration Locke specifically addressed those students with whom he had conducted an extended disputation on natural law, presumably during a recent academic term: "During this year I played such a part in your disputations [*velitationibus*] that I always departed at once vanquished and enriched." It is also clear from this valedictory address that the topic of the disputation was "That law, which was the object of all our strife I would have sought in vain [*quaesiveram*], and often lost had not your way of life restored that very law which your tongues had wrested from me. Hence it can be doubted whether your disputations [*disputationes*] assaulted or your behavior defended the law of nature the more keenly."[72]

The character of Locke's comments makes it unlikely that we shall ever precisely establish the relationship between these disputations with his students and preparation of the initial draft of his manuscript on the law of nature.[73] The nature, indeed the very existence, of this relationship is unclear. The evidence suggests that the initial draft of this work was composed no later than 1664, though it might have been written somewhat earlier, as von Leyden conjectures. Locke penned the first draft of this material in a notebook designated variously by him as *Lemmata* or *Lemata*. [This draft, in Locke's hand, is MS A.] *Lemmata* are the titles designating subjects or themes for consideration or explanation, and the term provides an accurate description of the notebook's contents. Locke had used this notebook for years for just such a variety of purposes before he decided to make use of the space that remained to record in it his reflections concerning the law of nature. The reader will find a more detailed

[72]Ibid., pp. 237–39 (translation by Diskin Clay).

[73][It seems, however, that Locke penned his autograph version of the *Questions* during or at the end of his term as moral censor at Christ Church; he ends MS A with the telling notation *Sic cogitavit J. Locke* 1664. His *Censorial Address* of that year contains clear references to the disputations he conducted that year concerning the law of nature; these are discussed in the "Translator's Introduction," below. It is also telling that Locke dated the octavo notebook in which an unknown amanuensis copied his text of both the *Questions* and the *Censorial Address* to 1663; cf. *John Locke: Essays*, ed. von Leyden, p. 7. DC]

description of *Lemmata* in our separate treatment of the manuscripts.

The Latin text of the manuscript is extremely difficult to decipher in MS A, but fortunately Locke had it transcribed (we do not know when) by an amanuensis into a partially filled but much less cluttered notebook. [This notebook is dated to 1663, and the folios containing the questions concerning the law of nature are dated by the colophon: Sic cogitavit J. Locke 1664.] Again, following von Leyden's usage, this version is identified throughout our work as MS B. This manuscript was far more clearly written than MS A. Although it may well be that these were John Locke's thoughts on these matters in 1664, one is by no means warranted in concluding that 1664 was necessarily the year in which the amanuensis prepared MS B.[74]

It was not until 1681 or 1682, nearly two decades after Locke penned the initial draft of his reflections on the law of nature, that he charged his amanuensis, Sylvanus Brownover, with preparation of what von Leyden designated MS C. Brownover's writing is remarkably even, regular, and perfectly legible. In those instances where he was unsure of a word or phrase, he left carefully measured spaces to be filled in by someone else or perhaps in his own hand under Locke's supervision. This painstaking procedure suggests a studied concern for avoiding strikeovers or other corrections that might have misled typesetters. Brownover used both recto and verso

---

[74]On this point von Leyden informs us that "after having written the draft version of these essays, in his own hand, Locke had it copied by an amanuensis in a notebook bearing the date 1663, and along with it, from papers now lost, the first three essays which are missing in MS. A" (*John Locke: Essays*, ed. von Leyden, p. 11). Among the "papers now lost" were part of the missing portion of *Lemmata*, which was divided into two portions, as is clear from the internal system of pagination that one can still discern within its remaining papers. Precisely when Locke had an amanuensis prepare MS B is an important and difficult matter on which more research can be done. Von Leyden is apparently persuaded that the work was copied before Locke's departure from Oxford. This is possible, although he provides no evidence in support of his assertion. One should also consider the possibility that MS B was prepared much later, possibly in conjunction with the preparation of MS C in the early 1680s, as Locke prepared to seek political exile in Holland and was forced to make a judicious division of his papers and manuscripts among several recipients, lest some of them were seized by the authorities or intentionally destroyed at his injunction or that of someone else.

of each folio, suggesting that the manuscript was being put into final form as fair copy. No space was left for additions to the text. Whatever Locke may have had in mind, he did not put the finishing touches on MS C, which, like the surviving half of MS A and all of MS B, was to remain for two and a half centuries concealed among his papers.

There is yet another aspect of MS C that invites comparison with Locke's practice in the preparation of his manuscripts intended for anonymous publication, for example, the *Epistola de Tolerantia* and his *Two Treatises of Government*. In both instances he took exquisite pains to conceal his authorship. Thus, although the *Epistola de Tolerantia* was completed during Locke's political exile in Holland, it was not published until his return to England in 1689, nearly four years later. When inquiries were made of Locke's Dutch publisher regarding the identity of the author, he could only reply " 'that the *Epistola* had been sent to him, joined to a short covering letter, which was unsigned and addressed in an unknown hand. Hence he could not even make a good guess from where it had come.' "[75]

Locke was hardly less careful in making arrangements for the anonymous publication of his *Two Treatises of Government*, which was published in London in 1690, again, shortly after his return from political exile. He concealed its genesis and authorship in a fashion that has sorely tried the patience of Peter Laslett, the most widely read twentieth-century editor of the work. Laslett complains that Locke

persisted in all his . . . exasperating attempts to conceal [his authorship] . . . in a way which can only be called *abnormal, obsessive*. He destroyed all his workings for the book and erased from his papers every recognizable reference to its existence, its composition, its publication, printing and reprinting. All the negotiations with both printer and publisher went on through a third party, who was instructed to refer to the author as "my friend". This in spite of the fact that the publisher was a personal acquaintance both of Locke and his agent, and handled nearly all of his other books. In Locke's own library, this book in all its editions was catalogued and placed on the shelves as

[75]*John Locke: Epistola de Tolerantia. A Letter on Toleration*, ed. by Raymond Klibansky, trans. by J. W. Gough (Oxford: Clarendon Press, 1968), p. xx.

anonymous, so that even a casual browser should find nothing to compromise the secret.[76]

Many of these observations regarding the publication of the *Epistola* and the *Two Treatises of Government* apply to the preparation of MS C, about which more will be said in the introduction to the manuscripts.

To summarize: a total of three manuscripts of Locke's reflections concerning the law of nature were penned over a period of some sixteen or more years between 1664 (or earlier) and 1681–1682. No title was affixed by Locke to any of these three manuscripts, all of which were destined to remain in total obscurity among his papers. Whatever his ultimate intention may have been with regard to his reflections on the law of nature, it is evident that he had no intention of publishing them early in life, certainly not while he was a tutor at Oxford, and, as one may gather, at no point during his lifetime.

3. The Manuscripts and Politics

The year 1665 marked a decisive turning point in Locke's life. Less than a year after delivering his Censorial Address at Christ Church College, he took temporary leave of Oxford to test his skills in the realm of international diplomacy. In 1665 he accepted a post as secretary to Sir Walter Vane, who shrewdly and rightly calculated that Locke could render valuable service on a mission to the elector of Brandenburg. This enterprise took him abroad for the first time. Such was the quality of his service that, on his return, he was offered a far more important assignment as secretary to the English ambassador to Spain. Locke rejected this offer, choosing instead to return to Oxford. Having decided against becoming a cleric, he instead pursued medical studies, which might have enabled him to remain at Christ Church College as a medical don.[77]

For reasons that are not clear and that may or may not have any connection with Locke's political or philosophical views, he was

[76]Locke, *Two Treatises*, ed. Laslett, p. 18; emphasis supplied.
[77]See Cranston, *John Locke*, pp. 96–97.

rebuffed in this aspiration by the Oxford authorities. So once again he took leave of the university, this time to enter the service of one of the extraordinary political figures of the era, Anthony Ashley Cooper, who was subsequently to become the earl of Shaftsbury and leader of the Whigs. Locke took up residence in Shaftsbury's London household where he served in many capacities: tutor to Ashley's son, family physician, advisor, and confidant on a broad range of political and economic affairs. These responsibilities did little to divert him from serious study and writing. During his early years of residence at Exeter House he initiated the basic work that underlay the publication, some twenty-five years later, of his brilliantly innovative work on economics, *Some Considerations of the Consequences of the Lowering of Interest and Raising the Value of Money* (1692). It was at Exeter House, probably in 1671, that James Tyrrell and others joined Locke for discussions that pointed to the famous *Essay concerning Human Understanding*. A phrase from a letter of Tyrrell's regarding the genesis and intention of that work is relevant to our concerns. Tyrrell reports that it was in an Exeter House gathering that Locke observed that the issue of human understanding was about "'the principles of morality and reveal'd religion,'"[78] a position contrary to that taken in Locke's exchanges with James Tyrrell and his "thinkeing friends" at Oxford some years later.

Locke remained for many years at Exeter House, but this productive and presumably pleasant period in his life was terminated by a precipitous decline in the political fortune of the Whigs and the consequent imprisonment of Shaftsbury in the Tower of London. In 1674, therefore, Locke returned briefly to Oxford, where he managed at last to obtain the long-sought degree of bachelor of medicine. Shortly after receiving this degree, he departed abruptly for France for several years to engage in travel and study. It was, we should observe, during this sojourn in France in 1678 that Locke engaged as his servant Sylvanus Brownover, who long served as his amanuensis.

By 1678 Shaftsbury had regained his political strength, and Locke returned to London to take up residence at his lord's new home, Thanet House. He again immersed himself in a variety of activities

---

[78]Cited in *John Locke: Essays*, ed. von Leyden, p. 61.

on Shaftsbury's behalf, including the close supervision of the education of his grandson, who was to become the third earl of Shaftsbury. But, as his journals reveal, he continued to pursue a broad array of scholarly interests. Among other things, he spent short periods in Oxford, where in 1680 he collaborated with James Tyrrell in composing a response to Edward Stillingfleet's sermon on the "Mischief of Separation."

Had Locke in fact been considering publication of his reflections on natural law some time in 1681 or 1682, he may well have been deterred by prudential political calculations to which we must now direct our attention. His patron, the earl of Shaftsbury, once again became locked in deadly political combat with King Charles II, a continuation of the fatal (for many) struggle over the succession issue. The Exclusion Act, by which Shaftsbury and his supporters had sought to disqualify the Catholic duke of York from the throne, passed the House of Commons easily, but it was defeated by the Lords in November 1680. Shaftsbury's other proposals designed to ensure that the throne of England be occupied by none other than a Protestant monarch also failed. But Shaftsbury had by then pushed too persistently and too far. The king's patience was exhausted. Charles dissolved Parliament early in 1681 and ordered the arrest of Shaftsbury in July of that year. Imprisoned again in the Tower, the courage of that intrepid political warrior finally gave way to despair. He offered to emigrate to the New World and to abandon politics forever, but Charles rejected this surrender and Shaftsbury remained incarcerated.[79] Though finally released, he was a broken man. He died in January 1683, as a political refugee in Amsterdam some eight months before Locke found sanctuary in Holland in September of that year. Those movements in the political firmament that had effectively eclipsed Shaftsbury's career cast ominous shadows across Locke's prospects and augured ill for his personal safety. Under the circumstances, it is hardly surprising that Locke was widely rumored to be contemplating a "voyage abroad." Specifically, Sir Thomas Lynch suggested that he accompany him on a voyage to Jamaica. Locke declined, and Sir Thomas graciously, though rather naively, responded that "he was not surprised that

[79]Cranston, *John Locke*, p. 201.

Locke should prefer the tranquillity and conversation of Oxford to the dangers of a journey to the New World."[80] Tranquility indeed! In England the pervasive political-theological controversy was fanning anew the searing flames of intolerance that had consumed the lives of countless Protestant and Catholic adversaries for more than a century and a half. Those Whigs who, like Locke, had been close to Shaftsbury were under suspicion, or, more precisely, under very close surveillance.

The historian Macaulay describes Locke's difficult situation at that time in a passage worthy of extended quotation:

> John Locke hated tyranny and persecution as a philosopher; but his intellect and his temper preserved him from the violence of a partisan. He had lived on confidential terms with Shaftsbury, and had thus incurred the displeasure of the court. Locke's prudence had, however, been such that it would have been to little purpose to bring him before even the corrupt and partial tribunals of that age. In one point, however, he was vulnerable. He was a student of Christ Church in the University of Oxford. It was determined to drive from that celebrated college the greatest man of whom it could ever boast; but this was not easy. Locke had, at Oxford, abstained from expressing any opinion on the politics of the day. Spies had been set about him. Doctors of divinity and masters of arts had not been ashamed to perform the vilest of all offices, that of watching the lips of a companion in order to report his words to his ruin. The conversation in the hall had been purposely turned to irritating topics, to the Exclusion Bill, and to the character of the Earl of Shaftesbury, but in vain. Locke never broke out, never dissembled, but maintained such steady silence and composure as forced the tools of power to own with vexation that never man was so complete a master of his tongue and of his passions. When it was found that treachery could do nothing, arbitrary power was used. After vainly trying to inveigle Locke into a fault, the government resolved to punish him without one. Orders came from Whitehall that he should be ejected, and those orders the dean and canons made haste to obey."[81]

Laslett, Cranston, and other twentieth-century commentators supplement Macaulay's account by observing that during his brief

---

[80]Ibid.
[81]Macaulay, *History*, I:505–6.

return to Oxford, Locke was observed in particular by the "good and scholarly Dr. Fell, head of the house since 1660 and seemingly a man trusted by Locke."[82] Dr. Fell, having cooperated with the activities of agents provocateurs, reported to the secretary of state as follows: "Mr. Locke being 'a student of this house' . . . and 'suspected to be ill-affected to the Government, I have for divers years had an eye upon him . . . he could never be provoked to take any notice, or discover in word or look the least concern; so that I believe there is not in the world so great a master of taciturnity and passion.' "[83] During his final months at Oxford, Locke was also closely observed by the Reverend Humphrey Prideaux, librarian of Christ Church College. Prideaux reported on Locke's movements to a government official, an under secretary of state named John Ellis.[84] Ellis's dispatches reveal considerable frustration. His wily quarry, he complained, " 'lives a very cunning unintelligible life. . . . Certainly there is some Whig intrigue amanaging, but here not a word of politics comes from him.' " Further, " 'where J[ohn] L[ocke] goes I cannot by any means learn, all his voyages being so cunningly contrived; sometimes he will go to some acquaintances of his near the town . . . but other times, when I am assured he goes elsewhere, no one knows where he goes, and therefore the other is made use of only for a blind.' "[85]

Locke unquestionably was a grand master at making use of "a blind," throwing off his trail those who sought to detect his ultimate intentions in a variety of enterprises. Although quite successful in dissembling his personal movements, Locke found it more difficult to conceal the transfer of his possessions, especially his books, manuscripts, and other papers, as he placed them in the hands of various

[82]Locke, *Two Treatises*, ed. Laslett p. 36. Laslett is citing the well-known correspondence of 8 November 1684 between Dr. Fell and Sunderland, as quoted in the interesting biography of Peter King, who, as the seventh Lord King in direct descent from the founder of the dynasty, had access to the rich legacy of notebooks, manuscripts, and other materials bequeathed by Locke to his ancestor. Lord Peter King, *The Life and Letters of John Locke, With Extracts from his Correspondence, Journals and Common-place Books*, 2 vols. (London, 1884). The first edition appeared in London in 1829.

[83]Laslett, in his edition of *Two Treatises*, p. 36, quoting Peter King.

[84]Cranston, *John Locke*, p. 202. Cranston adds in this passage that "Prideaux was thus, in effect, an unpaid Government Spy."

[85]Ibid., p. 221.

friends before executing his carefully planned escape from England. Another of the royal agents stationed in Oxford, having identified Locke in his dispatch as "a great confidant if not secretary, to the late Earl of Shafsbury," reported that papers were being moved from his chambers:

> "Several handbaskets of papers are carried to Mr. James Tyrrell's house at Oakely . . . or to Mr. Pawling's, the mercer's, house in Oxford. Though Mr. Tyrrell is [the] son of a very good man . . . yet he and Mr. Pawling are reported to be disaffected. It is thought convenient to make a search by a deputy lieutenant at Oakely . . . and if you at the same time direct a search by our Lord Lieutenant or one of his deputies at Mr. Pawling's, and that the Bishop of Oxford and Vice-Chancellor then search Mr. Locke's chamber it may conduce to his Majesty's service."[86]

If any such searches were made, they undoubtedly proved disappointing to the deputy lieutenant, for Tyrrell's and Pawling's homes by no means served as the major repositories of Locke's most important manuscripts and papers. In a letter of 26 August 1683, addressed to his close friend, Edward Clarke, Locke wrote pointedly: "I have herewith sent you *many* papers. You will know how and how far and in what occasions they are to be made use of better than I. *What you dislike you may burn*."[87] In the same letter Locke hinted to Clarke the possible hideaway of yet another portion of his papers. "You remember the word *papers*," said he. "This enclosed will guide you to a gentlewoman in whose hands are lodged the writings concerning my annuity."[88] Aside from his "annuity," whatever that may have meant in this context, Locke did not specifically mention such other papers as he may have placed in the hands of this particular gentlewoman, though he did reveal the gravity of his situation

---

[86]Ibid., p. 228.

[87]*Correspondence* 2:600; emphasis supplied. Locke instructed Tyrrell specifically to burn some of his papers. In a letter to Locke dated 6 May 1687 Tyrrell reported: "I have sent A. all the bookes you bad me as allso that you would have had burnt" (ibid., 3:194).

[88]Ibid., p. 601.

toward the end of a long letter in which he added, "Upon consideration I have thought it best to make a will."[89]

Locke's clandestine preparations to escape persecution in England took account of a pressing concern, one that proved fully justified, viz., that royal agents might seek to intercept letters written to or by him and thereby implicate his friends. To safeguard his correspondents from this threat, he wrote to Edward Clarke in the autumn of 1683 to inform him:

> There may possibly be some occasion for this following cypher
> Countesse of Shaftsbury 1. 11. 21. 31. etc.
> Dr Thomas 2. 12. 22 and soe on
> Your self 3. 13
> my self 4.
> Mr Tyrrell 5
> Mrs Mary Percivall 6
> Mr Prince 7
> Mr Pawling 8
> R S 9
> My Cosin Stratton 10
> All being but ten you may put what figures you will to make up any number but tis the last will be the Cypher as 165. will be Mr Tyrrell because of the last figure 5.[90]

[89]Ibid., pp. 601–3. I have been unable to discover in Locke's account books or any other sources information about any "annuity" that he may have been receiving at this point in his life. To be sure, he inherited from his father some parcels of farm land, and there are precise records on the small rental payments received from them. But such income would hardly have been rightly described as an annuity. It may be worth considering the possibility that "annuity" is a code word, though its significance is not yet clear to me.

[90]Ibid., pp. 603–4. Locke's instructions for the cipher were part of a letter, the text of which has been cut away. One must remain curious regarding such other instructions of this sort that Locke may have given Clarke on the eve of his flight from England. Readers of Locke's correspondence will be familiar with other devices habitually used by him to conceal authorship of his letters as well as intended recipients. Von Leyden makes note of one such device used by Locke when he was twenty years of age: "about the year 1652 he wrote several letters and poems . . . to a certain P.A. Allowing for Locke's habit of transposing initials, this person may have been Colonel Alexander Popham, who acted as Locke's patron in his early days at Westminster and Oxford" (*John Locke: Essays*, ed. von Leyden, p. 15). The editor adds, "most of Locke's early correspondents are anonymous or only indicated in his

Even as Locke busied himself perfecting these and other elaborate security arrangements, a number of prominent Whigs were arrested and summarily tried, and some were swiftly executed. They were accused of having plotted to assassinate King Charles and his brother at Rye House. The plot, whatever it may have been actually, was "exposed," and a number of Whig leaders were brought to trial. Among them was Algernon Sydney, whose chief offense, as it seems, was his authorship and publication of a work attacking the position of Sir Robert Filmer, an enterprise in which Locke had himself been engaged for some years, and which he published anonymously only after the fall of the Stuart monarchy.[91] In this connection, one can hardly fail to recall the extraordinary care exercised by Locke in releasing the *Two Treatises of Government* for publication *after* the Glorious Revolution. Locke, as we have seen, protected himself most effectively from incrimination on the basis of his writings by publishing almost nothing. Hardly less important under the circumstances, he sought to safeguard his manuscripts from prying eyes with all the care that human ingenuity could muster. Nevertheless, as one who had been long and closely associated with the politically odious earl of Shaftsbury, he remained in imminent danger of arrest and the threat of extremely harsh forms of interrogation, including torture, and the ultimate threat of execution should he have returned to England.

Being a man who never took lightly, either in theory or practice, the indispensable goods of life, liberty, and property, Locke secured refuge in Holland, at that time a sanctuary for numerous political and religious dissenters. He landed in Rotterdam in September 1683 and was to remain in Holland for more than six years. He had departed England not a moment too soon. The persecution of Shaftsbury's former adherents had intensified, and Locke's varied services to the Whigs in general and to Shaftsbury in particular were neither forgotten nor forgiven by the king and his partisans. Within a year of his departure from England, he was illegally stripped of his

---

draft letters by initials. Again, it can be found that names of several addresses were marked by him by transposed initials (e.g., U. W. for William Uvedale), presumably for reasons of disguise" (ibid., n. 2).

[91]More precisely, he did not publish until it appeared absolutely certain that William and Mary securely occupied the throne.

permanent place as a medical don at Christ Church College by direct order of Charles II.[92] Though ordered by the king to return to England to "defend himself," he was far too canny to be drawn into such a trap. His refusal to return voluntarily led the English government officially to seek his extradition. Locke responded by going into hiding in the home of a Dutch friend, where he briefly assumed the name Dr. van der Linden.[93] Despite these precautions, he was unable to shake the relentless pursuit of English agents stationed in Holland. They continued to report his movements and may have had a hand in convincing the authorities of Utrecht to force Locke to give up residence in that city. His situation became increasingly precarious, as did that of other Whig refugees, with the accession of James II to the English throne in 1685. The target of the Exclusion Act now ruled, and Locke's life remained in jeopardy until James was forced from the throne in 1688.

Even as Locke moved furtively through Holland seeking respite from his persecutors, a number of his close friends and associates in England were subjected to direct and more severe persecution. One recalls that Locke had placed a considerable portion of his papers in the hands of his most trustworthy friend, Edward Clarke, before his departure abroad. Unfortunately, Clarke's ties with Locke were well known to the authorities, and "an order for [Clarke's] apprehension was issued on 4 June . . . 1685."[94] He was arrested and imprisoned, but, according to de Beer, Clarke petitioned the king and was ultimately released on bail. During this period two of Locke's other close friends, Sir Walter Yonge[95] and John Freke,[96] were also ar-

---

[92]Laslett, in his introduction to the *Two Treatises of Government*, characterizes the "Royal order to remove Locke from his Studentship in 1684 [as] the first move against the universities in the final Stuart bid for personal government" (p. 36).

[93]Locke also used the pseudonym "Dr. Lynne" in corresponding with certain friends in England; with some of his Dutch correspondents, he occasionally used the pseudonym "Lamy." Cranston, *John Locke*, pp. 257 and 255.

[94]*Correspondence* 2:738, n. 1.

[95]Yonge's brother-in-law was also probably taken into custody together with him. Ibid., 3:7.

[96]According to de Beer, Freke was taken into custody "at the time of Monmouth's rebellion." Some years after the success of the Glorious Revolution, John Freke, along with Edward Clarke and Sir Walter Yonge, became members of Locke's informal "College," through which the latter sought to influence Parliament on issues of national importance. Ibid., 3:58. On this point, see also Cranston, *John Locke*, p. 393.

rested and taken into custody. A major charge against Clarke was that he had been "in correspondence with traitors in Holland," especially Locke. Perhaps the authorities had "cracked" Locke's cipher code. In any event, it is evident that Locke had not exaggerated the perilousness of his situation when, with reference to his papers, he had emphasized to Clarke that "what you dislike you may burn." Clarke's generous exercise of that authority may have facilitated his release by the authorities, even as it probably deprived posterity of some considerable portions of Locke's most revealing and important writings.[97]

That portion of Locke's papers, manuscripts, and books left in the care of his old friend, James Tyrrell, was treated with much less care and circumspection, especially as regarded their circulation. This may help to explain why, late in 1686, Locke wrote to Tyrrell instructing him to turn over (possibly to Edward Clarke) many of the papers that had been left at Oakley. Tyrrell was indignant and, true to character, dispatched one of his aggressive and impatient letters to Locke.[98] One should have thought that he would have been grateful rather than aggrieved to have been relieved of some portion of his dangerous responsibilities, but even at the height of the ferocious and bloody political persecution of that time, he seems to have been naively unaware of the dangers to himself and the perils to which he was subjecting his friend. Tyrrell evidently pored over

[97]One cannot but be reminded of the very beginning of Locke's Preface to the *Two Treatises of Government*: "Reader, Thou hast here the Beginning and End of a discourse concerning Government; what Fate has otherwise disposed of the Papers that should have filled up the middle, and were more than all the rest, 'tis not worth while to tell thee" (Locke, *Two Treatises*, ed. Laslett, p. 171). Laslett contends that the greater part of Locke's critique of Filmer was lost; that originally he had planned and perhaps written a book "similar in size and in purpose to Sidney's unmanageable *Discourses*. But it is quite understandable that he should have been unwilling to repeat the performance" (ibid., p. 61).

[98]*Correspondence* 2:766. In his anger Tyrrell reminded Locke that he could not help "but call to mind that I heard you say that you liked not to leave your papers, and writeings in London, because of fire, and other accidents: and yet you could send for all you had left with me; to be consigned to a hand that had no place els at that time to keep them in. whether they have bin since removed to any safer place I never inquired. since it is none of my businesse. but if that Gentlemans papers had bin seized (as they were not long since like to have bin) I know not in what condition yours might have been in likewise." De Beer speculates that the gentleman in question was Edward Clarke, although Clarke's estate was not located in London.

Locke's books and manuscripts painstakingly, a possibility that he inadvertently revealed years later in the course of a bitter exchange regarding an allegedly missing inventory of materials that Locke was certain he had left with him. In response to Locke's caustic questioning, Tyrrell responded somewhat ambiguously that he had found "no catalogue of your bookes amongst your Manuscripts. for I have looked over them all with great care."[99]

On this score, von Leyden goes so far as to argue that Tyrrell's perusal of Locke's manuscripts evolved into what he describes as an unconscious assimilation of some portion of their contents. He illustrates his contention by reference to Tyrrell's *Disquisition on the Law of Nature*, which was published in 1692. Specifically, he suggests:

In many places of this book Tyrrell acknowledges his indebtedness to Locke's *Essay* and quotes from it. However, we get the impression that his indebtedness to Locke extends further than what he owes to the *Essay*. Several of Tyrrell's chief arguments concerning natural law, to which there is in fact no parallel in Locke's *Essay*, are so much like those in Locke's essays on natural law that there can be little doubt about their derivation. Tyrrell makes no mention of the essays [on the law of nature] in his *Disquisition* and in some places where his arguments resemble Locke's he even intimates that he is the first to set them forth. The suspicion that we are here face to face with a case of plagiarism is strong enough to make it necessary to look farther.[100]

Looking farther, von Leyden concludes that

there is only one explanation that I can suggest to show how this part of Locke's essays [on the law of nature] found its way into print under Tyrrell's name, though without Tyrrell's intention. A notebook on the law of nature, possibly the one we have named MS B . . . is listed in an inventory of 1680 of Locke's belongings in Christ Church. . . . If, as is not unlikely, the notebook on the law of nature was among the things in Tyrrell's hands for the nine years preceding the publication of his *Disquisition of the Law of Nature*, there would have been ample time and

---

[99]*Correspondence* 4:284.
[100]*John Locke: Essays*, ed. von Leyden, pp. 85–86.

every reason for him to consult it and possibly to take notes from it for future reference.[101]

I find these suggestions somewhat persuasive. They could explain Tyrrell's professed intimate familiarity with Locke's reflections on the law of nature that informed and encouraged his continuing and intensive efforts to convince Locke that he should publish his manuscript. This part of Tyrrell's campaign began no later than 1685, less than two years after Locke's abrupt departure from England. It continued during his absence, reaching its peak shortly after his return. By 1687 Tyrrell may well have perused Locke's manuscripts thoroughly, for he observed: "I should be glad to hear you would resolve to print your papers: or at least to communicate them to those you can trust to see how much of them is new; and fit for it: and now you have finisht that discourse [*An Essay concerning Human Understanding*] I should be glad to hear whether you have done what you intended concerneing the Law of nature: which you have so often promised to review."[102]

As we have observed, there is no evidence to suggest that Locke ever responded directly to this further urging, but, undeterred, Tyrrell continued to push the issue still harder in yet another letter just three months later. "I am sorry you will not promise me to *finish your Essay of the Law of nature*: and doubt there is somewhat of lazynesse: more then the fear of being thought to savour of the short perruke; and plain Cravat: since I never thought either good morality: or good manners can be suspected of Quakerisme."[103] Should one infer that in response to Tyrrell's earlier letter, Locke had expressed reluctance to provoke theological controversy and exacerbate his political difficulties through publication of his reflections on the law of nature? Tyrrell's efforts subsided for a time, but not for long. Following Locke's return to England, he fired his final salvo: "I could wish you would publish your owne thoughts upon this excel-

---

[101]Ibid., pp. 87–88.

[102]*Correspondence* 3:191.

[103]Ibid., 3:256; emphasis supplied. It is revealing that Tyrrell, like von Leyden nearly three centuries later, assumed that Locke's *"Essay on the Law of Nature"* was *incomplete*. Among other things, one is led to conjecture that he, too, may have regarded Questions III, VI, and IX as the titles of "essays" that Locke had not finished, a matter discussed below.

lent; and material subject; since I know you have made long since a Treatise or Lectures upon the Law of nature which I could wish you would revise, and make publick, since I know none more able, than your self to doe it. and which would likewise make a second part to the former worke: and I have heard you say more then once that you intended it."[104] It is not impossible of course that Locke had commented in passing to Tyrrell that he "might" sometime consider publication of his reflections on natural law. For that matter, as I have suggested in the discussion of MS C, Locke may have taken a tentative step toward preparation of the manuscript for possible publication about 1681–1682. Nevertheless, it is also clear that by 1690 he had no intention whatsoever of publishing it, or indeed, of revealing the very existence of the manuscripts. By that time, Tyrrell and his "thinkeing" friends at Oxford, along with rather more strident critics like John Edwards, served to remind a man, who of all men living was perhaps least in need of such reminders, of the risk inherent in publishing a potentially controversial treatise on natural law, or, for that matter, on any subject that challenged received opinion and dogmas put forth by the powerful and accepted by an unthinking public. Publication of his reflections on the law of nature could well have affected the clergy and its flock in such a fashion as to raise serious doubts about the orthodoxy of his religious views— to say nothing of the time and energy that would be lost to one who, as previously observed, described himself as "no friend to controversy." The issue of publication was closed. On his return to England, Locke finally recovered from Tyrrell and others what remained of his papers, manuscripts, and books. He took elaborate pains to conceal with special care the manuscripts of his reflections on the law of nature and wrote or published nothing definitive on this subject during the remaining fifteen years of his life.

4. Reflections on von Leyden's Views of the Text

The publication in 1954 by von Leyden of Locke's hitherto unknown reflections on natural law has had considerable influence on

---

[104]Ibid., 4:109.

contemporary interpretation of the great philosopher's thought. One may say that it opened the way for a potentially revolutionary transformation of our understanding of Locke's natural law teaching. The potential usefulness of the editor's presentation of Locke's manuscript concerning natural law is enhanced through the inclusion in his volume of an emended version of Locke's Latin text based on MS B, along with an introduction of some ninety pages in which he seeks to explicate the character of Locke's natural law doctrine.[105] Speaking generally, it is fair to say that he locates Locke's doctrine squarely within the Christian natural law tradition, and he takes Locke to be substantially in accord with major elements of that tradition.[106]

Von Leyden tentatively traces the roots of Locke's reflections on natural law to a protracted, youthful discussion (accompanied by an exchange of letters and manuscripts) between Locke and another young scholar, Gabriel Towerson.[107] He suggests that, although their collaborative work may have been initiated as early as the 1650s, "it is unlikely that Locke completed all or even most of his essays before 1660, since there is evidence to show that in the last essays of the series *he was largely under the influence of authors whose works he did not study until after 1660.*"[108]

---

[105]Von Leyden includes in his volume an "Analytical Summary" of eight of Locke's "essays" concerning the law of nature. He also provides an analysis of "Locke's Shorthand," which he may have been among the first in our time to decipher. It seems that Locke understandingly acquired skill in shorthand in preparation for diplomatic service. Of this skill he writes as follows: "*Shorthand*, an Art . . . may perhaps, be thought worth the Learning, both for Dispatch in what Men write for their own Memory, and Concealment of what they would not have lie open to every Eye. For he that has once learn'd any Sort of Character may easily vary it to his own private use or phansy" (*Some Thoughts concerning Education*, in *The Educational Writings of John Locke*, ed. James Axtell [Cambridge: Cambridge University Press, 1968], pp. 265–66, emphasis original).

[106]Again, I am necessarily abstracting from the many important differences within that tradition. Note my earlier explication of this point.

[107]*John Locke: Essays*, ed. von Leyden, p. 8.

[108]Ibid., pp. 10–11; emphasis supplied. At one point von Leyden observes that "the voice of Culverwel can again be recognized, this time in connexion with the doctrine of faith and reason, a topic not discussed by Locke in his essays, despite the fundamental treatment afforded to it in Culverwel's *Discourse of the Light of Nature* and the substantial influence of his work on the young Locke" (p. 79). Nor did the editor see these "influences" as constituting a transitory phenomenon. For example, he

He reiterates the view that in these manuscripts one finds Locke writing "under the influence of" well-established authorities on natural law. Specifically, he contends that Locke's "youthful" understanding of the law of nature was strongly influenced by such famous natural law teachers as Richard Hooker, *Of the Laws of Ecclesiastical Polity* (London, 1593); Robert Sanderson, *De Juramenti Promissorii Obligatione* (London, 1647) and *De Obligatione Conscientiae* (London, 1661); James Usher, *The Power Communicated by God to the Prince, and the Obedience Required of the Subject* (1640);[109] Nathanael Culverwel, *An Elegant and Learned Discourse of the Light of Nature* (London, 1652); Hugo Grotius, *De Jure belli ac pacis* . . . ; and others. Von Leyden seems to understand Locke's "early" work essentially as an imperfect reflection of their analyses or, more precisely, as some

---

laments that "the soundness of [Locke's] teaching in . . . the *Essay* is largely *impaired* by what we can now recognize as the survival of very early, *immature* notions of his" (ibid.; emphasis supplied). I further understand von Leyden as specifically suggesting that Locke's most mature and famous work was rendered permanently defective and "impaired" by what he takes to be the alleged insufficiencies of his "youthful" reflections on natural law. Paradoxically, the editor discerns a destructive reciprocal relationship between Locke's most youthful and his most mature work. Even as the defects in the *Essay* are said to be explained in part by inadequacies in Locke's youthful reflections on natural law, so, too, did problems raised by publication of the *Essay* stand in the way of rectification of the deficiencies inherent in the revision and publication of his "Essays" on the Law of Nature. "Therefore," the editor speculates that the decision to suppress the early "essays" may "be explained perhaps by Locke's original intention to reserve his early thoughts on this topic for special publication" (MS C perhaps?). It may be that the controversies following the publication of his writings on philosophy and theology made him change his mind and leave his fuller, detailed thoughts on those controversial questions unpublished (ibid., pp. 13–14). Von Leyden adds that the development of Locke's doctrines of "hedonism and his philosophy of language . . . made it difficult for him to attempt a full exposition of natural law" (p. 77). Further, "in view of all the novel teaching in the *Essay* and of Locke's new lines of approach in matters of morality it is not surprising to find that the thought of publishing his early work on natural law receded from his mind and that the moral doctrines of his youth were not wholly absorbed in the writings of his maturity" (p. 78). He concludes that these and related "statements in Locke's published works . . . have puzzled or dissatisfied readers" (p. 82). No doubt. I would tentatively suggest at this point that these difficulties stem from what I take to be the failure of the editor to grasp, among other things, the essential unity of Locke's work.

[109]Von Leyden adds, "James Tyrrell . . . edited the manuscript of this book in 1661, prefixing a dedication to Charles II, while Sanderson . . . supplied a lengthy preface. Both the preface and the book itself deal with the problems occupying Locke's mind during the years following the Restoration" (ibid., p. 33).

sort of inadequately articulated synthesis of these views. He denies therefore that Locke's views on the law of nature were original in any significant sense at this early point in his development. While granting that the establishment of certain causal connections between the views of these writers and Locke's thought is at best an uncertain and speculative enterprise, he nonetheless seeks to discover what he terms the "filiation" of Locke's "youthful" views on the law of nature.

With this goal in mind, von Leyden analyzes portions of Locke's earliest writings. These include his two early treatises on the civil magistrate, which Locke also left unpublished. Rather curiously, von Leyden regards it as profitable to explore these early writings, despite his characterization of their "rather desultory treatment . . . of law in general and of natural law in particular."[110] Of immediate interest to us is his problematic observation that "throughout his Latin treatise Locke employs scholastic terms which he may have derived directly from St. Thomas or Suarez."[111] He submits that in this early work Locke holds that divine law "can be subdivided into natural and positive [law], according as it is made known to men either by a natural and innate light of reason, or by supernatural revelation."[112] This statement is of the utmost importance, for it

[110]Ibid., p. 29.

[111]Ibid., p. 27, n. 3. Although the editor observes that there is but a single direct reference via Hooker's *Ecclesiastical Polity* to "Aquinas . . . we are justified, it seems, in assuming that Locke did read St. Thomas in the original, for a number of Thomistic arguments, especially in his seventh essay, can be traced to definite passages in the *Summa Theologica*. Besides, the opening paragraph of the first essay, where Locke discusses man's nature and his relation to God and the universe, and also the way in which he formulates the titles of his essays [as disputations] all this betrays Thomist influence. Surely we need not be surprised at finding scholastic influences in Locke's essays, which were written early and for the most part in a conventional style: we find such influences even in his mature writings, in which his thought is more independent and novel. Admittedly, however, it is difficult to decide whether for any of his scholastic notions Locke was indebted to St. Thomas rather than to Hooker or Suarez" (p. 36). He goes on to add, "it is possible, however, that he derived the material of his discussion from various books on conscience such as those written by William Perkins (1608), William Ames (1630), Henry Hammond (1645), Joseph Hall (1649), Jeremy Taylor (1660). His main inspiration . . . was Robert Sanderson's lectures on obligation. . . . Locke's library contained the books of all the authors mentioned" (p. 27, n. 3).

[112]Ibid., p. 28.

suggests that both natural law and positive law may properly be *subsumed under divine law*—rather than being *distinguished* from it.[113] This, I submit, is the basic premise from which the editor consistently misunderstands Locke's reflections on the law of nature. Whether Locke in fact held this view is, therefore, a crucial issue, and one that will be discussed at length.

Von Leyden continues his analysis of Locke's understanding of natural and positive law by suggesting:

> Together they constitute the eternal foundation of morality and, by the intervention of inferior laws derived from divine law, introduce moral values even into things indifferent, so that these become either good or bad. It follows that, in respect of their binding force, *all laws, no matter whether political, fraternal, or monastic, are divine*, for they constrain men in virtue of the divine law on which they are founded and which alone binds by its intrinsic force. Accordingly, the commands of the civil power have a binding force for no other reason than that God wills that every man should be subject to a magistrate's jurisdiction; they must be obeyed not for fear of punishment but for conscience' sake.[114]

On the basis of this understanding of law, as explicated by von Leyden from Locke's early Latin treatise on the civil magistrate, one may better apprehend his contention that, "from the mere appeal to natural law at the outset," Locke "passed to the fairly detailed attempt at classifying laws and obligations, and, thence, to a full inquiry into natural law itself. Thus, much in Locke's eight essays on natural law . . . is best understood if seen in the light of his previous writings on the civil power and the nature of obligation."[115] The editor does not, however, make any attempt to establish this thesis.

To reiterate, from this brief account of von Leyden's analysis, it is increasingly clear that he, like many of Locke's contemporaries, seeks to interpret Locke's understanding of natural law squarely within a Christian natural law framework. Locke was not altogether unwilling to have his position so interpreted, so it seems, and he made no attempt to disabuse those who did so. In his response to

[113]The position of Tyrrell and the "thinkeing men" of Oxford?
[114]*John Locke: Essays*, ed. von Leyden, p. 28; emphasis supplied.
[115]Ibid., p. 30.

friends and critics alike, he obfuscated all of the major issues and failed to supply any definitive answers regarding his position. He might have clarified his views by publishing his *Questions concerning the Law of Nature*, but he stubbornly refrained from so doing.

What was true in the seventeenth century continues to be the case among interpreters of Locke today. They continue to reach strikingly opposed conclusions on the most basic issues. These divergent interpretations rest on what appear to them to be solid, Lockean foundations, and various opposed positions can be supported by copious quotations drawn directly from his various writings. Despite this, one should not conclude that all analyses are equally valid, or that no definitive formulation of Locke's views on the law of nature is possible. In what follows it will be seen that my views on these matters differ in many decisive respects from those of von Leyden. Which of these interpretations, if either, better assists one in grasping Locke's position must be left to the determination of the reader.

Turning to these differences, I begin with two matters that may initially appear utterly trivial: first, the title given by the editor to Locke's reflections on natural law, and second, his capitalization of the Latin *deus*, both in the Latin text and in his English translation.

Von Leyden terms his edition of Locke's hitherto unpublished and untitled manuscripts on natural law as *Essays on the Law of Nature*. This title is in perfect harmony with his understanding of their contents and of his view of Locke's intention in having written them. To repeat, he and other scholars interpret these "essays" as Locke's initial, inadequate, didactic explication of his "youthful" understanding of natural law.

Regarding von Leyden's title, I draw attention first to his characterization of Locke's manuscripts as "essays." I believe that this is inapposite, and that such a designation ensnares both the editor and his readers in problems that are far from trivial. For example, in describing the contents of MS B, the editor comments that the "booklet" in which it was written "contains nine essays on the law of nature. . . . Between the second essay and the third and between the sixth and the seventh there are titles for yet two others which were never written. In a continuous series Locke attached a number to each title, to those he merely contemplated as well as to those which have essays corresponding to them. Thus there are twelve titles in

all, and nine completed essays."[116] Bluntly put, among the editor's serious errors is that he has miscounted; his enumeration is simply incorrect. The most cursory examination of MSS B and C, guided by the editor's own criteria and terminology, reveals that there are three "essays," rather than two, which, in his terminology, "were never written."[117] The third "unwritten" "essay," numbered and titled by Locke, lies between what the editor designates as the fourth and fifth "essays." Furthermore, because the editor assumes that Locke's intention was that of writing "essays," he is, ipso facto, led to dismiss as formal empty "titles" three of Locke's questions. This is far from a trivial matter.

There is a further and deeper problem with the editor's enumeration. If one counts correctly, one will discover that there are only eight, not nine, completed "essays" on the law of nature. The editor arrived at his incorrect total of "twelve titles in all" by mistakenly including in his total enumeration the *Oratio Censoria Funebris*, the address delivered by Locke at Christ Church College in December 1664. On that occasion Locke addressed himself to the issue *"An secundum naturam quisquam potest esse faelix in hac vita?"*—can anyone by nature be happy in this life? Locke's exploration of this matter is absorbing and cleverly composed, but, at the same time, it is abundantly clear that this discussion has no direct connection whatsoever with his thematic reflections on natural law and was not intended by him to be included as one of his "essays" on the law of nature. In the entire course of the *Oratio* he refers only twice, and only in passing at that, to the law of nature. First, he mentions the *"disputationes"* or disputations in which he had been engaged with some of his students among the *Baccalaurei* during the academic year.[118] Second, he makes an inconsequential reference to the law of nature near the conclusion of the address.[119] It cannot be emphasized too strongly that Locke took elaborate precautions to separate those numbered "essays" that deal explicitly with the law of nature from the Cen-

---

[116]Ibid., pp. 7–8.

[117]See Questions III, VI and IX, below. I have followed Locke's enumeration of his questions as written in his own hand rather than that of von Leyden, a matter discussed below.

[118]*John Locke: Essays*, ed. von Leyden, pp. 236–39.

[119]Ibid., pp. 240–43.

sorial Address. Among other things, in MS B and MS C he wrote (or had his amanuensis write) at the conclusion of the "essays" proper, *Sic Cogitavit* J. Locke, "So thought John Locke." By so doing, he made it altogether clear that he was marking the termination of these questions on natural law. It should be added that the Censorial Address is separated from his "essays" by virtually the entire length of the *Lemmata* in which we find portions of MS A. Given Locke's manifold efforts to separate these manuscripts, the burden of proof that they are in any way connected is the responsibility of the editor. Nowhere in his book does von Leyden attempt to establish such a connection; he only asserts it.[120]

As for von Leyden's title, one must ask then if Locke's reflections on natural law are not "essays," exactly what are they? The answer is evident. It can be easily discovered simply by looking at the manuscripts themselves. What one immediately observes is that Locke has penned a number of questions concerning the law of nature. The first question raised by Locke, as translated by us, is: "Does there Exist a Rule of Conduct or Law of Nature?" Locke answers "*Affirmatur*," yes, there does. There follows an extended and complex discussion of this issue which points toward the next and related question, "Is the Law of nature Knowable by the light of nature?" Locke again answers "*Affirmatur*," yes, it is thus knowable, and again an extended discussion of the issue follows. The third question follows readily from the second, as those familiar with the Christian natural law tradition will surely know. It asks: "Does the law of nature become known to us by tradition?" Locke answers "*Negatur*," it is not, and immediately moves on to the fourth question, without

---

[120]As a matter of fact, von Leyden manages to mire himself in something of a quandary on this matter. He observes that "at the end of the eighth essay Locke added the remark *Sic cogitavit J. Locke, 1664* and at the beginning of the ninth he wrote *Oratio Censoria funebris, '64.*" (ibid., p. 8). Three pages later in speaking of the date of the composition of the *Oratio*, 1664, von Leyden reports that "this last essay cannot have been composed by him until then. Moreover, in MS. B, the title of the essay, instead of the phrase 'according to the law of nature', has the more general phrase 'according to nature'. In a superscription in MS. B Locke specified that this essay was to be the Censor's 'funeral' speech of 1664 and, by affixing at the end of the *preceding* essay the observation that *Sic Cogitavit J. Locke, 1664,* he indicated that the last essay was to be kept separate from the main body of his essays and to be intended for a special purpose, a Censor's valedictory speech" (p. 11; emphasis added). Precisely my point.

developing the issue of "tradition" in Question III, although he does in fact deal with this controversial and important matter at considerable length in Question II. By dropping Question III from any consideration, the editor obviously assumed that those questions to which Locke responded in a single word should be disregarded, even discarded, on the ground that they were not "essays." He is, of course, perfectly right in his judgment that they are not "essays," and it is possible that these questions answered so tersely by Locke are unimportant. Yet the opposite could be equally true; a short answer is not necessarily an insignificant answer.

How, then, should Locke's reflections on the law of nature be titled? Simply put, they are questions in the tradition of late scholasticism as it still held sway over much of the instruction at Oxford. Recalling what may have been Locke's only publicly recorded reference to the origin of his systematic reflections on natural law, in his *Oratio*, he spoke of *velitationes*, "wranglings," and *disputationes*, "disputations," conducted over these vexed matters.[121] Within the manuscripts themselves, in discussing the issue of whether the will of God is binding "of itself and by its own force," Locke responds in part by asking whether *"lumine naturae cognoscibilis et tunc est de qua disputamus lex naturae,"* whether it is knowable by the light of nature, and is thus the law of nature that is the object of our *disputation?* (folio 87, lines 8–9, emphasis supplied). Locke posed eleven questions concerning the law of nature, and he dealt with them by providing responses that ranged in length from one word to many pages. Therefore, we have chosen "questions" as the word that appeared to us to convey most clearly the immediate character of Locke's work. The Latin phrase *quaestiones disputatae* might have served equally well. In *quaestiones disputatae* a proposition is stated. It is typically followed by objections to which responses are made. Thus, for centuries the term had a precise meaning, although the *quaestiones disputatae* are no longer in widespread use as a mode of instruction and writing.

Moreover, the precise sense of these terms was totally familiar to Locke and his contemporary readers. The disputation was, from the end of the twelfth century through most of the seventeenth century,

---

[121]Ibid., pp. 237–39 and p. 12.

an integral part of the curriculum of the university. It served both as a means of instruction and as the form for many written presentations.[122] The oral disputation was a more or less structured form of public debate. At Oxford, for example, "a Statute of October 1583 regulated the public exercises in theology, Civil Law, and medicine. They were to be held every term in the School of Theology from the first hour to the third, theological disputations ten times a year, those in Civil Law and medicine once only in alternate terms. Under the rules of conduct of a formal disputation, the Respondent opened with his thesis: he was allowed half an hour for this but not more. The Opponents criticized and answered; they were limited to a quarter of an hour each. The Moderator presided and summed up."[123] A less highly structured form of disputation, the *disputatio de quo libet*, was a "free" discussion whose subject was directly suggested by the audience.[124]

What is uniquely valuable about this form of inquiry is the fashion in which it forces the hearer or reader to ponder seriously all sides of the issue under examination. One must reflect on what one's own position and conclusions would be. This is surely why the disputation has long served as a valuable device for the investigation of controversial issues and, as such, an eminently useful vehicle of higher education.

By the end of the seventeenth century, there was increasing dissatisfaction with the disputation, especially when it degenerated into hairsplitting and purely formalistic wrangling. Hegel once referred to it as "intellectual gymnastics for display and for amusement,"[125] and Descartes complained that he had never "noticed that the arguments carried on in the schools have ever brought to light a truth which was previously unknown."[126] Nevertheless, some would-be reformers who were impatient with its abuses "still believed in dis-

[122]Josef Pieper, *Guide to Thomas Aquinas* (New York: New American Library, 1964), pp. 74–76. Saint Thomas, for example, wrote more than five hundred *quaestiones disputatae* and regularly held oral disputations at the University of Paris.

[123]Charles Edward Mallet, *A History of the University of Oxford*, 2 vols. (New York: Longmans, Green, 1924), 2:127.

[124]Pieper, *Aquinas*, pp. 76–77.

[125]Cited in ibid., pp. 74–75.

[126]René Descartes, *Discourse on Method, and Meditations* (New York: Liberal Arts Press, 1960), pt. 6, p. 44.

putation as the best method of developing the resoning powers of men."[127]

It should come as no surprise that Locke would use such a vehicle for exploration of the thorny issue of the law of nature. As we shall see, the elements of the disputation are all present in his questions: the question, the response, objections, and replies. Even when they are not explicitly labeled, they would be recognized as such by those familiar with the form of a disputation. The structure of Locke's questions is designed to force serious readers to engage actively in the argument in precisely this fashion. One thing is certain: Locke's reflections on the law of nature yield remarkably different meanings if one analyzes them as a work consisting of carefully articulated *quaestiones disputatae* integrated into an artfully structured disputation, rather than as disparate didactic "essays" that were left unfinished by their "youthful" author.

Turning now from the general issues of the title and the overall character of the work, we must consider our second point, the author's attempts to "help" Locke through his persistent replacement of *deus* by *Deus*. The editor freely acknowledges that "the spelling of this word in MS. A . . . and also in some of Locke's corrections in MS. B is *deus*; [but] in this edition the word is capitalized wherever it stands for a truly theistic conception,"[128] which, in the editor's view, is most of the time. That is to say that the editor is unwilling to accept Locke's own consistent use of *deus* because he evidently believes that he understands the author's position better than did Locke himself, and he insists on extending a helping hand to assist Locke with his "problem."

Accordingly, it is essential to establish the facts regarding Locke's use of *deus*, for much depends on this. In MS A, the only one of the three manuscript texts penned solely in Locke's own hand, he consistently wrote *deus*. Someone may rightly object that the text of the first three questions is missing in MS A. The notebook, *Lemmata*, in which Locke composed his reflections on the law of nature was subsequently divided into two portions, one of which "disap-

---

[127]Mallet, *Oxford*, 2:148.
[128]*John Locke: Essays*, ed. von Leyden, p. 108, n. 1.

peared."[129] Still, neither common sense, nor any available evidence, suggests that Locke would have consistently written *deus* in two-thirds of MS A while departing from this practice in the now missing opening third of the work.

But what of MS B: is it not the case that *Deus* consistently appears in place of *deus* throughout much of the Latin manuscript? True, but what conclusions should one draw from this? The unidentified amanuensis who struggled through the complicated task of transcribing Locke's nearly indecipherable *Questions* from *Lemmata* did in fact consistently replace *deus* by *Deus*. This amanuensis is, however, described and dismissed by von Leyden as "an illiterate man, obviously not versed in Latin."[130] Accordingly, one might have expected such a scribe to follow the established orthographic conventions of his age by writing *Deus*. He, like von Leyden and others subsequently, probably assumed that Locke could not have intended anything else.

But this is not the decisive point. Locke did not attempt to correct errors of detail committed by his poor struggling amanuensis. This would have been a wasteful and time-consuming enterprise, and pointless, moreover, since MS B was obviously neither suited nor intended for publication, given its rough form and many corrections. It was evidently intended chiefly for Locke's private use. Perfectly compatible with precisely such use were the limited corrections and additions made by Locke, who, as von Leyden rightly reports, filled "in some lines missed out by the amanuensis in the process of transcription. He also added passages and remoulded others, thereby transforming the copy into something slightly dif-

---

[129]See ibid., p. 11. One portion of *Lemmata*, one must conclude, is irretrievably lost. The most assiduous inquiries into Locke holdings outside the Bodleian have secured no information whatsoever on the missing section of the notebook. If, as I have speculated, the notebook was divided by Locke before his self-imposed exile in Holland, perhaps part of it might have been among the papers and manuscripts left with Edward Clarke, who, as we know, was given ultimate discretion: "what you dislike you may burn." There may well have been other politically sensitive materials in the missing section of *Lemmata*. We will probably never know. What we do know from the *Correspondence* is that Clarke used his discretionary authority freely, and the first third of *Lemmata*, whether destroyed by him or not, was far from being the only work of Locke's to be sacrificed to the flames. On this point, see n. 93, above.

[130]Ibid.

ferent from the original draft."[131] The critically important information that von Leyden fails to convey to us is that wherever Locke
corrected passages in which the amanuensis had written *Deus*, Locke
himself changed the spelling back to the original *deus*. The editor
inadvertently, as one gathers, furnishes his readers with some perfect examples of just such corrections by having reproduced folio 62
from MS B as a plate that appears opposite the title page in his
edition and at the beginning of Question VII in ours. The title to
Question VII is at the top of folio 62. It was, one judges, written in
Locke's own hand, as was the numeral "7" by which he identified this
as the seventh question concerning the law of nature, although von
Leyden persistently insists on referring to it as the fifth "essay."
Again, the editor is attempting to "help" Locke.

Glancing at the beginning of Question VII, one observes that the
amanuensis badly botched the beginning of the opening paragraph.
Locke crossed out his flawed transcription and, on the verso of the
folio, wrote his corrected version of the passage. As the editor explains the matter, "the passage from *Vox* to *Deum* was added by
Locke on f. 61^v, in place of the amanuensis's version of it in MS B,
which is a faulty and incomplete transcription from MS A."[132] The
beginning and the ending of Locke's correction in his own hand in
Latin reads as follows: *Vox populi vox dei . . . adeo ut si huic voci tanquam
legis divinae praeconi auscultare velimus vix aliquem tandem crederemus
esse deum.*" We have translated as follows: "The voice of the people is
the voice of god. . . . were we willing to harken to this voice as if it
were the herald of divine law, we should finally hardly believe in the
existence of any god at all."

Locke wrote *dei* and *deum* in lower case, as is unambiguously clear
from the plate. Despite Locke's consistent practice, the amanuensis
and then von Leyden changed the Latin text to read "*Vox populi vox
Dei*," and concluded with "*crederemus esse Deum.*" Locke corrected the
amanuensis, and then von Leyden corrected Locke. Once again,
the editor's explanation of the principle underlying his changes in
Locke's orthography is not complicated: "*Deus* is capitalized by me
throughout, except where the word stands for 'deity' in general or

[131] Ibid.
[132] Ibid., p. 160, n. 1.

for a non-Christian god."[133] One is led to conclude from this that when the editor replaces *deus* by *Deus*, he intends us to understand that Locke is speaking of the God of Sacred Scripture, the God of whom Aquinas, Culverwel, Sanderson, Cumberland, and countless others in that host of Christian natural law writers were speaking, and "under whose influence" Locke's work is understood by the author to have been fundamentally shaped. This transformation of Locke's work by the editor does not end with the mere substitution of *Deus* for *deus*. He carries it considerably further in his English translation than in the Latin text, since the necessity of supplying personal pronouns in English affords him far greater latitude. For example, in those passages referring to the deity in the opening paragraph of Question I, the editor writes "Himself" twice, "His" twice, "He" twice, and "Almighty God" once—in addition to translating *deus* twice as "God," a total of nine unwarranted uses of misleading majuscules injected into the translation of slightly more than one folio of Latin text. Consequently, the phrase "Almighty God" is his translation of the Latin contraction, *Deum O. M.*, which, as the editor suggests in a footnote, means literally *Deum Optimum Maximum*, "God, Best and Greatest." The Roman pagans who used the term were thereby paying reverence to Jupiter, best and greatest, who was neither omnipotent nor omniscient, though ruler of their pantheon of gods. One is deeply puzzled in trying to understand how this term of worshipful respect, as used by pagan polytheists to denote the king of their multitudinous deities, can be understood by the editor as revealing a "truly theistic conception" of God. This is indicated by von Leyden's surprising translation of *Deum O. M.* as "Almighty God,"[134] even if, as some assert, this was not an

---

[133] Ibid., p. 90.

[134] I infer that Locke, himself, would have been puzzled by the editor's use of this pagan term of respect taken from a religion condemned by Locke in no uncertain terms in the *Questions* as atheism masquerading in the guise of polytheism. Speaking of "the opinion of the Greeks and Romans and the entire Pagan World concerning the gods," Locke asks, "what . . . are these people except atheists under another name? For it is as impossible for many divinities to be, or to be conceived to be, as none" (Question VII, fol. 76, line 15 to fol. 77, line 10). In Question VIII, Locke uses the term *a "Deo enim optimo maximo obligamur"* in the context of his discussion of obligation. Von Leyden translates the passage containing this phrase as follows: "we are indeed bound by Almighty God because He wills, but the declaration of His will

unusual practice among writers in Latin at that time. However that may be, it is evident that the general effect of the editor's alteration of the Latin text, together with the innumerable further distortions induced by his capitalization of personal pronouns referring to the deity, gives Locke's work an uncompromisingly theistic tone. Not surprisingly, it has been taken in precisely this fashion by a good many of those Locke scholars who have relied heavily on the editor's work during the past quarter-century.[135]

---

delimits the obligation and the ground of our obedience" (*John Locke: Essays*, ed. von Leyden, pp. 184–85). We have translated this more literally: "For we are bound by god, who is best and greatest, because he wills; in effect, the declaration of his will defines the principle of [our] obligation" (fol. 87, lines 2–4). One should also observe that *Deo* is capitalized by the editor, although Locke wrote it in lower case in MS A. His rendition of this passage gives it a theistic tone that is not apparent in Locke's original. Such distortions on the part of the editor tend to obfuscate key issues in the *Questions*, both for himself and for his readers. The lively and open questions raised in the disputation are frequently transformed into a statement of theological dogmas by von Leyden's translation, and the intention of Locke's work is gravely distorted, to say the least.

[135]We translate "god" where Locke wrote *deus*, yet I think we have to recognize that, had Locke seen his *Questions* into print, even anonymously, he would likely have printed "God," as is the case in all of his published writings.

But two points must be made. He *didn't* publish his questions, and *in his corrections* to MS B *he* wrote *deus* rather than *Deus* whenever it was necessary to correct a given passage. [For the two apparent exceptions to this rule, see "Translator's Introduction," sec. 3.] Furthermore, one must consider whether Locke wrote *god* in the lower case in other writings during the period when MS A was being composed, that is, between 1640 and 1664. I undertook such a quest at the Bodleian and found, among other things, a thirty-six-page manuscript written in Locke's hand (MS Locke 4.7) of a "question" penned in English. Probably completed in 1660, it bears the title: "Question: *Whether the Civill Magistrate may lawfully impose and determine the use of indifferent things in reference to Religious Worship?*" One finds in this manuscript that Locke wrote "god" rather than "God."

But this consideration would hardly be seen as decisive by those who might contend that had Locke published his *Questions concerning the Law of Nature* in Latin, he would have written *Deus*, rather than *deus*. Though the issue is open, I again submit that Locke went to the greatest pains throughout the *Questions* to make it clear that his inquiry into the law of nature specifically excluded revelation. Inasmuch as Locke makes it amply clear throughout the disputation that it is a strictly philosophical, not a theological, inquiry, it is difficult to see how or why any difficulties would have been raised by his use of *deus* in a manuscript written solely in Latin. If Locke had published the *Questions*, there is no reason to believe that it would have been in any language other than Latin. It is pointless, I think, to speculate regarding his use of majuscules had he written the *Questions* in English. The critical point is that he did *not*

Still, it must be said in the editor's defense that his theistic interpretation of the text is neither original nor surprising. In this regard, he finds himself treading firmly in the footsteps of Locke's
contemporary, James Tyrrell. It was the latter, one should not for-
get, who repeatedly urged Locke to equate divine law with natural
law and thereby to harmonize his friend's view of the relationship
between natural law and Sacred Scripture. One recalls that Tyrrell
had strongly urged upon Locke his opinion that much of the criticism of him as a "Hobbist" could have been avoided had he "more
clearly expresse[d] what you meant by a divine Law: since it had bin
easy for you to have added, in a Parenthesis, *which others call the Law
of nature*."[136] Reiterating essentially this very point some two and a
half centuries later, von Leyden informs us, "The best way to understand what Locke *means* by the binding force of natural law is to keep
in mind the relationships which he believes to exist between God,
natural law, and human nature . . . *natural law, together with divine
revelation, is the expression of God's will*. . . . natural law is in keeping
with human nature, or, in other words, God's will is in conformity
with what He has created."[137]

Perhaps the most demanding task facing those seeking seriously
to understand Locke's complex and vexing *Questions* is that of deter-
mining the adequacy of the currently dominant theistic interpretation of his work. Above all, one must weigh the soundness of this
interpretation, as compared with an alternative analysis that, as will
be seen, flatly contradicts it. Locke scatters the fundamental tenets
of these alternative arguments "up and down" throughout his disputation. Still, some of these principles are very plainly stated. In
Question II, for example, one encounters an extended passage

---

do so, together with the fact that he chose not to publish any part of them in any form
whatsoever. Under the circumstances, I would take it that the duty of faithful editors
is to present Locke's unpublished texts in exactly the form in which he left them to us.
Locke was an extraordinarily careful writer, and we are bound to follow his decisions
respecting the choice of majuscules, rather than making alterations in his work that
have the effect of interposing ourselves between him and the reader who, after all,
must determine his interpretation of Locke's intention, unhindered by unwarranted
assistance on the part of an editor.

[136]*Correspondence* 4:108; emphasis original.

[137]*John Locke: Essays*, ed. von Leyden, p. 50; emphasis supplied.

reminiscent of Locke's harsh response to Tyrrell's suggestion that Sacred Scripture and the law of nature be equated. Locke explicitly and firmly rejects this possibility when in Question II he observes:

> there are three means of knowledge which, without excessive scrupu-lousness in my choice of terms, I might call: inscription, tradition, and sense; to these supernatural and divine revelation can be added as a fourth. This does not pertain to our present argument, since we are inquiring, *not into what man has the power to know when filled by the divine spirit,* [or] *what he has the power to behold, illuminated by a light come down from the heavens,* but what, by the power of nature and his own sagacity, man, equipped with mind, reason, and sense, can unearth and investi-gate. (folio 23, line 10 to folio 24, line 3; emphasis supplied)

To conclude this introduction, I submit to the reader as a working hypothesis that Locke's *Questions* may best be understood as a dis-putation characterized by a pervasive tension between two or more opposed understandings of the law of nature. These perspectives present themselves to the reader initially as containing many blatant contradictions, but this should not be surprising if, as I hold, the *Questions* were composed as a disputation.[138] Many readers will observe that arguments for and against each of several positions are presented. Even more careful readers may discern that many of these arguments are strikingly defective and contradictory, and that some are presented implicitly rather than explicitly.

The Latin text that follows is designed to serve the reader most faithfully by presenting Locke's *Questions* in a form as nearly identi-cal as possible to that in which he bequeathed it to us. By the same token, the English translation takes no liberties with Locke's text,

---

[138]The manifold contradictions that characterize Locke's *Questions*, as well as his other works, have long been a subject of extended comment in the secondary litera-ture. Von Leyden posits various explanations regarding these contradictions. He suggests, for example, that Locke may have "changed his mind" on key issues as he developed his manuscript incrementally over the years and fell successively under the influence of a series of diverse writers on natural law. We have, I think, afforded this suggestion sufficient consideration and may conclude without concurring with his observation that "with the reappearance of the manuscript of his essays it is possible to show that several of these statements are the products of his early thought, and that in relation to their early context they can be explained as perhaps justified" (ibid., p. 82).

nor is it based on any a priori assumptions about the intention of his work. Thus, when Locke writes *deus* in Latin, it is faithfully rendered here as "god." Every effort has been made to express Locke's arguments in the form and idiom of his other works composed during the period roughly from the 1660s to the 1690s in preference to the "modern idiom" chosen by von Leyden.[139] We have sought to remain true to the letter, form, and spirit of Locke's work. This is to say that, above all, we have sought to avoid joining the ranks of Locke's "helpers." We do not try to assist him in any way. The goal we have set ourselves throughout our work, simple and unsophisticated as it may seem to some, has been that of intruding ourselves minimally between Locke and his readers—an objective we believe that Locke would have expected of those who seek to be numbered among his true friends.

[139]Speaking of his translation, the editor describes the dilemma he faced: "I had a choice between two alternatives, namely, either to adopt modern idiom and terminology, or to follow that used by Locke in his published writings—which in fact would have been the idiom and terminology of his essays, had he decided to write them in English. For the most part I have preferred to adopt modern idiom" (ibid., p. 91).

The Manuscripts

Jenny Strauss Clay

The following pages offer descriptions of the extant manuscripts of Locke's *Questions concerning the Law of Nature*. Such description possesses an intrinsic interest for the light it throws on Locke's methods of composition, especially since Locke's drafts and revisions of many of his other works are not preserved. They were probably destroyed by him or on his instructions. Furthermore, the accounts of the manuscripts already in print (the catalogue of the Lovelace Collection and that contained in von Leyden's edition) do not focus adequately on some of the problems the manuscripts present and ignore some of the clues that might lead to their solution.

Perhaps the first question must be, What materials did Locke intend to include in his *Questions*? Second, to what extent do the manuscripts present a finished product? Do we have merely a sketch or something approaching a final version of Locke's thoughts concerning natural law? Finally, do the manuscripts give any possible indications of Locke's intentions with respect to the publication of the *Questions*? An examination of the manuscripts does, I believe, suggest some answers to these substantive issues.

MS A

MS A (Bodl. MS Locke e.6) is contained in a notebook, 18 by 14 cm., of 91 leaves. The present binding is late. The first folio gives the title, *Lemmata: ne*, and Locke's signature three times:

John Locke	puor
John Locke	svine
John Locke	Gum (?) = Glm. (?)

A list of books, none with a publication date later than 1654, follows on folio 2. The title, *Lemmata*, is repeated in red at the top of folio 6, and Locke's reading notes begin on the seventh folio and continue through to the end of the notebook (which is clearly incomplete). Almost all the references are drawn from the list of books on the second folio. Pages 21–91 of Locke's original pagination are missing.

At a later date Locke reused the notebook, starting at the back and turning it upside down. First comes a draft of a Latin treatise on the civil magistrate (fols. 91^{v}rev.–69^{v}rev.), another version of which can be found in the Bodleian MS Locke c.28. On the following leaves Locke includes a cast of characters and a synopsis of a play called "Oroz King of Albania" (fols. 68^{v}rev.–64^{v}rev.). Third, folios 64^{v}rev.–17^{v}rev. contain five questions concerning natural law and one title without text, all in Locke's hand. This is our MS A.

Subsequently, Locke started again at the front of the notebook and wrote a draft of the *Oratio Censoria Funebris* (fols. 3–16), which can be dated to 1664. It is important to note that the layout of the notebook indicates no connection between the natural law questions and the Censorial Address. On the contrary, Locke seems to have taken pains to separate these two works. We must remember that, although at present only one folio separates these works, seventy pages of Locke's original pagination once lay between them. The *Questions* end on Locke's page 93, whereas the Censorial Address concludes at Locke's page 19.

The text of MS A snakes in and around the reading notes and contains many deletions and additions. It is not a tidy production but rather shows signs of having been worked over carefully until Locke got just the phrasing he wanted.

The titles in MS A read as follows:

An Ratio per res a sensibus haustas devenire potest in Cognitionem legis naturae. Affirmatur.

An firma animi persuasio probat legem naturae. [title only]

An Lex naturae cognosci potest ex hominum consensu? Negatur.

An Lex naturae homines obligat? Affirmatur.

An obligatio Legis naturae sit perpetua et Universalis? Affirmatur.

An privata cujusque utilitas sit fundamentum legis naturae? Negatur.

MS A, then, does not contain the first four questions found in subsequent versions, and no autograph of these has turned up. Probably, they were written on the missing pages of this same notebook. The general plan of the *Questions* as it emerges in later copies is not clearly evident from MS A.

MS B

Bodleian MS Locke f.31, which contains MS B of the *Questions,* is a leather notebook, 14.5 by 8.5 cm., of contemporary binding, with "I. L." (Iohannes Locke) stamped on the front and back covers. The inside front cover contains the number 63 (1663?), and the first folio has Locke's signature along with various doodles, including a personal sign that Locke used extensively in his account books. The inside back cover contains Locke's signature and the words "I then, there came."

A number of pages have been cut or torn out of an earlier notebook or gathering of quires to introduce the present notebook. It appears to have been used for various purposes at different times. Folio 2^v begins with notes for the vocalization of Hebrew; folio 3 gives the beginning of an alphabetized list of reading notes and citations. The back of the notebook was used in a similar fashion, for alphabetized notes, again beginning with an "A" entry, starting out on folio 159rev. and continuing sporadically to folio 9^v with the letter "eta." Hebrew-Latin vocabulary lists entitled "Anomola [*sic*] ex Psalmis" occur on folios 5^v–7^v, while at the end, folios 158^{v}rev.–

142^{v}rev. likewise contain Hebrew word lists drawn from the Psalms with the occasional dates for the entries, beginning July 7 (fol. 154) to October 28 (fol. 141).[1] "Anomala ex Genesi" begins on folio 139^{v}rev. Amid all these notes is found a short address in Locke's hand, "Principi Daniae Oxonium ex Itinere divertenti [16]62" (fols. 136^{v}rev.–134^{v}rev.). Finally, folios 9–119 contain eleven questions on the law of nature (= MS B) in the hand of an unknown amanuensis whom we will call B. The Censorial Address in the same hand, but with title and date (1664) added by Locke, follows immediately on folios 120–138.

MS B is neatly written with numerous corrections and deletions in Locke's hand. The verso of each folio was left blank by B, as if to leave room for Locke's additions. The numbering of the questions, often in Locke's hand, stops at 8. The titles in MS B, many of which are again in Locke's hand, run as follows:

1. An Detur Morum Regula sive Lex Naturae? Affirmatur.

2. An Lex naturae sit lumine naturae Cognoscibilis? Affirmatur.

3. An lex naturae per traditionem nobis innotescat? Negatur. [title only]

4. An Lex Naturae hominum animis inscribatur? Negatur.

5. An Ratio per res a sensibus haustas pervenire potest in cognitionem legis naturae? Affirmatur.

---

[1]Professor Delbert Hillers of The Johns Hopkins University has generously examined these lists for us and reports: "The list starts with Psalm 2:7 and moves on, touching scattered forms in the Psalms up to 51:4, then shifts back to 3:7 and goes to 33:6, gives a few earlier forms, then proceeds in order to 59:5, and concludes with four entries from earlier Psalms. I cannot think of any significance in the *portion* of the psalter dealt with. Most of the items chosen exhibit peculiarities in spelling, form, or the like, but there are certainly others in this part of the psalter. They are not all difficult forms, by any means. Some of the forms gathered as "anomola" are not unusual at all. . . . The interest, then, seems to have been linguistic, but there is much that can only have been of personal, private interest, to someone with a very uneven grasp of Hebrew, betraying a combination of apparent sophistication and very elementary errors."

6. An ex inclinatione hominum naturali potest cognosci lex Naturae? Negatur. [title only]

7. An lex naturae cognosci potest ex hominum consensu? Negatur.

8. An Lex naturae homines obligat? Affirmatur.

9. An Lex naturae obliget bruta? Negatur. [title only]

10. An obligatio legis naturae sit perpetua et Universalis? Affirmatur.

11. An privata cujusque utilitas sit fundamentum legis naturae? Negatur.

The end of the *Questions* is clearly indicated by "Sic cogitavit John Locke" and the date, 1664. The following Censorial Address is clearly not to be considered as an integral part of the same work.

MS C

MS C is found in a small parchment box, Bodleian MS Locke f.30, containing 187 leaves and measuring 15.5 by 9.0 cm. This curious box, perhaps homemade, is labeled *Biblia* on top with "in" on one side and front, and finds its companion in MS Locke f.32, labeled *Biblia* and "out," and containing notes on the Old Testament. Our MS Locke f.30 is similarly filled with orderly notes on the New Testament, beginning with Matthew and continuing through Revelations (fols. 1–121ᵛ). The *Questions* on natural law, MS C, occupy folios 122–173ᵛ, and the Oratio Censoria again follows on folios 174–184ᵛ.

All the leaves of MS Locke f.30 are now loosely sewn together, but the biblical notes were sewn only recently when the manuscript was acquired by the Bodleian. The *Questions,* however, show signs of an earlier sewing. In addition, both the paper and the watermarks of the *Questions* differ from that of the preceding leaves, and the first folio of the *Questions* is stained and weathered, as if it had been exposed.

MS C is in the hand of Sylvanus Brownover, Locke's secretary and

amanuensis. It is neatly written on both recto and verso of each folio. Occasionally words are omitted and space is left to fill them in. The titles of the *Questions* follow those of MS B, and the numbering of the *Questions* leaves off with 8, as in MS B. Signatures are clearly indicated at the bottom of the appropriate folios (A, A2, A3, A4, and on through H) as well as the title "Lex Naturae." The end of the *Questions* again reads "Sic cogitavit John Locke" but gives no date.

It is worth noting that Locke nowhere assigns a general title to his work and that all three manuscripts of the *Questions* are found in the context of notebooks and reading notes that do not at first glance suggest the presence of the *Questions*.

Dates and Relations of MSS A, B, and C

The three manuscripts of the *Questions* have a simple and linear relationship. MS B is a copy of MS A, corrected and augmented by Locke. Their direct filiation is proved by B's misinterpretation of certain paper flaws in A as punctuation marks and by his occasional omission of lines of A. The writer of B had the formidable task of deciphering Locke's hand and acquitted himself rather well, although occasionally committing the usual types of scribal errors. He clearly knew some Latin, as some of his mistakes present attempts to interpret or "normalize" Locke's usage. MS C is a copy of B and an inferior one at that. It was not revised by Locke although copied in the expectation that someone would go over it, as the lacunae left for illegible words testify. Brownover sometimes left space for the insertion of Greek or mechanically and badly attempted to copy it. As a poor and uncorrected copy of B, C has no independent authority, and its variant readings are not recorded in the apparatus.

MS B is the only manuscript of the *Questions* to bear a date: 1664. MS A must have been written between 1654 and 1664, and there is no reason not to suppose a date close to the last year. Locke may have had the *Questions* copied only shortly after he had completed his original draft. The date of MS C must lie within the period of Brownover's service as Locke's secretary (1678–1699), or at least fifteen years after MS B.

The date of MS C can be further narrowed. The Department of Micro-Beta Photography of the Bodleian Library was able to match the watermarks of MS C with the paper Locke used in his journal for

the year 1681. Since we know from other sources that it was Locke's habit to purchase a fresh ream of paper toward the beginning of each year, the coincidence in watermarks suggests a date around 1681 for MS C. Evidently, Brownover had access to this paper and used it in preparation of what appears to be a fair copy of the *Questions*. Though of no value for the establishment of the text of the *Questions*, MS C is significant insofar as its existence demonstrates Locke's continued interest in the *Questions*. If Locke intended to publish them, the first step would have been to put them in a publishable form. MS B with Locke's additions and corrections could not be sent to the printer. A clean, complete copy was necessary. Could that copy be MS C? Nothing in the format of C would contradict this hypothesis. Rather, some of its peculiarities would tend to support the view that it may have been intended for the printer, a hypothesis explored at length in the Introduction.

If MS C attests to Locke's intention to publish his *Questions* on natural law, the project was never carried out. Furthermore, posthumous publication does not seem to have been contemplated, since Locke did not correct C.

Conclusions

The examination of the manuscripts suggests some answers to our opening questions. The evidence supports the exclusion of the Censorial Address argued elsewhere on substantive grounds. In MS A the address is distinctly separated from the *Questions*. In MSS B and C the end of the *Questions* is unambiguously marked. Although MS A lacks the first four questions and contains the text of the five questions found in B, the overall plan of the *Questions* as it emerges in MS B is not yet evident in the draft of MS A. Finally, the format of MS C suggests that Locke envisioned possible publication of the *Questions* around 1681, but the project was subsequently dropped.

Principles of the Edition

The Latin text presented here is a diplomatic edition of Locke's *Questions* on the law of nature and is essentially a collation of MSS A and B. MS C, as has already been noted, has no value for the establishment of the text.

The text of the *Questions* attempts to follow Locke's practice faithfully in all respects. As a result, we have given somewhat greater weight to Locke's autograph, MS A, than heretofore in respect to Locke's own habits of spelling and capitalization. On the other hand, we have not tried to improve or regularize Locke's Latin.[2] Though all abbreviations have been expanded, consistency has *not* been imposed on Locke's syntax or spelling. For to impose Ciceronian standards on Locke's Latin can only be anachronistic. Locke's Latinity is discussed in the Translator's Introduction.

In keeping with the general principles of this edition, we reproduce the Greek as Locke wrote it and as it was printed in contemporary editions of Hooker and Aelian. Thus in folio 18, we print ἐπὶ τὸ μῆζον καὶ ἐπὶ τὸ μῆον rather than ἐπὶ τὸ μεῖζον καὶ ἐπὶ τὸ μεῖον; in folio 74, γεγηρακῶτας and ὑπεργήρον rather than γεγηρακότας and ὑπεργήρων; and in folio 71, λῃστεύην rather than λῃστεύειν.

Capitalization

Locke is extremely sparing of capital letters, whereas the writer of MS B is somewhat more liberal in the use of majuscules. In general, capitals begin new paragraphs but rarely sentences. The present edition retains the occasional capitalization of important words but gives preference to MS A in these matters. Divergences between the two manuscripts are noted in the apparatus. *Deus* presents a special problem, which is discussed in the Introduction.

Paragraphing

The paragraphing of the printed text generally follows that of MS B. But as Locke did not indent at a new paragraph but simply began a new line, it is occasionally unclear whether a break is intended, especially when the preceding line extends to the right-hand margin or when a new leaf begins just at the break. Often divisions, which having been eliminated in B left only tell-tale majuscules, can be recovered from MS A. Such paragraphs, based on the evidence of

---

[2]With one exception: the convention of writing *ij* for *ii* has not been retained.

MS A, have been printed as such in our text and indicated in the apparatus.

Punctuation

We have painstakingly reproduced in our edition the punctuation of the *Questions* from MS B. Von Leyden notes (p. 90) that the punctuation of B "is abundant and most haphazard," ascribing it to the amanuensis, whereas he remarks that in MS A "it is too sparse." In his edition, he "preserves neither that of MS B nor that of MS A." An examination of both manuscripts has, however, revealed that the writer of B reproduced Locke's punctuation from A, and that Locke then revised the punctuation when he went over MS B, often changing existing commas to semicolons and adding colons and question marks. The punctuation of MS B is therefore Locke's own.

In following Locke's punctuation of the Latin text, the reader and translator have a considerably more difficult task. Peter Nidditch has rightly emphasized that some changes in pointing may be more significant than verbal variants for an understanding of Locke's meaning.[3] Certain particles such as *enim, igitur,* and *autem* often indicate the beginning of a new thought, but as Locke's sentences are generally long and full stops rare, proper punctuation becomes critically important. The comprehension of Locke's meaning can be substantially enhanced by careful attention to his punctuation.

Punctuation is occasionally dropped by inadvertence in both MSS A and B, usually at the end of lines. We have supplied punctuation in brackets only rarely and only when clearly necessary for the sense. Problems arising out of the punctuation of the manuscripts are taken up in the notes.

Apparatus

The critical apparatus records the variants between MSS A and B, as well as Locke's final corrections and additions in MS B. As a rule,

---

[3]P. H. Nidditch, "The Forthcoming Critical Edition of Locke's Works: A Report by the General Editor," *Locke Newsletter* 5 (1974): 16, n. 5.

deletions in A are not recorded unless they present special interest. Lengthy deletions by Locke in MS B are, however, printed in the text in angle brackets and, if longer than a phrase or two, indented. The apparatus also takes note of the emendations of von Leyden, but not his modernizations, and includes occasional explanatory notes and discussions of grammatical problems.

To conclude, we have attempted to provide the readers of Latin with an accurate rendering of the manuscript evidence and with a reliable foundation on which to construct an interpretation of Locke's *Questions* on the natural law and to draw their own conclusions.

Translator's Introduction

DISKIN CLAY

1. Locke's Latin Works

Locke drafted and delivered his untitled questions concerning the law of nature in Latin, inevitably, since Latin was the language of instruction in theology and philosophy at Oxford, and Latin was the language in which he disputed with his undergraduates when he was senior censor of moral philosophy at Christ Church in 1664.[1] Latin was still the language of learning in Europe. It was the language in which Robert Sanderson as the first professor of divinity at Oxford had delivered his lectures in 1646 and 1647 on the binding nature of promises and the obligation of conscience—lectures Locke knew and exploited in his discussion of obligation in Questions VII and VIII.[2] It was the language of Hobbes in *De Cive* (1647) and of Descartes in *Meditationes de prima Philosophia* (1641), thinkers who left their impression on Locke and on his questions concerning the law of nature.[3]

---

[1]Von Leyden gives a brief account of Locke's career as censor of moral philosophy at Christ Church in 1664; see *John Locke: Essays on the Law of Nature*, ed. W. von Leyden (Oxford: Clarendon Press, 1954), pp. 11–12.

[2]For an indication of the importance of Sanderson's lectures on obligation—both his *De Juramenti Promissorii Obligatione* (London, 1647) and *De Obligatione Conscientiae* (London, 1661)—to Locke's treatment of the same theme, see n. 38 to Question IV, n. 81 to Question VII, and nn. 84 and 85 to Question VIII.

[3]In his first version of Question IV (in which he addresses the question "Is the law of nature inscribed in the minds of men?"), Locke both named and praised Descartes as a proponent of the argument that the human mind has been stamped with some innate ideas at birth (fol. 38; cf. n. 37, below). As for the more delicate matter of

In Holland, Latin was the language of Hugo Grotius in *De Jure Belli ac Pacis* (1625) and in Germany it was the language of Samuel Pufendorf in *Elementorum Jurisprudentiae Universalis* (1660).[4] In Oxford, Locke not only wrote and taught in Latin; he was interested in the Latin language itself and the style of the Renaissance and early modern writers who wrote in it. In a notebook of 1667 he lists the modern writers of a pure Latin style (*Purioris Latinitatis Scriptores moderni*)—a list that includes Lorenzo Valla and John Milton.[5] And as he set down his *Some Thoughts concerning Education* (1693), he could state categorically of Greek and Latin that "a Man can have no place amongst the Learned in this part of the World who is a stranger to them."[6] And he could insist on the crucial importance of learning Latin from a speaker of Latin, something he knew from his experience at Oxford and his exile in Holland, which began a decade before.[7]

Hobbes, Locke was clearly inclined later in life to disown any direct knowledge of his writings (cf. Introduction, sec. 1). Hobbes is never named in the *Questions* (nor is any contemporary), but it seems likely that Locke had Hobbes's conception of right (*jus*) in mind in Question I (cf. n. 7). Locke takes pains to conceal any possible allusion to Hobbes's distinctive thinking on the state of nature as a state of war by describing this thought as the thought of "some men"; cf. n. 102 to Question XI and n. 59 to Question VII.

[4]The influence of Grotius's *De Jure Belli ac Pacis* is most evident in Question I, where one of the definitions of the law of nature as a "dictate of right reason" is that of Grotius (cf. nn. 7 and 9 to Question I). In folio 14 Locke actually quotes from the *Prolegomena* to Grotius's *De Jure* without acknowledging the authority for his distinction between nature and convention (cf. nn. 16 and 17 to Question I). Later, in Question VII, Locke confronts Grotius's a posteriori argument that the agreement of the more civilized nations of the earth points to a universal cause in the law of nature (cf. nn. 57 and 75 to Question VII). In Question X Locke adopts Pufendorf's distinction between absolute and hypothetical obligations, again without acknowledging his source in the *Elementorum Jurisprudentiae Universalis* (cf. n. 91 to Question X). Later in life Locke would recommend Grotius's *De Jure* and Pufendorf's *De Officio hominis et civis* (of 1673) and the larger work of which this is an abridgment, the *De Jure Naturali et Gentium* (of 1672), along with "Tully's Offices," as the sources for instruction "in the natural Rights of Men . . . and the Duties resulting from thence"; *Some Thoughts concerning Education*, in *The Educational Writings of John Locke*, ed. James L. Axtell (Cambridge: Cambridge University Press, 1968), p. 294.

[5]Locke MS. f.14, fol. 16. Similar are his comments in Locke MS. d.10, fol. 91, on the Latin language.

[6]*Some Thoughts concerning Education*, ed. Axtell, p. 279.

[7]Ibid., p. 269. In Holland, Locke produced his anonymous *Epistola de Tolerantia*,

The questions concerning the law of nature were not Locke's first Latin work. In 1660 at the age of twenty-eight he composed a *quaestio disputata* with the title *An Magistratus Civilis possit res adiaphoras in divini cultus ritus asciscere, easque populo imponere?*[8] His answer to this vexed question was *Affirmatur*. Then in September 1662 he wrote and seems to have delivered a Latin address to Prince Christian of Denmark on the occasion of his visit to Oxford.[9] His untitled questions concerning the law of nature, the work we are presenting here, were the record of his teaching as censor of moral philosophy at Christ Church in 1664, and at the end of his year's term he delivered in Latin his valedictory or "funeral" address to the members of his college.[10] This, too, takes the form of a *quaestio disputata*. Its original title was *An secundum legem naturae quisquam potest esse faelix in hac vita?*[11] The dying censor's answer to this disputed question was *Negatur*. Latin too was the language he chose for his anonymously printed *Epistola de Tolerantia* (of 1689)—a work he dedicated anagrammatically to his close friend Philippus von Limborch, with whom he conducted a long and fascinating correspondence in Latin.[12]

---

which was published in Gouda in 1689. In his edition of the only work in Latin Locke published during his lifetime, Klibansky provides a useful survey of Locke's knowledge and use of Latin; *John Locke: Epistola de Tolerantia: A Letter on Toleration*, ed. Raymond Klibansky (Oxford: Clarendon Press, 1968), pp. xlii–xliv. As Klibansky notes, "The *Epistola* certainly was composed at a time when Locke was obliged to use Latin daily" (p. xliii).

[8]Edited by Philip Abrams: *John Locke: Two Tracts on Government* (Cambridge: Cambridge University Press, 1967).

[9]Preserved in Locke MS. f.31, fols. 136^v–134^v; cf. *John Locke: Essays*, ed. von Leyden, p. 19, n. 4.

[10]First edited and published by von Leyden in his *John Locke: Essays*, pp. 220–43, as the "ninth" of Locke's "essays."

[11]This is the title of Locke's autograph (MS A); MS B reads *An secundum naturam . . .*; cf. ibid., p. 220, n. 2.

[12]Locke's long Latin correspondence with van Limborch (1633–1712) began with a letter of 20/30 November 1684 and an elegant adaptation of Martial, *Epigrams* II 5.7–8 (no. 792 in *The Correspondence of John Locke*, ed. E. S. de Beer [Oxford: Clarendon Press, 1976–], 2:652). More than a decade later Locke complained of his lack of practice in writing Latin, but in a limpid Latin style (in his letter to van Limborch of 29 October 1697, no. 2340, *Correspondence* 6:244).

2. The Title and Form of the Questions

Locke left his questions concerning the law of nature untitled. Their first editor, Wolfgang von Leyden, gave them the title *Essays on the Law of Nature*, thinking, evidently, of the title of Locke's *An Essay concerning Human Understanding* and that of his second treatise on government, "An Essay concerning the True Original, Extent, and End of Civil Government." And, indeed, this is how Locke's old associate from his Oxford years, James Tyrrell, referred to the unpublished manuscript that Locke had entrusted to him as he left England for Holland, with still other possessions. We have reviewed the correspondence between Locke and Tyrrell that concerned the notebook which contained Locke's questions in the Introduction to this volume, but it is well to review some of these letters in order to establish more firmly the literary character of Locke's manuscript on the law of nature.

First, we note Tyrrell's letter to Locke of 29 August 1687. Here Tyrrell writes: "I am sorry you will not promise me to finish your *Essay* of the Law of nature." "Essay" is Tyrrell's word for Locke's thoughts on the question that had been absorbing him for years and that led to his own *A breif Disquisition of the Law of Nature* of 1692. But he offers a different and, it would seem, more accurate description of the work that had long been in his safekeeping in a letter of 27 July 1690: "I could wish you would publish your owne thoughts upon this excellent; and material subject; since I know you have made long since a Treatise or Lectures upon the Law of nature which I could wish you would revise, and make public, since I know none more able then your self to doe it."[13] Tyrrell's language sug-

---

[13]Cf. Introduction, sec. 4, for fuller excerpts from these letters. Locke's presentation copy of Tyrrell's *A Breif Disquisition* contains interleaved pages, in Locke's hand, with a list of passages from the *Essay* to which Tyrrell had referred in his *Disquisition;* cf. John Harrison and Peter Laslett, *The Library of John Locke,* 2nd ed. (Oxford: Clarendon Press, 1971), no. 3000. Locke might have noticed some passages in Tyrrell's work that incorporated some of the material from his own unpublished questions concerning the law of nature. Von Leyden has presented a convincing case for Tyrrell's borrowings from Locke's questions (*John Locke: Essays,* pp. 85–88)— borrowings that are not out of keeping with the derivative character of a work whose full title is *A Breif Disquisition of the Law of Nature, According to the principles and Method laid down in the Reverend Dr. Cumberland's (now Bishop of Peterboroughs) Latin Treatise on*

gests that he knew Locke's treatise or lectures on the law of nature from MS B, which bore Locke's corrections, but which was quite obviously not yet ready for publication. And still another letter, of 6 May 1687, makes it clear that Locke and Tyrrell had discussed a revision of this work.[14]

Treatise or lectures? Tyrrell could have known that Locke's questions originated as lectures. He was closely associated with Locke during his friend's term as censor of moral philosophy at Christ Church, and, as the product of the same education as Locke, he would have recognized the scholastic character of these questions.

Three other pieces of evidence bear on the problem of recovering the form of these questions. The first is the most immediate. Like his two "tracts" of government, as their editor entitled them, and like the Censorial Address that followed the instruction recorded in the questions themselves, Locke's questions are just that: *quaestiones* or, in a fuller description, *quaestiones disputatae*. These are the familiar verbal combats held at Oxford and other universities of the period. Locke took part in them himself as an undergraduate, and in later life he looked back on them with keen displeasure.[15] Only less apparent than the evidence of the titles of his eleven questions and the conduct of the eight questions he elaborated in writing is the syntax of the questions itself. Locke's style is unmistakably the emergent, spontaneous, and involved style of oral delivery. Last, we have the evidence, now familiar, of Locke's Censorial Address, which looks back on his disputations with the undergraduates to whom he was bidding farewell.

These were the students who challenged the series of theses he propounded on the law of nature during his instruction in 1664. As

---

that subject: As also His confutations of Mr. Hobb's Principles put into another Method. With the Right Reverend Author's Approbation (London, 1692).

[14]"I should be glad to hear whether you have done what you intended concerning the Law of nature: which you have so often promised to review," no. 932, *Correspondence* 3:191. I would endorse von Leyden's conjecture (*John Locke: Essays*, p. 87) that Tyrrell knew Locke's questions from MS B.

[15]The essential evidence for Locke's attitude toward his philosophical education at Oxford is well presented by Axtell in *The Educational Writings of John Locke*, pp. 31–33. For Jean LeClerc's recollection of Locke's distaste for the "Peripatetick" philosophy he studied at Oxford, cf. sec. 4, and n. 25, below.

he takes his leave of these bachelors of arts, Locke recognizes the familiar character of his teaching. The passage has been given in English (Introduction, section 2). Here is its Latin form: *Sic ego Vestris hoc anno interfui velitationibus ut victus simul et locupletatus semper abirem; ea enim fuit Vestrae victoriae humanitas ut quantum argumenta Vestra, quibus toties succubui, famae meae detraharent tantum adderent cognitioni. Legem illam de qua omnis dimicatio saepius amissam frustra quaesiveram, nisi quam lingua Vestra mihi extorsit eandem restitueret vita; adeo ut dubitari possit utrum disputationes Vestrae legem naturae acrius oppugnarent an mores defenderint.*

In Locke's Latin the terms to attend to are *velitationes, dimicatio, quaesiveram, disputationes.* They come as close as Locke ever came outside his questions to suggesting the title he would have given them had he ever decided to publish them. Within the questions the evidence points in the same direction. He employs the telling terms *quaerimus* and *disputamus* (fol. 32, line 3; fol. 37, line 11; fol. 40, line 8; and fol. 87, line 8) and *quaestio* (in fol. 25, line 14). We have already recalled the form of the academic disputations held at Oxford in Locke's time (Introduction, section 4). The combatant or challenger would propose a thesis in the form of a response, positive or negative, to a disputed question. In Locke's *Questions concerning the Law of Nature* (as I will now refer to them), the term *thesis* (fol. 25, line 10) is true to form. The disputant would then offer the arguments in support of his thesis for an hour, and then he would respond to objections brought against his thesis by members of his audience.

Locke's written *quaestiones* differ from this venerable model of university instruction and testing in that they anticipate and incorporate, as did Saint Thomas Aquinas, the objections to the thesis propounded. Thus, in his first question, "Does there Exist a Rule of Conduct or Law of Nature?" Locke first states his thesis, defines his terms in a series of definitions, and offers his first argument for the existence of a law of nature. He then faces an objection (fol. 15, line 14): "At this point, some object to the law of nature." He then replies and offers two counterarguments: *Respondemus.* This same pattern of thesis, objection, response holds for other questions. In the second question, for example, "Is the Law of nature Knowable by the light of nature?" Locke anticipates and counters an objection to his argument (fols. 33–34): "Against this opinion of ours the following

objection readily presents itself. . . . We reply, however . . ." *Respondemus*. The procedure is the same in other questions.[16]

His last question, "Does the private interest of each individual constitute the foundation of the law of nature?" comes closest to the distant, and for Locke lost, model of the Thomistic *quaestio disputata*. Here a question is propounded, objections are urged against it, and the thesis implicit in the question emerges to answer the objections to it and to establish its truth by a marshaling of arguments, which is to say authorities, in its support. In his final question, Locke first deploys the authority of Carneades to make a case for the argument he would deny—that an individual's self-interest is the foundation of the law of nature. He then defines the relation between self-interest and the primacy of the obligation of the law of nature and gives three arguments in support of his position. None of these is supported by authority. He finally anticipates a last challenge to his thesis for the primary obligation of the law of nature (fol. 118): "To these objections we make this response" (*Ad haec sic respondemus*).

Locke's syntax we will consider in section 4 below.

3. Locke's Two Voices

The form of Locke's *Questions concerning the Law of Nature* evokes the world in which they originated—the *quaestiones disputatae* in which he engaged his students at Christ Church and more remotely the forms of scholasticism and of medieval education. But Locke's language is rarely that of the schools. This might surprise, for Locke refers to the authority of Aristotle and Aquinas in his first question, and, unlike his procedure in the following questions, he summons them as authorities for the traditional argument he would make. Locke cites Aristotle twice, and in Greek. It is clear from the peculiar form of his citation of a crucial passage from Book V of the *Nicomachean Ethics*[17] that Locke is drawing Aristotle into the terms of his

---

[16]Question X, fol. 93, lines 11–12: *His nequicquam obstantibus, asserimus Legis naturae obligationem perpetuam esse et universalem;* fol. 102, line 12: *Ad hoc respondemus, negando minorem . . . ;* Question XI, fol. 113, line 6: *Regeret hic fortasse aliquis . . . ,* and fol. 114, line 1: *quo posito sequitur 1° . . .* (Locke's response).

[17]In fol. 13, lines 10–11; cf. n. 14 to Question I.

own discussion; and it is equally clear that he depended on Richard Hooker's *Laws of Ecclesiastical Polity* for his citation from Aquinas.[18]

If the form of Locke's *Questions* derives from the *quaestio disputata* of the schools, and if his language is occasionally that of medieval and contemporary scholasticism, the voice of tradition and authority is not one of the voices of the *Questions*. One of his voices is that of a Christian who occasionally evokes the Old and New Testaments to support his attitude toward the law observed by the natural world and the relation of humans to their creator. We hear it at the opening of the first question as Locke alludes to the order of the natural world and the God of Proverbs 8.29: "he gave to the sea his decree, that the waters should not pass his commandment" (fol. 9). It is the voice that recalls God's creation of humanity and authority over creation in Question V: "Hath not the potter power over the clay, of the same lump to make one into a vessel of honor, and another into dishonour?" (Romans 9:21, fol. 58). It cries out against polytheism (fol. 87), as well as the monstrous absurdities of pagan worship (fol. 88), and speaks of the pagans as *Ethnici* (fol. 77).

The other and more sustained voice is what can be called Locke's pagan voice. It is the cultured voice of a scholar who had served at Christ Church as lecturer in Greek three years before he became censor of moral philosophy and whose citations and allusions to Classical texts far outweigh his allusions to the Bible.[19] Of Greek authors, he explicitly cites Aelian, Aristotle, and Didymus;[20] of Romans he cites Aulus Gellius, Juvenal ("the poet"), Pomponius Mela, Seneca, Solinus, and alludes to Cicero, Horace, Ovid, and Terence.[21] By contrast, his use of contemporaries such as Hobbes,

---

[18]In fol. 18, lines 8–9; cf. n. 23 to Question I.

[19]The only other significant biblical allusion I detect in the *Questions* is in Question II (fol. 34, line 10), where Locke seems to evoke Job 28.1–28 (cf. n. 35 to Question II). There is a reference to God's original *Fiat* in Question VII (cf. n. 58 to Question VII); and Locke refers to the Israelites' theft of the gold and clothing of the Egyptians in Question X (cf. n. 92 to Question X).

[20]Aelian (cf. nn. 70–71 to Question VII); Didymus (cf. n. 62 to Question VII); Aristotle (cf. nn. 12–14 to Question I). In this same question, Locke's quotation of Hippocrates, *On Diet* I 5, derives from Hooker; cf. n. 24 to Question I.

[21]Aulus Gellius (cf. nn. 63–64 and 66 to Question VII); Juvenal (cf. n. 86 to Question VIII); Pomponius Mela (cf. n. 68 to Question VII); Seneca (cf. n. 4 to Question I); Solinus (cf. n. 67 to Question VII). For Locke's allusion to Cicero's

Robert Sanderson, Hugo Grotius, and Descartes goes unacknowledged. Speaking in his pagan voice, Locke can style God *Optimus
Maximus,* applying the cult title of the Roman Jupiter.[22] He can
express his amazement at the thought that the light of reason could
have been dimmed or extinguished with the fall of the "first man"
(fols. 38–39); he can express indignation at the outrages done to the
temples of the *gods* (fols. 62 and 92). He can speak familiarly of
Saturnalia (fol. 93) and call the marriage bed the *genialis torus* (fol.
72). Roman is his admiration for the *virtus* of Hercules (whom he
styles Alcides, fol. 110), Marcus Curtius, Gaius Fabricius Luscinus,
and Cicero (fols. 111–112).[23] And pagan is his conception of the
gods as urging humans to happiness (fol. 47); his use of the phrase
"fear of divinity" (*timor numinis,* fol. 95, line 9) rather than fear of
God; and his only reference to Christian religion (fol. 78).

Usually it is not difficult to identify the voices within this poly-
phonic work, but in two cases especially Locke's reader and translator face difficulties. In his own copy of the *Questions* (MS A) and in
his corrections, Locke never capitalized *deus* except in two cases,
which seem to prove the rule he had adopted to write the word in
lower case. In MS B Locke corrected the phrase of his unknown
amanuensis (*adeo*) by *a Deo,* obviously to make his meaning clear (fol.
87, line 2); and in folio 88, line 5, he writes *Deus* in upper case at the
beginning of a sentence. Yet he did capitalize Dog (*Canis*) in folio 77,
line 7, where he is referring to the Egyptian god Anubis. The editor
is left with three choices. Locke's first editor, von Leyden, capitalizes
the word *deus* "whenever it stands for a truly theistic conception of

---

description of the law of nature in his *Republic* (as this was known through Lactantius), cf. n. 6 to Question I; and for Cicero as *pater patriae* cf. n. 101 to Question XI.
Locke's phrase for the treason of Catiline (*nec timuit hostile ipsius Romae muris aratrum
imprimere*) recalls Horace, *Odes* I 16.20–21 (*imprimeretque muris hostile aratrum exercitus
insolens*); cf. n. 100 to Question XI. Locke alludes to Ovid in Question I (cf. n. 5 to
Question I) and to Terence in Question VII (cf. n. 61 to Question VII), but again
without attribution.

[22]Locke had already adopted this style in his Latin "tract" on government of 1660
(*John Locke: Two Tracts,* ed. Abrams, p. 186), as had Hobbes before him in the letter
to the Count of Devon which prefaced his *De Cive* of 1 November 1646 (*Thomae
Hobbes . . . Opera . . . latine,* ed. William Molesworth [rpt. Darmstadt, 1961], p. 140);
cf. n. 3 to Question I.

[23]Cf. nn. 97, 99 and 101 to Question XI.

divinity."[24] Von Leyden also capitalizes *Deus* in his Latin text. A second choice is that of Philip Abrams in his edition and translation of Locke's Latin "tract" on government and Esmond de Beer in his exemplary edition of Locke's correspondence; both retain Locke's choice of lower-case *deus* in their edition of Locke's Latin but translate *God*. The third choice is the choice of this edition and of Henry Shankula in his edition of Locke's journals, 1675–1704, and that is to respect Locke's choice of upper or lower case in both his original texts and in translation. Lower-case "god" will be disquieting to the reader, but it represents *deus* in our original. (We capitalize *God* only at the beginning of a sentence.)[25]

My other problem is concealed in the phrase *vitae futurae spem* (fol. 43, line 10; cf. *futurae vitae* in fol. 44, line 5). If Locke is speaking in his pagan voice, he must mean hope for one's future life on this earth; but if he is speaking as a Christian, he means hope for that life which is to come. I have chosen to translate literally and to note the difficulty. Another version of this problem arises when he speaks of divinity as *numen* (as in *timor numinis*, fol. 95, line 9), or of *charitas* and *fides* as virtues (in fol. 98, line 1), where it is unclear whether he has the theological virtues of charity and faith in mind.

4. Locke's Latinity

Locke's language in the *Questions* does not respond to their form; his Latin is not on the whole that of the schools. We know just how much he detested the "wrangling" of the schools and of Oxford in later life. And we know the estimate of intellectual life at Oxford that he expressed to Jean LeClerc and thus preserved for his biography: "the only Philosophy then known at Oxford was the Peripatetik,

---

[24]*John Locke: Essays*, ed. von Leyden, p. 108, n. 1; cf. Ibid., p. 90, and our Introduction, sec. 4.

[25]One example of Locke's practice in Latin is the letter to Philippus van Limborch (mentioned in n. 12 above) of 29 October 1697, where Locke speaks of the excitement his *Essay* had stirred up among "the cassocked tribe of theologians" and refers to the question of the unity of God (*Ad unitatem dei quod attinet* . . .); no. 2340, *Correspondence* 4:245. The editor of Locke's *Correspondence* prints *dei* but translates "God." Another example of Locke's practice, which seems nearly consistent in his journals, comes from his *Lemmata Ethica* (Bodleian Locke MS d.10) of 1659 and the entry on *Traditio*, where he writes "god" (cf. n. 3 to the translation of Question I).

perplex'd with obscure Terms and stuff'd with useless Questions."[26]
Locke's own *Questions concerning the Law of Nature* are remarkably
free of the "obscure Terms" of the schools, and they are far from
"useless." But the language of the schools and of Aristotle as he was
incorporated into late antique and medieval Latin philosophy leaves
its imprint on the language of the *Questions,* especially on the language of Questions X and XI. We have seen how Locke twice quoted
Aristotle in Greek, and we have noted his single, and derivative,
reference to Aquinas. In one case, where he adopts with a certain
wry reluctance the scholastic qualification *ad semper* ("forever" or
"for forever," fol. 95, lines 2 and 10), he adds "as the Schoolmen like
to say."

But he employs the forms of argumentation accepted in his day,
and his language is familiar from the formulas of scholastic argumentation: *quo posito necessario sequitur* (fol. 32, line 10); *hoc enim
supposito necessario sequitur* (fol. 33, line 14); *his ita positis necessario
sequitur* (fol. 55, line 12); *his ita positis dicimus* (fol. 87, line 16); *quo
posito* (fol. 115, line 12). He disposes of a counterargument by revealing its syllogistic structure and negating its minor premise (*negando
minorem,* fol. 102, line 12). And he recognizes the *argumentum a posteriori* (fol. 102, line 1). He evokes the distinction (as he does in his
Essay) between speculative and practical principles (the *principia
practica et speculativa* of fol. 46, line 3; cf. fol. 49, line 9; fol. 51, line
11; fol. 76, line 9; fol. 81, line 1). He opposes positive to natural (as
in fol. 63, line 1, and fol. 99, line 7). But his most clearly scholastic
terminology is derivative, although he makes no gesture to identify
its source. In his treatment of the obligation of the law of nature (in
Question X), he distinguishes between an obligation that is "effective" and "terminative" (and here his translator can only English his
Latin), and he also distinguishes between obligations that are "absolute" and "hypothetical" (fol. 86, line 12, and fol. 96, line 13). He
takes his terms from Robert Sanderson and Samuel Pufendorf, both
of whom had employed them only years before he composed his
Questions.[27]

---

[26]Quoted from LeClerc's *Life and Character of Mr. John Locke* (from *La Bibliothèque
Universelle* of 1706) by Axtell in his edition of *The Educational Writings of John Locke,*
p. 33.
[27]Cf. n. 81 to Question VII and nn. 84, 85, and 87 to Question VIII.

But the fast impression one gains from reading Locke's Latin is that he does not owe much to the schools or to scholasticism. Even as he was involved in the *velitationes* of Oxford in 1664, Locke had gone a long way to discharging his debt to Descartes for "the great obligation of his first deliverance of the unintelligible way of talking philosophy" of his formative years.[28] Unlike many of his contemporaries, his opinions were not formed by his tutors and fellows; nor was his language.

He uses, inevitably, non-Classical terms or terms that appear only in late Latin: *conceptus animi*, fol. 52, line 1; *discursus*, fol. 50, line 10; cf. *discurrere*, fol. 50, line 12; *existentia*, fol. 55, line 4; *identica*, fol. 66, line 3; *intellectus;* fol. 33, line 16; *moraliter*, fol. 116, line 7; *positivum* (as of *jus* in fol. 99, line 7; cf. fol. 63, line 1). But in his choice of the words *honestum, inhonestum, rectum,* and *utilitas*, Locke is speaking in his pagan voice, and this is the voice of Cicero. His pagan voice is not only Latin; he quotes Greek, Aristotle, Hippocrates, and Didymus, as well as Aelian, and domesticates the Greek terms that had become current in the Latin of his day: *axioma*, fol. 46, line 2, and fol. 51, line 6; *characteres*, fol. 25, line 2, and fol. 38, line 3; *ideas*, fol. 48, line 7; fol. 49, line 6; and fol. 57, line 3; *Mathesis*, fol. 51, line 7; *methodus*, fol. 25, line 7; fol. 46, line 3; fol. 51, line 8; and fol. 57, line 4; *oeconomia*, fol. 32, line 8; *pandectas*, fol. 25, line 6; *politia*, fol. 29, line 4; and *thesis*, fol. 25, line 10—to give only a partial list.

More significant are the terms *adventitius* and *mutuatitius* to describe notions or ideas that derive from some external source. They were current in Locke's day, but they point to a break with authority in distinguishing as they do between what we learn from others and what we learn from our own powers of reason.[29]

Locke's philosophical terminology draws the attention of the reader who looks forward to his later works and especially his *Essay*. But his orthography is of interest to the humanist who is concerned with neo-Latin, and it presents a delicate problem for his editor. Any Latinist concerned with the purity of Classical Latin would want to castigate his Latin text before bringing it into print, as did von

---

[28]Cf. *The Works of John Locke* (London, 1823), 3:48.

[29]For *adventitius*, cf. Descartes's language in his third *Meditation* (quoted in n. 37 to Question III); *mutuatitius* Locke would have translated as "borrowed"; cf. *John Locke: An Essay concerning Human Understanding*, ed. Peter H. Nidditch, I 2.27, p. 63.

Leyden.[30] Our sense as editors is that Locke wrote as he spoke and that often he spoke without due reverence to the rules of Latin grammar. And when he wrote, he often failed to write in a Latin justified by a sense either of phonetics or of etymology. Something has been said about the problems of editing Locke's imperfect text (MS B, essentially) in The Manuscripts, but Locke's spelling is of interest for his mastery of Latin as he wrote and spoke it as censor of moral philosophy in 1664, and his syntax is of interest not only to the Lilys of our age, but as an indication of how Latin served him as a teacher and how his *Questions* had their origins in the "emergent" style of his *disputationes* with his undergraduates at Christ Church.

Locke's Latin orthography is that of his age, and it is sometimes inconsistent. Some diphthongs are shortened (*pene* for *paene* in fol. 16, line 17; fol. 26, line 15; and fol. 33, line 10), and some long vowels are represented as diphthongs (*caeteras* for *ceteras* in fol. 37, line 4, and fol. 54, line 8; *faelix* and *faelicitas* for *felix* and *felicitas* in fol. 56, line 5; fol. 113, line 8; and fol. 118, line 2; but MS A has *felicitatem* in fol. 78, line 3. We also read *infelici* at fol. 62, line 3, *foemina* for *femina* in fol. 72, line 8; fol. 74, line 8; and fol. 75, line 10). Locke writes *sydera* for *sidera* at fol. 9, line 8; *lachrymis* for *lacrimis* at fol. 76, line 2; and his spelling of *piratae* is inconsistent: *piratae* in fol. 70, line 14, but *pyratae* in fol. 86, line 8, and fol. 90, line 4. He has a tendency to simplify some double consonants (*acerimum* for *acerrimum* in fol. 105, line 8; *acuratius* for *accuratius* in fol. 24, line 7, and fol. 57, line 5, but *accuratius* in fol. 106, line 11 [MS A]; *celeberimum* for *celeberrimum* in fol. 45, line 11; and *imo* for *immo* in fol. 17, line 6; and *liberimus* for *liberrimus* in fol. 20, line 16; and fol. 41, line 1); in compound verbs a variation is apparent: *aloquitur* for *alloquitur* in fol. 62, line 12, where the amanuensis is at fault; *tolere* for *tollere* in fol. 56, line 10, where Locke is at fault. Locke writes *author* and *authoritas* for *auctor* and

---

[30]Von Leyden's corrections are recorded in the notes he appends to his Latin text. Some are necessary and are acknowledged in our apparatus, but we have chosen not to classicize or regularize Locke's orthography, and we have allowed him the use of the indicative where the subjunctive would be required in Classical Latin. This was the editorial decision of Raymond Klibansky in his edition of Locke's *Epistola de Tolerantia:* "In his use of moods also Locke often departs from classical norms. Yet it obviously would be both futile and presumptuous for an editor to alter either Locke's vocabulary or his syntax for the sake of conformity with some pseudo-classical pattern" (p. xliii).

auctoritas throughout; also *chara* for *cara* in fol. 55, line 8, and *lethum* for *letum* in fol. 75, line 10. The termination *-cius* is sometimes written *-tius* as in *aventitiis* in fol. 40, line 15, *Fabritii* in fol. 111, line 7, and *mutuatitius* in fol. 28, line 4, and fol. 35, line 11. He writes *Quum* for *cum* at the beginning of a paragraph or sentence, apparently as a flourish, in fol. 29, line 4; fol. 37, lines 1 and 5; and fol. 82, line 1.

Perhaps the most striking feature of the Latinity of the *Questions* is Locke's erratic use of the subjunctive. Often he uses the indicative where the subjunctive is required in Classical (and later) Latin; sometimes he uses both the subjunctive and the indicative. The very titles of his *Questions* display a fluctuation in the use of the subjunctive. All of these titles involve indirect questions and require the subjunctive, which is the mood of Questions I–IV and X–XI. But the same verb appears in the same grammatical context but in different moods in the titles to Questions VIII and IX: *An Lex naturae homines obligat?* (VIII) and *An Lex naturae obliget bruta?* (IX).[31] From this last example it is clear that Locke knew that an indirect question requires a verb in the subjunctive mood (cf. fol. 10, line 2, fol. 22, line 4; fol. 37, line 12; and fol. 80, line 5 for the proper usage); but he also writes the indicative (as in fol. 29, line 3) or combines the indicative with the subjunctive (as in fol. 15, lines 2–4), *quid liceat . . . quid oportet;* fol. 24, lines 6–7, *quid sint, quid agant . . . quibus legibus tenentur;* and fol. 41, line 7, *quam longe . . . mores distent, quam alieni sunt*). Locke's corrections in MS B show that he went to pains to correct the grammar of his amanuensis and restore the subjunctive where he had written an indicative.[32] We have followed von Leyden in correcting what appear to be inadvertencies on Locke's part, but we have left him to the solecisms in his use of the indicative for the subjunctive; obviously, they were acceptable to him as he argued in Latin with his undergraduates at Christ Church.

He uses *licet,* for example, with its proper subjunctive for the most part (as in fol. 28, line 1; fol. 42, line 3; fol. 58, line 5; and fol. 76, line

---

[31]Locke's Latin "tract" on the powers of the civil magistrate is entitled *An Magistratus Civilis possit res adiaphoras in divini cultus ritus asciscere easque populo imponere*— with the required subjunctive.

[32]These corrections are recorded in the apparatus to our Latin text. Note fol. 64, n. 7; fol. 82, n. 9; fol. 92, n. 4; fol. 100, nn. 1 and 2; fol. 101, n. 5; and fol. 112, n. 1.

8), but in fol. 17, line 3, he wrote *licet ipsa sanior pars hominum . . . non . . . consentiunt,* offending against the mood and agreement of subject and verb; cf. fol. 34, line 1. He uses *quod* instead of *ut* and with the indicative in a clause of result in fol. 33, lines 7–10: *quomodo evenit . . . quod . . . tot sunt caeci? qui fit quod plurimi mortales hanc legem ignorant?;* cf. the usage of fol. 38, line 6, and fol. 87, line 15. He uses the indicative for an object clause introduced by *dubito quin* in fol. 28, line 3, *nec dubito, quin maxima hominum . . . pars . . . mores suos componunt* (and makes the error of agreement we have already noticed). When he uses a relative clause of characteristic, as he rarely does, he can mix the indicative with the subjunctive, as in fol. 61, lines 7–8: *nemoque repertus sit qui se negligit se ipsum abdicet.* He writes *quis* for *aliquis* with a verb in the indicative, fol. 96, line 9.

5. The Translation

None of this robust inelegance in Locke's orthography and predilection for the indicative is visible in translation. But the translation that faces Locke's Latin text illustrates a striking feature of Locke's Latinity—what can be called its "emergent" style. The style of the *Questions* resembles Locke's rapid hand as he penned MS A and reminds us of Lord Peter King's judgment of Locke as a writer (in the two senses of this word): "It appears from the character of the handwriting in Mr. Locke's original sketches, that after having well considered his subject, he was able at once, without the least hesitation, to draw upon his own ample resources, and striking out his work, as it were, at a heat, to write down his thoughts, *currente calamo,* without difficulty, hesitation or impediment."[33]

Locke could write as rapidly as he did because he knew exactly what he wanted to say, and what he wanted to say he had already said in Latin and in the dramatic form of oral presentation in his *disputationes* with his students at Christ Church. His Latin style is very much the style of oral delivery. At times he will begin a sentence, stray from its syntax as his thought develops into distinctions

---

[33]Lord Peter King, *The Life and Letters of John Locke, With Extracts from his Correspondence, Journals, and Common-place Books* (London, 1884), 1:vi–vii.

and qualifications, and then return abruptly to his train of thought by repeating the beginning of his sentence anaphorically. His treatment of the question of tradition in Question II[34] is a good example (fol. 26, lines 8–13). His thought can be reduced to the simple statement "We say that tradition is not the means by which the law of nature becomes known to us." But to the term "tradition" Locke appends a relative clause to distinguish tradition from sense experience, and he goes on to qualify this distinction by adding two parenthetical clauses that elaborate the relation between tradition and sense experience. At this point, he is forced to recover his syntax and sentence structure by returning to his opening words—"tradition, I say . . ."—a phrase that develops into still another parenthetical clause. Von Leyden pointed to the difficulties of the argument and syntax of folios 79–80.[35] I would point to the ramshackle structure of the sentence I translate from Question IV (on folios 48–49, "So long as reason and the senses serve one another," fol. 48, line 5 to fol. 49, line 3) and the anaphora of fol. 47, line 6, and fol. 69, line 7, as still other examples of the emergent style of Locke's oral presentations.

At times, however, I have respected the character of English and reduced a long periodic sentence of my original to two sentences. But when confronted with the significant syntactical elaborations of Locke's emergent style, I have chosen to be faithful rather than elegant. I have attempted a literal rather than literary translation of Locke's *Questions*. Where Locke writes in asyndeton, as he often does, I have followed him at the cost of a certain abruptness (as for example in fol. 61, line 7; fol. 77, line 2; and fol. 87, line 15); often his asyndeton involves a repetition of the same word three times (as in fol. 98, line 2; fol. 102, line 2; fol. 104, line 6; and fol. 109, lines 12 and 14). Where I have had to expand on his Latin, I have indicated my minor supplements to clarify his sense by enclosing them in square brackets.

My English is neither that of Locke's *Essays* or *Two Treatises*, although both these works have guided me in my translation, nor that of contemporary Anglo-American philosophy. I have faced a num-

---

[34]Cf. n. 31 to Question II.
[35]*John Locke: Essays*, ed. von Leyden, p. 177, n. 1.

ber of difficulties my reader should be aware of. Locke is careful to distinguish *jus* in its meaning of a right to the enjoyment of something and *jus* in its common meaning of law.[36] But at times he uses *jus* not as right but as law. I have given his terms in square brackets to clarify his usage and my translation when this seemed helpful to the reader. And reluctantly I have departed from von Leyden as well as Locke and his contemporaries in my translation of the key term *consensus* in Question VII. Locke and his contemporaries would have certainly chosen "consent" over "general agreement" or "consensus" to express the meaning of *consensus*.[37] But, since the word "consent" now suggests agreement to an order or proposition rather than an agreement in thinking about the same matters, I have chosen to translate the term as I do.

The notes to the translation have only three purposes, and they have been made easier by the painstaking research of Wolfgang von Leyden, to whom my debt in elaborating these notes is considerable and evident. I have tried to identify the sources of Locke's allusions and quotations and, since some of his sources are now inaccessible (in American libraries at least), I have tried to give a significant sample of the language Locke is responding to. His most significant allusions are unacknowledged, and this makes the task of his commentator the more difficult. When I have had the guidance of Locke's English in translating his Latin, I have recorded this in my notes; and at times I have recorded the difficulties I have faced as a reader of the *Questions* and as their translator.

[36]Cf. nn. 2 and 8 to Question I and n. 96 to Question XI.

[37]As he did in speaking of the argument for innate principles in the mind from "Universal Consent," see *Essay*, ed. Nidditch, I 2.3, p. 49.

Questions concerning the Law of Nature

THE LATIN TEXT
AND TRANSLATION

I An Detur Morum Regula sive Lex Naturae? Affirmatur.

II An Lex naturae sit lumine naturae Cognoscibilis? Affirmatur.

III An lex naturae per traditionem nobis innotescat? Negatur.

IV An Lex Naturae hominum animis inscribatur? Negatur.

V An Ratio per res a sensibus haustas pervenire potest in cognitionem legis naturae? Affirmatur.

VI An ex inclinatione hominum naturali potest cognosci lex Naturae? Negatur.

VII An lex naturae cognosci potest ex hominum consensu? Negatur.

VIII An Lex naturae homines obligat? Affirmatur.

[IX] An Lex naturae obliget bruta? Negatur.

[X] An obligatio legis naturae sit perpetua et Universalis? Affirmatur.

[XI] An privata cujusque utilitas sit fundamentum legis naturae? Negatur.

The Questions

I   Does there Exist a Rule of Conduct or Law of Nature? There does.

II   Is the Law of nature Knowable by the light of nature? It is.

III   Does the Law of nature become known to us by tradition? It does not.

IV   Is the Law of Nature inscribed in the minds of men? It is not.

V   Can Reason arrive at a knowledge of the law of nature through sense experience? It can.

VI   Can the law of Nature be known from the natural inclination of mankind? It cannot.

VII   Can the law of nature be known from the consensus of mankind? It cannot.

VIII   Is the Law of nature binding on men? It is.

[IX]   Is the Law of nature binding on brutes? It is not.

[X]   Is the obligation of the law of nature perpetual and Universal? It is.

[XI]   Does the private interest of each individual constitute the foundation of the law of nature? It does not.

I. An Detur Morum Regula sive
Lex Naturae? Affirmatur.[1]

Cum deus[2] se ubique praesentem nobis praestat, et se quasi oculis
hominum ingerit tam in constanti jam naturae tenore quam fre-
quenti olim miraculorum testimonio, neminem fore credo qui aut
ullam vitae nostrae habendam esse rationem, aut aliquid esse, quod
5 aut virtutis aut vitii mereatur nomen agnoscit, qui non deum[2] esse
secum statuerit, hoc igitur supposito, quod dubitare nefas esset,
scilicet numen aliquod mundo praesidere, cum caelum perpetua
rotatione volvi, terram stare, sydera lucere, jusserit, ipsi indomito
mari limites posuerit, omni plantarum generi et germinandi et cres-
10 cendi modos tempestatesque praescripserit, cum animantes omnes
illius voluntati morem gerentes suas habeant et nascendi et vivendi
leges, nec quicquam sit in tota hac rerum natura tam vagum, tam
incertum, quod[3] ratas fixasque non agnoscit operandi naturae suae

Sigla
MS A = Bodleian MS Locke e.6
MS B = Bodleian MS Locke f.31
MS C = Bodleian MS Locke f.30
vL = W. von Leyden, *Essays on the Law of Nature* (Oxford, 1954).

94

I. Does there Exist a Rule of Conduct or
Law of Nature? There does.

Since god shows himself everywhere present to us and, as it were, forces himself upon men's eyes, as much now in the constant course of nature as in the once frequent testimony of miracles, I believe there will be no one, who recognizes that either some rational account of our life is necessary or that there exists something deserving the name of either virtue or vice, who will not conclude for himself that god exists. Once it has been granted that some divine power presides over the world—something it would be impious to doubt, for he has commanded the heavens to turn in their perpetual revolution, the earth to abide in its place, the stars to shine, has fixed limits to the unruly sea itself,[1] has prescribed for every kind of plant the manner and season of its germination and growth; and all creatures in their obedience to his will have their own proper laws governing their birth and life; and there is nothing in all this world so unstable, so uncertain that it does not recognize authoritative and

Preliminary note: Where possible, when works cited are listed in John Harrison and Peter Laslett, *The Library of John Locke*, 2d ed. (Oxford: Clarendon Press, 1971), their entry number (LL) is also given. However, in some cases, they cannot have belonged to Locke's library at the time he drafted his *Questions concerning the Law of Nature*.

[1]Cf. Proverbs 8.29: "He gave to the seas his decree, that the waters should not pass his commandment"—a text often adduced by writers on the theory of natural law; Saint Thomas Aquinas, *Summa Theologiae* Ia2ae 93.5 and Francisco Suarez, *Tractatus de Legibus ac Deo Legislatore* (Antwerp, 1613) II. c. 3.37. Cf. Jeremiah 5:22 and Richard Hooker, *Of the Laws of Ecclesiastical Polity* (London, 1593, LL 1492 [1632]), I.3.sec.2; and Nathanael Culverwel, *An Elegant and Learned Discourse of the Light of Nature* (London, 1652), p. 46.

95

convenientes leges, merito quaerendum videtur, num solus homo
15 exlex

[1]Title in B's hand; numeral 1 in Locke's hand (?) follows title in B. [2]*Deus, Deum* B. Concerning the capitalization of *deus*, see the Introduction. [3]*quod* vL; *quae* B. (Perhaps Locke was thinking of *res* as an antecedent.)

(folio 10) sui omnino Juris, sine consilio, sine lege, sine aliqua vitae suae
norma in mundum prodierit, quod non facile credet quisquam qui
aut Deum Optimum Maximum[1] aut universum totius humani generis omni tempore et loco consensum, aut denique seipsum aut
5 conscientiam suam cogitaverit. sed priusquam ad legem ipsam et illa
quibus esse probatur deveniamus argumenta, operae pretium fac-
turus videar si varia illius nomina quibus insignitur indigitavero.

Primo igitur, hoc illud est bonum morale vel honestum, quod
tanto studio quaesiverunt, tantis laudibus prosecuti sunt olim Phi-
10 losophi, et inter eos praecipue Stoici, hoc unum illud Senecae[2]
bonum, quo contentum esse dicit debere hominem, cui inest tantus
splendor, tantus decor, ut illud[3] etiam agnoscat vitiis corrupta mortalium pars, et ipsum dum fugiunt probant.

2° Recta ratio vocatur quam quisquis se hominem putat, sibi

fixed laws which are suited to its own nature—once this has been granted it seems proper to ask if man alone has come into this world

(lio 10)   entirely outside some Jurisdiction, with no law proper to him,[2] without plan, without law, without a rule for his life—something he who has given thought either to god, best and greatest,[3] or to the universal agreement of the entire human race in every time and place or, finally, to himself or his own conscience, will not easily believe. But before we come to that law itself and those arguments by which its existence is demonstrated, it would seem worthwhile were I to set out the various names by which this law is signified.

First, then, it is that "moral good" or "virtue" [*honestum*] which Philosophers once sought with such zeal and which they strove after with such great glory—among them the Stoics especially. This is that "good" of Seneca, with which he says man ought to be content,[4] in which there is such splendor, such beauty, that even that part of mankind which is corrupted by vices recognizes and the very thing they approve even while shunning.[5]

Second, it is called "right reason,"[6] which whoever regards him-

---

[2]*Juris* in the sense of "jurisdiction," not *jus* in the narrower sense of "right," which Locke will define as the right to a free and unhindered use and enjoyment of a thing (cf. fol. 11 and n. 8, below).

[3]Here Locke is speaking of God in the terms reserved for Jupiter, *Optimus Maximus* (O.M.), in Roman religious language. For the pagan style of speaking of God as Jupiter O.M., see the Translator's Introduction, sec. 3.

[4]In his *De Vita Beata* 4.2; cf. 9.3–4 (LL 2612 and 2616).

[5]An allusion to the paradox articulated by Medea in Ovid *Metamorphoses* VII 20–21 (*video meliora proboque / deteriora sequor*, "A better course I see and approve of, a worse I follow"); Locke offers his commentary on it in *An Essay concerning Human Understanding*, ed. Peter Nidditch (Oxford: Clarendon Press, 1975), II 21.35 (p. 254).

[6]As it is termed by Hugo Grotius, *De Jure Belli ac Pacis* (Paris 1625, LL 1329ᵃ [1650]) I.1.sec.10.1, and by Hobbes in his *De Cive* I.15 (London, 1647), in *Opera Philosophica quae latine scripsit*, ed. William Molesworth (London 1839–1845; reprint, 1961), 2:169–70 and the note to p. 169, where Hobbes gives his own understanding of the term *dictamen rectae rationis*. It goes back to Cicero, *Republic* III 22.33, but Grotius could only cite it as it was transmitted in Lactantius, *Institutiones Divinae* VI.8.6–9. The text is: *Est quidem vera lex recta ratio, naturae congruens, diffusa in omnes, constans, sempiterna, quae vocet ad officium iubendo, vetando a fraude deterreat, quae tamen neque probos frustra iubet aut vetat, nec improbos iubendo aut vetando movet. huic lege nec obrogari*

15 vindicat, hoc illud est de quo tam acriter inter se digladiantur variae
hominum sectae, et quisque

[1]*Deum Optimum Maximum* B. Cf. fol. 87, n. 1. [2]*Senecae* B; *Seneca* vL. [3]*illud* vL; *illum* B.

(folio 11) opinioni suae praetendit. Per rationem autem hic non intelligendum puto illam intellectus facultatem qua[1] discursus format, et
argumenta deducit, sed certa quaedam practica principia e[2] quibus
emanant omnium virtutum fontes, et quicquid necessarium sit ad
5 mores bene[3] efformandos, quod ex his principiis recte deducitur id
jure dicitur rectae rationi conforme.
   Alii et plurimi vocant legem naturae qua appellatione hujusmodi
legem intelligunt, quam quisque eo solum lumine quod natura
nobis insitum est, detegere potest, cui etiam per omnia se morige-

self as human claims for himself; it is over this that the various sects of men contest so fiercely among themselves, and the guise in which everyone

ɪlio 11) presents his own opinion. By "reason," however, I do not think we should understand here that faculty of the intellect by which it articulates discourse and deduces arguments, but some definite practical principles from which flow the sources of all virtues and whatever might prove necessary to the proper formation of character. What is rightly deduced from these principles is properly said to conform to right reason.

Others, and these are the majority, speak of a "law" of nature, by which term they understand a law of this sort: a law which each individual can discover by that light alone which is implanted in us by nature; to which too he ⟨ought to⟩[7] show himself obedient in

---

fas est, neque derogari aliquid ex hac licet, nec tota abrogari potest, nec vero aut per senatum aut per populum solvi hac lege possumus, neque est quaerendus explanator aut interpres Sextus Aelius, nec erit alia lex Romae, alia Athenis, alia nunc alia posthac, sed et omnes gentes et omni tempore una lex et sempiterna et immutabilis continebit, unusque erit communis quasi magister et imperator omnium deus; ille legis huius inventor, disceptator, lator; cui qui non parebit, ipse se fugiet, ac naturam hominis aspernatus hoc ipso luat maximas poenas, etiamsi cetera supplicia quae putantur effugerit (Laelius: "In truth right reason is the true law. It is in accordance with nature, is infused in all men, and is unchangeable and eternal. By its commands this law can summon men to their duties; by its prohibitions it can restrain them from doing wrong. Its commands and prohibitions never fail to influence good men, but these are without effect upon the bad. To invalidate this law by human legislation is never sanctioned, nor is it possible to suspend any of its provisions, and to annul it entirely is impossible. Neither the senate nor the people can absolve us from our obligation to obey this law, and it requires no Sextus Aelius [Paetus Catus, the author of a treatise on the Twelve Tables] to expound and interpret it. It will not lay down one rule at Rome and another at Athens, nor will it be one rule today and another tomorrow. But there will be a single law, eternal and unchangeable, binding at all times upon all peoples. And god will be, as it were, one common master and ruler over all; he is the author of this law, its interpreter, and its sponsor. The man who does not obey it will abandon himself, and, in despising the nature of man, will by this very act suffer the severest of penalties, though he has escaped all the other consequences which men call 'punishment'"). After the translation of Cicero, *On the Commonwealth*, ed. G. H. Holland and S. B. Smith (Columbus, Ohio: The State University Press, 1929), pp. 216–17. Cf. *De Legibus*, I.6. 18.

[7]We have supplied *debet, quam* in the Latin text.

10 rum praestare ⟨debet, quam⟩⁴ officii sui rationem postulare sentit, et
hoc illud est, secundum naturam vivere quod toties inculcant Stoici.

Haec lex, his insignita appellationibus, a jure naturali distinguen-
da est, jus enim in eo positum est quod alicujus rei liberum habemus
usum, lex vero id est quod aliquid agendum jubet vel vetat.

15 Haec igitur lex naturae ita describi potest, quod sit ordinatio
voluntatis divinae lumine naturae cognoscibilis, quid cum natura
rationali conveniens, vel disconveniens sit,

---

¹*qua* B; *quae* vL. ²*e* Locke's correction for *in* B. ³*bene* vL.; *bena* B. ⁴*praestare* Locke's
correction for *praestat* B. We have supplied *debet, quam*, or possibly *quod*; cf. *praestare
debere sentiunt* B fol. 15; *cui nos nosmet morigeros praestare debere* B fol. 17. The sense
requires the addition of a relative pronoun.

(folio 12) indicans, eoque ipso jubens aut prohibens. minus recte enim mihi
videtur a nonnullis dici dictatum rationis, ratio enim legem hanc
naturae non tam condit dictatque, quam a superiore potestate san-
citam, et pectoribus nostris insitam[,] investigat detegitque, nec legis
5 illius author est sed Interpres,¹ nisi supremi legislatoris minuendo
dignitatem, velimus rationi illam legem acceptam referre, quam
solum quaerit, nec enim ratio cum facultas solum animi sit, et pars
nostri, nobis dare leges potest, ex his facile patet in ea omnia reperiri

everything, [and] which he perceives as demanding a rational account of his duty; and this is that famous precept "live according to
nature" which the Stoics urge upon us so insistently.

This law, denoted by these terms, should be distinguished from
natural right [*jus naturale*]; for right [*jus*] consists in the fact that we
have a free use of something, but law [*lex*] is that which either
commands or forbids some action.[8]

This law of nature can, therefore, be so described [as a law]
because it is the command of the divine will, knowable by the light of
nature, indicating what is and what is not consonant with a rational
nature,

lio 12) and by that very fact commanding or prohibiting. Less accurately, it
seems to me, some say it is a dictate of reason;[9] for reason does not so
much lay down and decree this law of nature as it discovers and
investigates a law which is ordained by a higher power and has been
implanted in our hearts. Nor is reason the maker of this law, but its
Interpreter—unless we are willing to diminish the dignity of the
supreme lawgiver and attribute to reason that received law which it
only investigates.[10] Nor can reason, since it is only a faculty of the
mind and a part of us, give us laws. From these considerations it is
readily apparent that all the conditions necessary to law are found in

[8]The background of this distinction between *lex* (law) and *jus* (right) is to be
discovered in Hobbes, *Leviathan* (London, 1651, LL 1465), pt. I, chap. XIV; cf. *De
Cive* I.7, *Opera latine*, ed. Molesworth, 2:163–64, and Samuel Pufendorf, *Elementa
Jurisprudentiae* (The Hague, 1660, LL 2404 [1660]), def. XIII, sec. 3.

[9]As did Grotius, *De Jure Belli ac Pacis*, I.1. sec. 10.1: *Ius naturale est dictamen rectae
rationis indicans actui alicui, ex ejus convenientia aut disconvenientia, inesse moralem turpitudinem aut necessitatem moralem, ac consequenter ab auctore naturae Deo talem actum aut
vetari aut praecipi* ("Natural law is a dictate of right reason, which indicates the
presence of either moral turpitude or moral necessity in a given act by reason of its
agreement or disagreement with our rational nature itself and which indicates, as a
consequence, that such an act is either forbidden or commanded by God, the author
of nature"). Hobbes, *De Cive* (see n. 6, above) articulates the practical principles
derived from the application of right reason in II.2–7.

[10]Cf. Cicero, *Republic* III 22.33 (cited in n. 6, above), who speaks of God as the
inventor, arbitrator, and legislator of the law of nature (*ille legis huius inventor,
disceptator, lator*).

quae ad legem requiruntur. Nam 1º declaratio est superioris volun-
10 tatis, in quo consistere videtur legis ratio formalis, quo autem modo
humano generi innotescat postea fortassis inquirendi locus erit. 2do
Quod legis est proprium; quid agendum sit vel omittendum praescribit. 3º homines obligat, omnia enim quae ad obligationem requiruntur in se continet, quamvis enim[2] eo modo quo leges positivae
15 non promulgatur, sufficienter tamen hominibus innotescit (quod
sufficit) cum possible sit solo lumine naturae, eam cognoscere.[3]

---

[1]*Interpres* Locke's correction for *scrutator* B. [2]*enim* Locke's correction for *nempe* B.
[3]*cognoscere* correction for *cognoscitur* B.

(folio 13)   His ita positis hujusmodi dari legem sequentia suadent argumenta.
I^{um} Arg[umentum] desumi potest[1] Ex Aristotelis testimonio ad
Nicom lib. 1. c. 7. ubi dicit quod ἔργον ἀνθρώπου ἐστὶ ψυχῆς ἐνέρ-
γεια κατὰ λόγον, cum enim prius variis instantiis probasset, esse,
5 cujusque rei proprium opus[,] quid sit illud etiam in homine quaesi-
vit, quod per rationem[2] omnium operationum facultatis et vege-
tantis et sentientis, quae hominibus cum brutis plantisque sunt com-
munes. tandem recte concludit officium hominis esse actionem
secundum rationem, adeo ut ea homini necessario agenda sunt quae
10 dictat ratio. Item lib 5º c. 7 Jus dividens in civile et naturale, τὸ δὲ[3]
νομικὸν φυσικόν inquit ἐστι τὸ πανταχοῦ τὴν αὐτὴν ἔχον δύναμιν,
unde recte colligitur, dari aliquam legem naturae cum sit aliqua lex
quae ubique obtinet,

this [law of nature]: For 1°, it is the declaration of a superior will, in which the formal definition of law seems to consist. But perhaps later there will be an occasion for inquiring into how it becomes known to the human race.[11] 2°, [It has] the property of law: it prescribes what is to be done and what is to be avoided. 3°, It is binding upon men, for it contains in itself all of the conditions requisite to obligation; [and] although, in fact, it is not promulgated in the manner of positive laws, it is, however, sufficiently known to men (and this meets what is required of law) since it is possible to know it by the light of reason alone.

)lio 13) Once these considerations have been laid down in this manner, the following arguments persuade that a law of this kind exists.

The first argument can be taken from the evidence of Aristotle at *Nicomachean Ethics* I c. 7[12] where he says that "the proper function of man is the activity of the soul according to reason"; for once he had proved by various examples that there is a proper function for each thing, he inquired what this proper function is in the case of man; this [he sought] through an account of all the operations of the faculties both vegetative and sentient, which are common to men along with animals and plants. He arrives finally at the proper conclusion that the function of man is activity according to reason; consequently man must necessarily perform those actions which are dictated by reason.[13] Likewise in Book V c. 7 in his division of law [*jus*] into civil and natural, he says that "this natural law is that law which has everywhere the same force,"[14] from which it is rightly

---

[11]That is, in Question II.

[12]1098a7, where Locke derives his definition from ἔργον ἀνθρώπου ψυχῆς ἐνέρ-γεια κατὰ λόγον, and is likely quoting from memory.

[13]*Nicomachean Ethics* I 7.1097b22–1098a20.

[14]1134b18. Neither of Locke's Greek texts of the *Ethics* (LL 120 [1632], 121 [1582]) contains Aristotle's distinction in this form. Aristotle distinguishes what is just politically into natural justice, on the one hand, and conventional justice, on the other, and characterizes natural justice as having everywhere the same force. Locke, evidently, read or remembered τὸ δὲ νομικὸν φυσικόν ἐστι τὸ πανταχοῦ τὴν αὐτὴν ἔχον δύναμιν instead of Τοῦ δὲ πολιτικοῦ δικαίου τὸ μὲν φυσικόν ἐστι τὸ δὲ νομικόν, φυσικὸν μὲν τὸ πανταχοῦ τὴν αὐτὴν ἔχον δύναμιν. Actually, Aristotle's division is not

15   ⟨cum[4] dantur aliqua morum principia quae agnoscit totum
genus humanum et unanimi consensu amplectuntur qui ubique sunt homines; quod fieri non poterat nisi esset a natura.
quamvis enim nonnulla sint de quibus inter se dissentirent[5]
homines, stabiles tamen fixique[6] apud omnes sunt

[1]*Ium* . . . *potest* added by Locke in margin of B. [2]*rationem* Locke's correction for
anotionem (?) B. [3]τὸ δὲ vL.; τόδε B. [4]The bracketed and inset passage was struck out by
Locke in B. [5]*dissentirent* Locke's correction for *dissentire videntur* B. [6]*plerumque* struck
out after *tamen*; *fixique* added by Locke in B.

(folio 14)   virtutum termini; quod si hae leges essent positivae, et ab hominibus prolibitu sancitae, sine aliqua praevia sui, aut notione aut

inferred that there exists some law of nature, since there exists some law, which obtains everywhere,[15]

⟨since there exist certain principles of conduct which the entire human race recognizes and which men everywhere embrace with unanimous agreement; which could not have come about unless it had its origin in nature. Even though there are, indeed, some [principles] concerning which men would disagree, yet the terms of the virtues are stable and fixed among all men.

(io 14)   But if these laws were positive, and established by men at their pleasure, without any prior notion of law itself or of obligation,

---

of law into civil and natural, but of political justice into natural and conventional. The text of Aristotle can be translated as follows: (1314b18–24): "There are two kinds of political [as distinguished from domestic] justice: the natural and the conventional. Natural justice has the same force everywhere and it does not depend upon its being agreed upon or not. Conventional justice is justice whose provisions are originally indifferent, but once these have been established they are important. For example, to set the ransom for a prisoner at a mina or to sacrifice a goat and not two sheep." The sequel is important for its formulation of the requirements for natural law—that it is everywhere one and the same (cf. fol. 30, line 7, *cum lex naturae ubique una eademque sit.*) "Some are of the opinion that all justice is of this nature [conventional], because what is natural is immutable and obtains in the same force everywhere, as fire burns here [in Greece] and in Persia. But they observe that what is thought to be just is mutable" (1134b24–28).

The confusion implicit in Locke's citation of Aristotle's Greek is clear. He treats the term *nomikon* as a substantive meaning "law" and not an adjective meaning "conventional." Thus he translates the term as *lex* (here and in fol. 13, line 12, and fol. 14, line 1). Saint Thomas had already assimilated Aristotle's clear-cut distinction between natural and conventional justice to the juristic distinction between natural and conventional law: *ius naturale* and *ius positivum: St. Thomae Aquinatis D. A. in X libros Ethicorum Aristotelis ad Nicomachum Expositio*, ed. P. Fr. Raymundi and M. Spiazzi, O. P. (Turin, 1964), p. 1016. And Averroes made precisely the same error or accommodation as does Locke in his commentary to the *Nicomachean Ethics: Iuris autem civilis, quiddam est naturale legale, et quiddam legale tantum.* See *Aristotelis Stagiritae libri Moralem totam Philosophiam complectentes, cum Averrois Cordubensis in Moralia Nicomachia Expositione* (Venice, 1574), p. 74.

[15]Fol. 13, line 15 to fol. 15, line 12 was corrected by Locke in B and then deleted. It is to be found as a note in *John Locke: Essays on the Law of Nature*, ed. W. von Leyden (Oxford: Clarendon Press, 1954), p. 282.

obligatione, non tam similes sui ubique essent, nec tam inter se consentirent, alia apud Indos alia apud Romanos esset virtus,

5   cum nihil sit in quo magis discrepant, in quo magis in diversum a se invicem abeunt homines, quam civitatum leges et morum positiva instituta. hoc inde etiam manifestum est, quod doctrina de virtutibus intra scientiae limites comprehendi possit, sic enim[1] *quae ex constituto veniunt a naturalibus recte separantur, nam*

10 *naturalia cum semper eadem sint, facile possint in artem colligi; illa autem quae ex instituto veniunt, cum et mutantur saepe et alibi alia sunt extra artem posita sunt,* ex quibus recte concluditur dari legem a natura. Neque enim vana res est et nullius prorsus momenti communis hominum consensus, qui aliunde deduci

15 non potest, nisi a communi aliquo omnibus hominibus principio, cujus fons sit ipsa natura. Nam *ubi multi diversis temporibus, et locis, idem pro certo affirmant, id ad causam universalem referri debet,* quae alia esse non potest quam dictamen ipsius rationis et communis natura, cum nihil aliud esse potest quod omnium

20 mentes iisdem principiis imbuere, et in eandem sententiam cogere

[1]*enim* Locke's correction for *nempe* B.

(folio 15)   potest, ex eo enim hominum inter se conspirantium universali consensu colligi potest non solum quid liceat homini agere, cum ea quae contra naturam sunt non videntur homines facturi, sed etiam quid oportet, cum plurimos non utilitate ducti, nec volup-

5   tatis alicujus suasu pellecti, id facere et faciendum praedicare

they would not so resemble one another everywhere, nor would they be in such close agreement with one another; virtue would be one thing among the people of India, something else among the Romans, since there is nothing in which men are more in discord, in which they scatter so far in different directions, than in the laws of cities and the positive regulations for conduct. From this it is clear that a doctrine of virtues could be included within the bounds of science. So indeed "those things which come from convention are rightly distinguished from things natural, for things natural, since they are always the same, could be easily brought together into a science. But those things which come from institutions, since they both often change and vary from place to place, lie outside of science."[16] From these premises it is rightly concluded that there exists a law which derives from nature. Nor, indeed, is the common agreement of men something empty and of no great moment. It can be deduced from no other source save some principle common to all men, whose source might be nature itself. For "when many men, in different times and different places affirm the same thing as certain, this ought to be referred back to a universal cause,"[17] which can be none other than a dictate of reason itself and our common nature, since nothing else is capable of instilling the same principles in the minds of all men, or of compelling them to the same judgment.

(lio 15)   Indeed, from this universal agreement of men, speaking with one voice, not only can it be inferred what man is allowed to do—since men do not seem bent on doing what is contrary to nature—but what they ought to do as well. We see most men, who are induced not by their private interest nor swayed by the urging of some pleasure, do this [what reason dictates] and

[16]A nearly verbatim, but unacknowledged, quotation from Grotius *De Jure Belli ac Pacis*, Prolegomena 30, p. xii; Locke has changed the mood of *separentur* and *mutentur* to the indicative, and the mood of *possunt* to the subjunctive *possint*.

[17]Again, a quotation from Grotius, *De Jure Belli ac Pacis*, Prolegomena 40, p. xiv; Locke has changed the mood of *debeat* to *debet*.

videmus.[1] cujus nulla alia reperiri potest causa, quam obsequium illud quod se legi naturae praestare debere sentiunt,
quod etiam factum omnes laudant, qua in re calculo suo hanc
esse legem comprobant, cum id laudant, quod dum non faciunt
10 ipsi, potius deridendum videretur: cum sine lege hac, aliis pro-
desse ita ut tibi noceas (quod in servanda fide saepe accidit) non
tam probi esset quam stulti.)

Obiicitur hic a nonnullis, contra legem naturae, scilicet nullam
15 omnino dari, quia nullibi reperitur, quod maxima pars hominum ita
vivit, quasi nulla omnino vitae esset ratio, nec ulla hujusmodi lex
quam[2] omnes agnoscunt, imo hac in re maxime dissentire videntur
homines, si enim esset lex naturae lumine rationis cognoscibilis, qui
fit, quod omnes homines quibus datur ratio eam non sciunt?
20 Respondemus 1⁰ quod uti in rebus civilibus non inde sequitur,
non esse aut promulgari legem, quia tabulam publice prostantem,
aut caeco legere impossibile

---

[1]*videmus* added by Locke in B. [2]Our correction for *quem* B.

(folio 16) sit, aut caecutienti difficile, quod aliis in rebus occupato non vacat,
aut otioso aut improbo non placet oculos ad tabulam attolere, et
inde officii sui rationem ediscere. Rationem omnibus dari a natura
concedo, et esse legem naturae ratione cognoscibilem dico, inde
5 tamen non necessario sequitur eam cuilibet esse notam, alii enim
lumine hoc non utuntur sed tenebras amant, nec se sibi ostendere
velint, sol autem ipse viam qua eundum est nulli monstrat nisi qui
aperit oculos et se itineri accingit, alii vitiis innutriti, vix inter honestum et turpe distinguunt, cum prava consuetudo diuturnitate[1] tem-
10 poris invalescens[2] peregrinos induxerit habitus, et mali mores prin-

declare that it should be done. No other cause can be discovered
for this than that obedience which men feel they ought to pay to
the law of nature—an obedience all praise, as well. In this, they
confirm the existence of this law by their own reckoning, since
to praise an action they do not perform themselves, would seem
more ridiculous [than praiseworthy]; without this law, to benefit others at the cost of harming yourself (which often happens
in keeping faith) would not be as much the act of an honorable
man as that of a fool.⟩

At this point, some object to the law of nature, claiming that no
such law exists at all, since it is discovered nowhere; for the greatest
part of mankind lives as if there were no guiding principle to life at
all, nor any law of the kind that all men recognize. Nay, in this men
seem to disagree most, for if there were, in fact, a law of nature,
knowable by the light of reason, how does it happen that all men
who are endowed with reason know it not?
We reply: 1°, as in the case of civic affairs, because a blind man
cannot read a notice displayed publicly, it does not follow that a law
does not exist or is not promulgated, nor because

[io 16) it is difficult for someone who has poor sight [to read it]; [nor]
because someone who is occupied with other matters does not have
the time, nor because it is not to the liking of the idle or vicious to lift
his eyes to the public notice and learn from it the statement of his
duty. I allow that reason is granted to all by nature, and I affirm that
there exists a law of nature, knowable by reason. But it does not
follow necessarily from this that it is known to each and all, for some
make no use of this light, but love the darkness and would not be
willing to reveal themselves to themselves. But the sun itself reveals
the way that must be taken to none but to him who opens his eyes
and girds himself for his journey. Some men who are nurtured in
vices scarcely distinguish between good and evil, since evil occupations, growing strong with the passage of time, have led them into
strange dispositions, and bad habits have corrupted their principles

cipia etiam corrupere; Aliis etiam vitio naturae acumen ingenii
hebetius est, quam ut sufficiat eruendis his naturae arcanis. Quotusquisque enim est qui in rebus quotidiani usus, aut scitu facilibus
rationis se permittit imperio? aut illius ductum sequitur, cum aut
15 affectuum impetu in transversum acti, aut per incuriam negligentes
aut consuetudine degeneres, non quid dictat ratio, sed quid suadet
voluptas, aut jubent pravi affectus proni sequuntur. quis pene est in
republica qui suae civitatis leges cognoscit promulgatas, publicis in
locis appensas, lectu et cognitu faciles et ubique oculis patentes?
20 quanto minus abditas et latentes naturae leges?

[1]*saepe* deleted after *diuturnitate* B. [2]*invalescens* vL.; *involescens* B.

(folio 17) Hac igitur in re, non major pars hominum sed sanior et perspicacior
consulenda est.
    2º Respondemus quod licet ipsa sanior pars hominum non pror-
sus inter se consentiunt quid sit lex[1] naturae, quae illius certa et
5 cognita decreta, non inde sequi nullam omnino dari naturae legem,
imo vero magis efficitur esse hujusmodi legem, cum omnes de lege
ipsa tam acriter contendunt; quemadmodum enim in civitate, male
concluditur nullas dari leges quia variae earum apud jurisperitos
interpretationes reperiuntur, sic etiam in Ethica, male sequitur nul-
10 lam dari legem naturae cum alibi hoc alibi illud pro lege naturae
habeatur[,] unde fortius astruitur legis existentia, cum de lege ipsa
omnes eandem tuentur sententiam, interpretando solum differunt,
cum omnes agnoscant natura dari turpe et honestum; sed altius
paulo hoc repetendum erit argumentum cum de modo cognoscendi
15 hanc legem erit agendum.
    2ᵐ Argumentum quo probatur dari legem naturae, desumi potest
ab hominum conscientiis: quod scilicet se judice nemo nocens absol-

as well.[18] Still others, because of a defect of nature, have a keenness of mind too weak to allow them to unearth these hidden secrets of nature. Indeed, how rare is the man who yields himself to the authority of reason in matters of daily life, or in things easily known, or follows reason's guidance? For men are often driven off their proper course by the onrush of their feelings or by their indifference and lack of concern or as they are corrupted by their habitual occupations, [and] follow passively not what reason dictates but what their low passions urge upon them. How rare is the man in a commonwealth who knows the laws of his city, which have been published, displayed in public places, easy to read and comprehend, and obvious to every eye? How much rarer is he who knows the hidden and unperceived laws of nature?

io 17) In this question, therefore, we must consult not the majority of mankind, but the sounder and more perceptive part.

2°, we reply that, even granted that this sounder part of mankind itself does not fully agree what the law of nature is, what its certain and known edicts are, it does not in truth follow from this that no law of nature exists at all. Nay, to the contrary, this strengthens [the conclusion] that a law of this kind exists, since concerning this very law all contend so fiercely. Indeed, just as in a state, it is wrong to conclude that there exist no laws since various interpretations of these laws are to be discovered among those expert in the law, so too in Ethics, it hardly follows that there exists no law of nature, since in one place one thing is considered to be a law of nature, in another, something else. Thus, the existence of the law is more firmly established, since concerning this law all hold the same opinion, and differ only in its interpretation; for all recognize that vice and virtue exist by nature. But we will return to this argument in some greater depth when we come to consider how this law is known.[19]

The second argument by which it is proven that a law of nature exists can be derived from men's consciences: that is, from the fact

[18]Cf. Cicero, *De Legibus* I 12.33.
[19]In Questions II and VII.

vitur. Judicium enim illud quod de se quisque fert testatur dari
legem naturae, si enim non detur lex naturae, cui nos nosmet[2]
20 morigeros praestare debere, dictat ratio, quomodo evenit quod
eorum conscientia, qui nullius alterius legis quibus aut diriguntur
aut obligantur

[1]*lex* vL.; *Lex* B. [2]*nosmet* added by Locke in B.

(folio 18) agnoscunt decreta, de sua quidem vita et moribus fert sententiam et
vel absolvit vel crimine alligat,[1] cum sine lege aliqua nulla fieri potest
sententia, quae lex non scripta est, sed innata.

3[m] deducitur[2] Argumentum, ab ipsa constitutione hujus mundi.
5 in quo reliqua omnia certam operationum suarum legem modum-
que naturae suae convenientem observant; id enim quod cuique rei
formam et modum et mensuram agendi praescribit id demum lex
est, id omne quod in rebus creatis[3] fit, materia est legis aeternae
inquit Aquinas, et τὴν πεπρωμένην μοίρην ἕκαστον ἐκπληροῖ καὶ
10 ἐπὶ τὸ μῆζον καὶ ἐπὶ τὸ μῆον dictante Hippocrate, unum quodque a
lege sibi praescripta ne latum quidem unguem discedit, quod cum
ita sit, non videtur, solum hominem legibus solutum esse, dum
reliqua tenentur, sed praescriptum habet suae naturae convenientem agendi modum, nec enim[4] primi opificis sapientiae con-
15 venire videtur perfectissimum formare animal et irrequietum,
mente intellectu, ratione et omnibus ad operandum necessariis
abunde prae reliquis instruere et tamen nullum ei opus destinare,
aut ideo solum legis capacem formare hominem ut nulli obtem-
peraret.

that "no one who is guilty wins acquittal when he himself is judge."[20] For that verdict which each pronounces upon himself is evidence that there exists a law of nature. For if the law of nature did not exist, to which reason dictates that we should show ourselves obedient, how does it come about that the conscience of those who recognize the commands of no other law, by which they are either directed or bound,

lio 18) passes judgment on their very life and conduct and either acquits or condemns them of crime? For without some law there can be no judgment; which law is not written, but innate.[21]

The third Argument is deduced from the very fabric of this world, in which all things [other than man] observe a fixed law of their operations and a measure suited to their own nature. For what prescribes to each thing the form and manner and measure of its activity proves to be a law:[22] "Everything which occurs in things created, is the matter of eternal law,"[23] Aquinas says, and as Hippocrates pronounces: "each thing in both small and in great fulfilleth the task which destiny hath set down,"[24] and each individual thing departs from the law set down for it not as much as a nail's breadth. Since this is the case, it does not seem that man alone is free of laws, while all other things are bound by them, but he has a prescribed mode of action which suits his nature. Nor, indeed, does it seem fitting to the wisdom of the first artificer to fashion a most perfect and ever active animal, to provide him abundantly in comparison with all other creatures, with mind, intelligence, reason, and all else necessary to his activity, and yet to assign him no [proper] function, or to fashion man alone with a capacity for law that he should obey none.

[20]From Juvenal, *Satires* XIII 2–3 (LL 1607 [1590]), quoted again in Question VIII, fol. 86.

[21]Cf. Romans 2: 14–15.

[22]The definition of Hooker, *Ecclesiastical Polity*, I 2. sec. 1.

[23]*Summa Theologiae* Ia2ae 93.4, as paraphrased by Hooker, *Ecclesiastical Polity*, I 3. sec. 1.

[24]Again, as taken from Hooker, *Ecclesiastical Polity*, I 3. sec. 1. I have adopted Hooker's translation of Hippocrates.

20   4ᵐ Argumentum, desumitur ab hominum societate, cum sine hac
lege hominibus inter ipsos nulla consuetudo, aut conjunctio esse
potest, duo enim sunt quibus niti videtur hominum societas

¹*alligat* vL; *alligit* B. ²*deducitur* added by Locke in B. ³*creatis* Locke's correction for
ornatis B. ⁴*enim* Locke's correction for *nempe* B.

(folio 19) certa scilicet reipublicae forma ac regiminis constitutio, et pacti
fides, quibus sublatis corruit omnis inter homines communitas, uti
sublata hac lege naturae, corruunt haec ipsa. Quae nempe civitatis
facies esse potest, quae reipublicae constitutio, aut rerum suarum
5 securitas, si¹ pars illa reipublicae quae maxime nocere valet,² omnia
pro libitu suo agere possit? si¹ in summa potestate maxima esset
licentia. Cum enim principes ⟨summa in Civitate Authoritas, sive
illi,⟩³ quos penes est leges pro libitu suo figere vel refigere et pro
imperio suo omnia agere aliorum domini, nec suis nec aliorum
10 positivis legibus astricti sint, aut esse possunt⁴ si alia superior non
esset lex naturae scilicet cui⁵ parere debent? quo tandem in loco
essent res humanae, quae societatis privilegiae, si ideo solum coirent
in civitatem mortales⁶ ut aliorum potestati fierent paratior praeda,
⟨si principes cum agerent, raperent, truderent, prosternerent oc-
15 ciderent subditos jure tantum suo uterentur.⟩⁷ nec melior sane principum quam subditorum esset conditio. Si nulla esset lex naturae
sine qua populus reipublicae legibus teneri non poterat, leges
nempe Civitatum positivae non per se et sua virtute, aut alio modo
obligant, quam vi legis naturae jubentis superioribus obtemperare⁸
20 pacemque publicam tueri, adeo ut sine

¹*si* Locke's correction for *ubi* B. ²*valet* Locke's correction for *praebet* B. ³*summa . . . illi,*
was struck out by Locke in B. ⁴*aut esse possunt* added by Locke in B. ⁵*cui* Locke's
correction for *quibus* B. ⁶*mortales* vL; *mortules* B. ⁷[*si . . . uterentur.*] was bracketed by
Locke in B. ⁸*obtemperare* vL; *obtemperari* (?) B.

(folio 20) hac lege, vi et armis principes forte ad obsequium plebem cogere
poterant[,] obligare vero non poterant. Alterum etiam humanae

The fourth Argument derives from human society, since without this law there can be no association or union of men among themselves. For there are two foundations on which human society seems to rest:

io 19) namely, the fixed form of a commonwealth and constitution of a regime, and [second] the keeping of covenants. These removed, all community among men collapses, just as, were the law of nature removed, these [foundations] collapse themselves. What, I ask, would be the face of a state, what the constitution of a common-wealth, or what the security of property, if that part of a common-wealth which has the greatest power to harm, could do anything at its own pleasure; if in supreme power there were the greatest [de-gree of] licence? Indeed, princes ⟨the supreme Authority in a State, or those⟩ in whose power it is to form or alter laws at their pleasure, and to do everything on behalf of their own rule, as lords over others, neither are nor can be constrained by their own positive laws or those of others, if there were not another law of nature superior to them, that is, [a law] they ought to obey. Where, I ask, would human affairs stand, what would the privileges of a society be, if mortals gathered together in a state only to become more readily prey to the power of others? ⟨if princes, when they acted, seized [the possessions of] their subjects by force, broke in upon them, threw them to the ground, murdered them, [and] relied only on their own [private] right.⟩ And the condition of princes would surely be no better than that of their subjects, if there were no law of nature, without which the people of a commonwealth could not be bound by laws. In truth, the positive laws of States do not bind of themselves and their own force, or in any other manner than by the force of the law of nature, which bids obedience to superiors, and keeping the public peace; and so, without this law

lio 20) princes could possibly compel the commoners to obedience by force and arms, but could not truly bind them. Without the law of nature

societatis fundamentum corruit sine lege naturae, scilicet rerum contractarum fides, non enim in pacto manere hominem expectan-
5 dum esset, quia promiserat, ubi alibi se commodior offerret conditio, nisi promissorum implendorum obligatio esset a natura, et non a voluntate humana.

5ᵐ Argumentum est, quod sine lege naturae nec virtus esset nec vitium, nec probitatis laus aut nequitiae poena, nulla culpa, nullus
10 reatus, ubi nulla lex. omnia ad voluntatem humanam referenda essent, et cum officium nihil postularet, non aliud agendum homini videtur, nisi quod suaderet aut utilitas aut voluptas, aut ni quod forte impingeret caecus et lege omni solutus impetus, recti et honesti interirent vana nomina, aut nihil omnino essent nisi nomen inane,
15 injurius esse non posset cum lex nulla aut juberet aut vetaret quicquam, homo suarum actionum liberimus et supremus arbiter. Intemperans vitae et valetudini suae minus forte consuluisse videatur, honestatem aut officium neglexisse minime. quamcunque nempe honestatem aut

(folio 21) turpitudinem habent virtutes et vitia[,] eam omnem legi huic naturae debent cum earum natura aeterna sit et certa, nec decretis hominum[1] publicis nec privata aliqua opinione aestimanda.

[1]*decretis hominum* Locke's correction in B.

the other foundation of human society collapses as well—that is, the keeping of contracts and agreements, for there would be no reason to expect a man to abide by an agreement, because he had made a promise, when a more advantageous arrangement offered itself elsewhere, unless the obligation to fulfill promises came from nature and not from the will of men.

The fifth Argument is that without the law of nature there would be no virtue or vice, no praise for probity or punishment for wickedness; where there is no law [there would be] no wrong, no guilt. Everything would have to be referred to the will of men, and, since duty would demand nothing, it seems that a man would have to do nothing except what either interest or pleasure urged upon him; or what some impulse, blind, and freed of all law, might happen to incite. The words "upright" and "decent" would perish as meaningless, or nothing would remain of them except an empty name. None could act against the law, since no law would make either commands or prohibitions. Man [would be] the supreme and absolutely free judge of his own actions. [In such a condition] the intemperate might possibly appear to have taken little thought for his life and health; [but] least of all [would he appear] to have neglected virtue and duty.[25] [But] in truth, whatever virtue

lio 21) or turpitude the virtues and vices possess they owe entire to this law of nature, since their nature is fixed and eternal, not something to be valued by the public decrees of men or some private opinion.

[25]Locke's meaning appears to be that in such a state "virtue" and "duty" would amount to no more than the most vigorous pursuit of one's own interest, pleasure, and fancies. And so the dissolute would seem to pay no more attention to these "virtues" than to one's own life and health. Locke uses a similar tactic, but without the advantage of quotation marks, in his discussion of the fate of the names of "justice" and "virtue" in the moral universe of Carneades, Question XI, fols. 105 and 110–112.

(folio 22)   ## II. An Lex naturae sit lumine naturae Cognoscibilis? Affirmatur.[1]

Cum turpis et honesti aliqua apud homines agnoscatur ratio, nec ulla gens sit tam barbara, tam ab omni humanitate remota, quae aliquam non habeat virtutis et vitii notitiam, laudis et vituperii conscientiam, proxime inquirendum videtur quibus modis innotescat
5 hominibus lex illa naturae cui unanimi adeo consensu praestant obsequium, nec illius omnem sensum exuere[2] possunt, nisi simul exuant humanitatem, amolienda enim prorsus natura est priusquam aliquis in omnimodam se asserere potest libertatem. modum autem, per quem in legis hujus cognitionem devenimus, dicimus
10 esse lumen naturae, ut opponitur aliis cognoscendi modis; dum autem lumen naturae hujus legis Indicem esse asserimus, non id ita accipi velimus, quasi aliqua esset homini interna lux

---

[1]Title and numeral in Locke's hand in B. [2]*exuere* vL; *execere* B.

(folio 23)   a natura insita, quae illum officii sui perpetuo admoneret, et quo illi eundum esset, recto tramite, et sine omni errore duceret: legem hanc naturae tabulis inscriptam in pectoribus nostris patere non dicimus, quae uti admota tabulae publice prostanti in tenebris face,
5 adventante aliqua luce interna, illius demum radiis, legitur, intelligitur et innotescit. sed per lumen naturae aliquid esse cognoscibile, nihil aliud velimus, quam hujusmodi aliqua veritas, in cujus cognitionem homo recte utens iis facultatibus quibus a natura instructus[1] est, per se, et sine ope alterius devenire potest.
10   Tres autem sunt modi cognoscendi quos sine scrupuloso nimis vocabulorum delectu, liceat mihi appellare, Inscriptionem, traditionem, et sensum,[2] quibus quartus addi potest, Revelatio scilicet[3] supernaturalis et divina, quae ad praesens non pertinet argumentum, dum inquirimus non quid homo divino spiritu afflatus scire,

---

[1]*instructus* vL; *instrustus* B. [2]*Inscriptionem, traditionem, et sensum* Locke's correction for *Inscriptio, traditio, et sensus* B. [3]*scilicet* added by Locke in B.

lio 22) ## II. Is the Law of nature Knowable by the
light of nature? It is.

Since some principle of virtue and vice is recognized among all men, and there is no race so barbarous, so removed from all humanity, that it does not have some notion of virtue and vice, some consciousness of praise or censure, it seems that we must next inquire by what means that law of nature, to which men offer obedience with such unanimous consent, is known to them. Nor can they put off all sense of that law, unless at the same time they cast off all humanity. Nature, indeed, will have to be abolished before someone can arrogate to himself every manner of liberty. The means, however, by which we arrive at a knowledge of this law is, we say, the light of nature, as opposed to the other means of knowing. But when we state that the light of nature is a Witness to this law, we would not want this to be understood as some kind of light internal to man,

lio 23) implanted by nature, which would perpetually urge his duty upon him, which would lead him to the path he ought to take, by the straight way, without any straying. We do not say that this law of nature stands inscribed on tablets in our breasts, which, at the approach of some inner light, is at last read by its rays, understood, and known, as when a torch is brought to a public notice board which stands in the darkness. But, when we say that something is known by the light of nature, we would signify nothing but the kind of truth whose knowledge man can, by the right use of those faculties with which he is provided by nature, attain by himself and without the help of another.

Now there are three means of knowledge which, without excessive scrupulousness in my choice of terms, I might call: Inscription, tradition, and sense; to these supernatural and divine Revelation can be added as a fourth. This does not concern our present argument, since we are inquiring, not into what man has the power to know when filled by the divine spirit,

(folio 24) quid lumine e caelis delapso illuminatus conspicere valet, sed quid
naturae vi, et sua ipsius sagacitate eruere et investigare potest homo
mente, ratione, et sensu instructus, quae omnis cognitio, quantacun-
que est, quae certe magnos fecerit progressus, quae totam per-
5 vadens rerum naturam, nec inter limites mundi circumscripta, caelum ipsum contemplatione ingreditur, et spiritus mentesque quid
sint, quid agant, quibus legibus tenentur accuratius inquisivit, haec
inquam tota cognitio uno[1] e tribus illis sciendi modis ad animum
pertingit, nec alia praeter haec dantur principia et fundamenta
10 cognoscendi; quicquid enim scimus, id omne vel beneficio naturae,
et quodam nascendi privilegio pectoribus nostris inscriptum est, vel
fando auditum, vel sensibus haustum.

(folio 23ᵛ)   Sed[2] cum de modis cognoscendi agere proposuerim, miretur hic
fortasse aliquis, cur rationem, magnum illud, et uti videtur praeci-
15 puum omnis cognitionis lumen omiserim. praesertim cum lex naturae, a plerisque vocetur ipsa ratio recta, et dictatum rectae rationis.
dicimus autem, nos hic inquirere de primis principiis et primordiis
omnis scientiae, quomodo primae notiones, et cognitionis fundamenta in animum illabuntur[,] illa autem a

[1] *uno*; our correction for *una* in B. [2] *Sed cum . . . jam investigamus* added by Locke on
verso of fol. 23 in B.

(folio 23ᵛ   ratione non accipi asserimus: vel enim per inscriptionem[3] impri-
cont.)   muntur animis nostris, vel traditione accipimus vel per sensus in-
trant, nihil enim agit ratio, magna illa argumentandi facultas, nisi
aliquo prius posito et concesso, utitur fateor hisce scientiae prin-
5 cipiis, ad majora et altiora eruenda sed ea minime ponit; non jacit
fundamentum etsi augustissimam saepenumero erigat structuram,
et ad caelum usque attollat scientiarum apices. aeque enim facile
poterit quisquam sine praemissis conclusionem inferre, ac sine aliqua prius cognita et concessa veritate, ratiocinari. ipsam autem[4]
10 originem cognitionis jam investigamus[.]

io 24) [or] what he has the power to behold, illuminated by a light come down from the heavens, but what, by the power of nature and his own sagacity, man, equipped with mind, reason, and sense, can unearth and investigate. All this knowledge,[26] however great its extent, has certainly made great progress. Penetrating the entire nature of things and not circumscribed within the limits of [this] world, it enters heaven itself in its contemplation and has with fair accuracy inquired of spirits and minds, their nature, their actions, by what laws they are bound. All this knowledge, I say, reaches the mind by one of these three modes of knowing. Nor are there other principles and foundations of knowing except these. For, all of what we know is either inscribed in our hearts by a benefaction of nature and some birth right, or by hearsay, or it is derived from our senses.

l. 23ᵛ)   But, since I have proposed to treat the means of knowing, some-one might wonder why I have omitted reason, that great, and, as it seems, principal light of all knowledge; especially since many call the law of nature right reason itself[27] and the dictate of right reason. Yet, we say that here our inquiry is into the first principle and the beginnings of all knowledge; how our first notions and the founda-tions of our knowledge gradually enter our mind. These, however, we assert are not known by reason, for either they are impressed on our minds by inscription, or we receive them through tradition, or they enter through the senses. For reason, that great faculty of argumentation, does nothing unless something has been established and agreed to beforehand. I confess that it does make use of these principles of knowledge in unearthing greater and deeper truths, but it is hardly the case that reason establishes them. Reason does not lay down a foundation, even though oftentimes it erects a su-perb structure, and raises as far as heaven the summits of the sciences. As easily will a man be able to arrive at a conclusion without premises as to be able to reason without truths first being known and agreed to. At present, however, we are investigating the very origin of knowledge.

---

[26]That is, knowledge deriving not from divine revelation, but from "inscription," tradition, and sense experience.

[27]As did Cicero, in a passage much evoked in the discussions of natural law, for which see nn. 6 and 9, above.

(folio 24   1º Inscriptionem quod attinet,⁵ quidam sunt, qui existimant, hanc
resumes)   legem naturae nobis innatam esse, et omnium animis ita a natura
infixam, ut

³*inscriptionem* vL; *inscripsionem* B. ⁴*autem* vL; *aut* B. ⁵*attinet* vL; *attinent* B.

(folio 25)   nemo sit, qui in mundum prodit, cujus mens nativos hosce officii sui
characteres et indices sibi insculptos non gerat, cujus animus practica haec principia, et vivendi regulas sibi connatas, notasque non
habeat, nec aliunde quaerere necesse sit, extraneas et mutuatitias
5   morum leges, cum homo suas intus semperque patentes habeat
pandectas, quae omne illius complectuntur officium. haec fateor
facilis est, et percommoda cognoscendi methodus, et optime cum
humano genere actum esset, si ita edocti essent homines, ita a natura
instructi, ita nati, ut quid deceret, quid minus, dubitare non possint.
10   hoc si concedatur stat certe theseos nostrae veritas: legem scilicet
naturae lumine naturae esse cognoscibilem. An vero aliqua hujusmodi detur¹ legis naturae in pectoribus nostris inscriptio, an hoc
modo humano generi innotescat, alibi fortassis inquirendi erit locus,
ad praesentem quod spectat quaestionem sufficiet probasse:

¹*detur* added by Locke in B.

lio 24   1°, in what concerns "Inscription," there are some who judge that
umes) this law of nature has been born in us and so graven in the minds of
all men that

io 25) there is no one who comes into the world whose mind does not carry
these very characters and marks of his own duty graven within
him,[28] whose mind does not have these principles of action and
rules for living born with it and known to it; nor is it necessary to
seek in any other source the external and derivative laws of morals,
since man has his own pandects[29] within, which always lie open
before him; which embrace all of his duty. This, I confess, is an easy
and very agreeable method of knowing, and it would be a perfect
arrangement for the human race if men were so taught—so instructed by nature, so born that they would not doubt as to what was
more fitting, what less than fitting. If this is conceded, the truth of
our thesis stands firm, which is, that the law of nature is knowable by
the light of nature. Whether in truth there exists in our hearts some
such inscription of a law of nature, whether it becomes known to the
human race in this manner, there will possibly be another place for
inquiring.[30] For the question at hand it will be sufficient to have
proved

---

[28]*characteres et indices sibi insculptos*. The metaphorical power of this notion of
"inscription" is well illustrated by Culverwel in his *Discourse*; he applies it first to
nature itself: "As for Nature, though it not be far from any of us; though it be so
intimate to our very beings; though it be *printed* and *ingraved* upon our essence; and
not upon ours only, but on the whole of Creation; and though we put all the *letters* and
Characters of it together as well as we can, yet we shall find it hard enough, to spell it
out, and read what it is" (p. 14); cf. pp. 42, 48, 62, and 54, where he considers the
extent of the law of nature: "There are *stampt and printed* upon the being of man, some
cleare and undelible Principles; some first and *Alphabetical* notions; by putting together of which it can *spell out* the Law of Nature" (emphasis added). Locke responds
to the metaphor of innate ideas "graven" in the mind in the *Essay*, ed. Nidditch, I 4.2,
p. 98.

[29]That is, in Roman jurisprudence, the title given the Justinian code of laws and, in
Locke's intellectual context, the metaphor Culverwel chose to describe the quasi-legal
"inscriptions" of the law of nature; *Discourse*, p. 99.

[30]In Question IV.

(folio 26) posse hominem si recte utatur ratione[1] sua, et nativis facultatibus,
quibus a natura instructus est, devenire in hujus legis cognitionem
sine praeceptore aliquo qui erudiret; sine monitore qui doceret
officium, si autem legem hanc alio modo cognosci praeterquam
5 traditione probaverimus, constabit illam lumine naturae, et interno
principio cognosci, cum quicquid sciat homo, id omne vel ab aliis vel
a se discat necesse est.

2[do] Itaque dicimus Traditionem, quam ideo a sensu distinguimus
non quod traditiones per sensum ad animum non ingrediuntur,
10 fando enim audimus, sed quod auribus[2] tantum sonum accipimus,
fide rem amplectimur; ut dum Ciceroni de Caesare loquenti[3] fidem
habemus, nos credimus fuisse Caesarem, quem cognovit Cicero
fuisse. Traditionem, inquam, dicimus non esse cognoscendi modum, quo ad nos pervenit lex naturae, non quod negamus aliqua,
15 etiam pene omnia illius praecepta nobis

---

[1]*ratione* Locke's correction for *vita* B. [2]*solum* crossed out after *auribus* B. [3]*loquenti*
inserted by Locke in B.

(folio 27) tradi a parentibus, praeceptoribus et illis omnibus qui juventutis
mores efformare, et teneros adhuc animos virtutis amore et cognitione imbuere satagunt, ne enim[1] animi in voluptatem nimium
proclives, vel corporis illecebris capti, vel[2] malis, quae ubique occur-
5 runt, exemplis seducti, saniora rationis dictata negligant, maxime
cavendum putant omnes, qui de erudiendis juvenum animis[3] quicquam cogitant, adeoque in prima adhuc aetatula, virtutum fundamenta jaciunt et omni opera, numinis reverentiam et amorem; erga
superiores obsequium, promissorum implendorum fidem, veracita-
10 tem, clementiam, liberalitatem, morum castitatem, reliquasque inculcant virtutes, quae omnes cum praecepta sint legis naturae, non

lio 26) that man, should he make right use of his reason and the native faculties with which he is provided by nature, can arrive at a knowledge of this law without a teacher to instruct him; without a tutor to teach him his duty. But, if we shall prove that this law is known by a means other than tradition, it will be established that it is known by the light of nature and by an inner principle, since it is necessary that whatever man knows, he learns entirely either from others or from himself.

2o[31], and thus we say that Tradition, which we distinguish from sense experience—not because traditions do not enter the mind through the senses—for we *hear* reports—but because our ears receive the mere sound, [and] we embrace the thing [reported] on faith; as, in the case of our faith in Cicero when he speaks of Caesar, we believe that Caesar lived, whom Cicero knew to have lived,— tradition, I say, is not the means of knowing by which the law of nature reaches us—not that we deny that some, and even nearly all, of the precepts of this law are handed down to

lio 27) us by our parents, teachers, and by all those who busy themselves in forming the character of the young and filling their still tender minds with the love and knowledge of virtue. For they think they should take the greatest care to prevent their minds, overly inclined to pleasure, or ensnared by the allurements of the body, or seduced by the evil examples which present themselves everywhere, from neglecting the sounder dictates of reason. All who have given any thought to educating the minds of the young, especially while in the earliest period of life, lay down as the foundations of their virtues, and with the greatest care, reverence and love for the divinity, and instill in them obedience towards their superiors, faith in keeping promises, truthfulness, clemency, liberality, purity of morals, and the other virtues. We do not deny that all of these, since they are

[31]Neither in Latin nor in English is this a coherent sentence. It would seem to be symptomatic of the origin of these questions in the oral debates between Locke and his students at Christ Church in 1664 (for which see the Translator's Introduction). The syntax of "And thus we say that Tradition" becomes clear only after the anaphoric "Tradition, I say, is not the means. . . ."

negamus, posse nobis ab aliis tradi, sed id solum asserimus, scilicet traditionem non esse primarium[4] et certum modum cognoscendi legem naturae; quae enim ab aliis fando audimus—si ideo solum

[1]*enim* Locke's correction for *autem* B. [2]*vel* Locke's correction for *aut* B. [3]*animis* Locke's correction for *moribus* B. [4]The scribe of B mistakenly started a new paragraph at *primarium*; Locke corrected the error.

(folio 28) amplectimur, quia alii honesta esse dictitarunt, haec, licet fortasse mores nostros recte satis dirigant, et intra officii nostri cancellos contineant, nobis tamen hominum dictata sunt, non rationis: nec dubito, quin maxima hominum pars mutuatitiis hisce morum regu-
5 lis quas a traditione accipiunt contenti, ad exemplum et opinionem eorum hominum inter quos nasci et educari contigit, mores suos componunt, nec aliam habent recti et honesti regulam[1] quam civitatis suae consuetudines, et communem hominum, quibuscum versantur, sententiam; ideoque legem naturae ab ipsis fontibus hau-
10 rire, et officii sui ratio, quibus nitatur principiis, quomodo obligat, unde primo promanat, investigare minime laborant opinione et laude, non naturae lege ducti. Legem autem naturae prout lex est, nobis traditione non innotescere sequentia probare videntur argumenta
15 1° quia in tanta traditionum inter

[1]*regulam* added by Locke in B.

(folio 29) se pugnantium varietate impossibile esset statuere, quid sit lex naturae, difficile admodum judicare quid verum quid falsum, quid sit lex, quid opinio, quid dictet[1] natura, quid utilitas, quid suadeat ratio, quid doceat politia. Quum[2] enim tam variae sint ubique traditiones,
5 tam contrariae plane et inter se pugnantes hominum sententiae, non solum in diversis nationibus, sed eadem civitate; unaquaeque

precepts of the law of nature, can be handed down to us by others; our only claim is that tradition is not a primary and certain means of knowing the law of nature. If we embrace what we hear from others only on word of mouth, simply because

lio 28) others have pronounced these things virtuous, possibly they can be allowed to direct our morals with sufficient rectitude and to keep us within the bars of our duty; in our opinion, however, they are the dictates of men, not of reason. Nor have I any doubt that the greater part of mankind, since they are content with these borrowed[32] rules of conduct which they receive from tradition, pattern their own conduct on the example and opinion of those men among whom they happen to be born and educated, and have no other rule for right and virtue than the customs of their state and the common opinion of the men among whom they dwell. And for this reason, since they are led by opinion and reputation, not by the law of nature, they do not stir themselves to draw the law of nature up from its very sources; or to investigate the basis of their duty, on what principles it rests, how it binds, from what sources it first flows. Yet the following arguments seem to prove that the law of nature, insofar as it is a law, does not become known to us by tradition:

1°, That in such a great variety of traditions,

lio 29) warring among themselves, it would be impossible to establish what the law of nature is, difficult even to judge what is true, what false; what is law, what opinion; what nature commands, what interest, what reason persuades us of, what civil society teaches. Since, indeed, traditions everywhere are so varied, men's opinions so manifestly contradictory and in conflict with one another, not only in different nations, but within the same state; [and since] every opin-

[32]*matuatitiis hisce morum regulis.* "Borrowed" is a key term in this discussion. Its fundamental meaning is extended to "inherited" and "acquired" or "external"; cf. the discussion which follows, fol. 30.

enim opinio quam ab aliis discimus traditio est, cum denique pro sua
quisque sententia tam acriter contendat, et sibi credi postulat, impossibile plane esset si traditio solum officii nostri dictaret rationem,
10   quaenam illa sit, cognoscere, vel in tanta varietate verum eligere,
cum nulla assignari potest ratio, cur huic homini, potius quam alteri
contrarium plane asserenti, major[3] traditionis deferenda sit authoritas, aut pronior[4] adhibenda fides, nisi ratio in ipsis rebus, quae
traduntur, aliquam reperiat differentiam

[1]*dictet* vL; *dictat* B. [2]Locke again corrected the copyist's error in beginning a new
paragraph at *Quum.* [3]*major* B; *majorum* vL. [4]*pronior* Locke's correction for *plenior* B.

(folio 30)   et ideo alteram amplectitur, alteram reiicit opinionem, quod in hac
minor in illa major sit evidentia, lumine naturae cognoscibilis; quod
sane non est traditioni credere, sed de rebus ipsis judicare, quod
tollit omnem traditionis authoritatem, aut igitur in cognoscenda
5   lege naturae traditione promulgata, adhibenda est ratio et judicium;
et tunc cessat omnis traditio, aut lex naturae per traditionem innotescere non potest, aut nulla erit. Cum enim lex naturae ubique

ion we learn from others is "tradition," [and], finally, since each contends so fiercely for his own opinion and demands that he be believed, it would be impossible to know what that "tradition"[33] is or to choose the truth in such a great variety, were tradition alone to dictate the principle of our duty, since no reason can be discovered why the preponderant authority of tradition should be granted or a more submissive belief given to [the claims of] one man rather than to another who claims the dead contrary, unless reason can discover some way of distinguishing between traditions themselves

olio 30) and, therefore, embrace the one opinion and reject the other on the grounds that there is less evidence in the one, more in the other—evidence which can be known by the light of nature. This, indeed, is not to trust tradition but to judge of things themselves, which does away with all the authority of tradition. Therefore, either reason or judgment must be applied in coming to know the law of nature as it is promulgated by tradition, and then all tradition loses its authority, or the law of nature cannot become known through tradition; or there will [prove to] be no law of nature. But, since the law of nature is everywhere one and the same, while traditions vary, it is necessary

[33]*Traditio* is literally a "handing down." Five years before Locke elaborated these questions, he entered into a notebook on ethical topics (*Lemmata Ethica*, Bodl. Locke MS d.10, 1659) his reflections on *Traditio* (p. 163): "*Traditio.* The Jews, the Romanists and the Turks, who all three pretend to guide themselves by a law revealed from heaven which shews them the way to happinesse, doe yet all of them have recourse very frequently to tradition as a rule of no lesse authority then their written law. Whereby they seem to allow, that divine law (however god be willing to reveale it), is not capable to be conveyed by writtings to mankinde distant in place time language and customs. And soe through the defect of language, noe positive law of righteousnesse can be that way conveyed, sufficiently and with exactnesse to all the inhabitants of the earth in remote generations, and so must resolve all into natural religion, and that light which every man has borne with him. Or els they give occasion to enquireing men to suspect the integrity of their princes and teachers, who unwilling that the people should have a standing rule of faith and manners, have for the maintenance of their own authority foisted in another of tradition, which will always be in their own power to be varied and suited to their own interests and occasions." A modernized transcript of this entry is printed by Lord Peter King in *The Life and Letters of John Locke, With Extracts from his Correspondence, Journals, and Common-place Books* (London, 1884; reprinted New York and London: Garland, 1984), pp. 296–97.

una eademque sit, traditiones autem variae, necesse sit, ut nulla
omnino sit lex naturae, aut hoc modo non cognoscibilis.

10   2do Si a traditione discenda esset lex naturae, fides hoc potius esset
quam cognitio, cum penderet potius ex authoritate loquentis, quam
ipsius rei evidentia, et ita demum mutuatitia potius esset, quam
innata lex.

3° Qui legem naturae traditione cognosci dicunt sibimet ipsis
15   contradicere videntur, qui enim retro oculos convertere velit, et ad
originem ipsam traditionem persequi, necesse sit, ut alicubi

(folio 31) gradum sistat, et aliquem tandem agnoscat primum hujus traditionis authorem, qui legem hanc, aut intus in pectore inscriptam
invenerit, vel ad ejus cognitionem, a rebus sensu haustis argumentando pervenerit. hi autem cognoscendi modi reliquis etiam homi-
5   nibus aeque competunt, nec opus est traditione, ubi quisque in se
eadem habeat cognoscendi principia, quod si author ille primus
hujus traditionis oraculo aliquo edoctus, spiritu divino afflatus mundo promulgaverit, haec lex ita promulgata, nequaquam lex naturae
est, sed positiva.

10   Concludimus[1] igitur, si qua sit lex naturae, quod nemo negaverit,
ea quatenus lex sit, traditione cognosci non potest.

3us[2] Et ultimus qui remanet[3] cognoscendi modus, sensus est, quod
principium constituimus hujus legis cognoscendae, quod tamen sic
accipi non debet,

---

[1]Numeral "3" crossed out before *Concludimus* in B. [2]*3us* added by Locke in the
margin of B. [3]*remanet* Locke's correction for *manet* B.

(folio 32) quasi ita alicubi prostaret lex naturae, ut vel oculis legere, vel mani-
bus explorare, vel sese promulgantem audire possimus, sed cum
jam de principio et origine hujus legis cognoscendae quaerimus, et
quo modo humano generi innotescat, dico fundamentum omnis

that there exists no law of nature whatsoever or that it is not know-able by this means.

2°, If the law of nature could be learned from tradition, this would be a matter of faith rather than knowledge, since it would depend more on the authority of the speaker than the evidence of the thing itself, and thus, in the end, it would be a derivative rather than an innate law.

3°, Those who say that the law of nature is known from tradition seem to contradict themselves. Whoever is willing to turn his eyes backward and to trace tradition back to its very source, would have to come to a halt somewhere

olio 31) and finally recognize some first author of this tradition, who will either have discovered this law inscribed in his heart or reached a knowledge of it by arguing from the evidence derived from his sense experience. Yet these means of knowledge are equally available to the rest of mankind, nor is there any need for tradition when each man would have in himself the same principles of knowledge. But if that first author of this tradition will have made it known to the world, instructed by some oracle, [and] inspired by the spirit of god, this law, so promulgated, is by no means a law of nature, but a positive law.

We conclude, therefore, that if there should exist a law of nature, something no one will deny, insofar as it is a law it cannot be known by tradition.

The third and remaining means to knowledge is sense, which we have established as the basis for knowing this law. This should not, however, be interpreted to mean

olio 32) that the law of nature manifests itself somewhere so palpably that we could either read it with our eyes, or explore it with our hands, or hear it proclaiming itself [to mankind]. But since we are now inquir-ing into the principle and the origin of the knowledge of this law and the way it becomes known to the human race, I say that the founda-

5 illius cognitionis hauriri, ab iis rebus quas sensibus nostris per-
cipimus, e quibus ratio et argumentandi facultas, quae homini propria est, ad earum opificem progrediens, argumentis a materia,
motu, et visibili hujus mundi structura et oeconomia necessario
emergentibus, tandem concludit, et apud se pro certo statuit, deum
10 esse aliquem harum rerum omnium authorem. quo posito, necessario sequitur universa lex naturae qua tenetur Gens humana, uti in
posterum patebit, ex dictis autem satis constat legem naturae esse
lumine naturae cognoscibilem; cum quicquid apud homines vim
legis

(folio 33) obtineat, necesse est ut[1] aut deum[2] aut naturam aut hominem agnoscat authorem, quicquid autem aut homo jusserit aut deus[3] oraculo mandaverit, id omne lex positiva est, lex autem naturae cum
traditione cognosci non potest, remanet ut solo lumine naturae
5 hominibus innotescat[.]

Contra hanc nostram sententiam, haec facile occurrit objectio,
scilicet si lex naturae lumine naturae cognoscatur, quomodo evenit
cum interna haec lex omnibus a natura insita sit, quod ubi omnes
illuminati sunt, tot sunt caeci? qui fit quod plurimi mortales hanc
10 legem ignorant, et omnes pene de ea diversa sentiunt, quod fieri
non posse videtur, si omnes lumine naturae ad illius cognitionem
ducerentur.

Haec objectio aliquam in se vim haberet, si diceremus legem
naturae pectoribus nostris inscribi, hoc enim supposito, necessario
15 sequeretur, eandem ubique de lege hac esse sententiam, cum lex
haec eadem in omnibus inscriberetur, et intellectui pateret.

[1]*est ut* inserted by Locke in B. [2]*Deum* B. [3]*Deus* B.

tion of all our knowledge of it is derived from those things we perceive by our senses. Beginning from these, our reason, or faculty for making arguments, which is proper to man, proceeds to the creator of these things by arguments necessarily springing from the matter, motion, and visible frame of this world, and its economy, and, finally, concludes and establishes for itself as a certainty that there is some god who is the author of all these things. This established, there necessarily follows a universal law of nature by which the human Race is bound, as will appear in what follows.[34] Yet, it is clear enough from what has been said that the law of nature is knowable from the light of nature, since whatever possesses the force of law among men,

lio 33) necessarily recognizes as its source either god or nature or man. Yet whatever man has laid down as a command, or god has delivered by an oracle, is positive law. Yet, since the law of nature cannot be known by tradition, the remaining possibility is that it can become known to men by the light of nature alone.

Against this opinion of ours, this objection easily presents itself: if the law of nature were known by the light of nature, how does it come about that, although this inner law is implanted in all by nature, when all are illuminated by it, so many are blind? Why does it come about that most mortals have no knowledge of this law, and nearly all have different opinions concerning it? This could not happen, it seems, if all were led to the knowledge of this law by the light of nature.

This objection would have a certain inherent force of itself, were we asserting that the law of nature is inscribed in our hearts. On this assumption, it would necessarily follow that there would be everywhere the same opinion concerning this law, since this law itself would be inscribed in the hearts of all and would be obvious to the understanding.

[34]In Questions V and VIII.

(folio 34)   Respondemus autem quod licet facultates nostrae intellectivae, nos in hujus legis cognitionem deducere possunt, non tamen inde sequi, omnes homines iis facultatibus necessario recte uti. figurarum numerorumque, natura et proprietates obviae videntur, et lumine
5   naturae sine dubio cognoscibiles, non tamen inde sequitur, quod[1] quicunque mente compos sit, Geometres evadat, aut artem Arithmeticam penitus calleat, attenta animi meditatione, cogitatione, et cura opus est, ut quis a rebus sensibilibus obviisque argumentando et ratiocinando in reconditam earum[2] naturam penetrare[3] possit.
10   latent in terrae visceribus auri et argenti ditiores venae, dantur etiam hominibus quibus effodi possunt brachia et manus, et machinarum inventrix ratio, non tamen inde omnes homines divites concludimus, operi se accingant prius necesse est, et multo labore eruendae sunt illae opes, quae in tenebris latent reconditae, otiosis
15   et oscitantibus sese

[1]*quod* correction for *ut* B. [2]*earum* vL; *eorum* B. [3]*penetrare* Locke's correction for *pervenire* B.

(folio 35)   non offerunt, nec vero omnibus qui quaerunt, cum aliquos etiam incassum sudantes videamus. quod si in rebus ad communis vitae usum pertinentes, paucos admodum inveniamus qui ratione dirigantur, cum homines raro admodum in sese descendunt, ut inde
5   vitae suae causam, modum, rationemque eruant, non mirandum est, quod tam diversae sint de lege hac non adeo cognitu facili mortalium sententiae, cum plurimi hominum de officio suo parum soliciti, aut aliorum exemplis aut patriis institutis et loci consuetudine, aut denique eorum,[1] quos bonos et prudentes viros judicant,
10   authoritate potius, quam ratione ducti, non aliam quaerunt vitae morumque regulam, sed mutuatitia illa contenti sunt, quam aliorum mores, opiniones aut consilia sine gravi aliqua meditatione aut studio incautis facile suggerunt, non igitur sequitur naturae legem naturae lumine

[1]*eorum* vL; *corum* B.

lio 34)   We reply, however, that even granted that our intellectual faculties can lead us to a knowledge of this law, yet it does not follow
from this that all men necessarily make right use of these faculties.
The nature and properties of figures and numbers seem obvious,
and doubtless knowable from the light of nature, yet it does not
follow from this that whoever is possessed of a sound mind, turns
out to be a Geometer, or has a knack for and mastery of Arithmetic.
For a man to penetrate into the hidden nature of these things by
reasoning and arguments based on sensible and obvious things,
there is need for the concentrated meditation of the mind, thought,
and care. Good, rich veins of gold and silver lie hidden in the bowels
of the earth, and moreover arms and hands and reason, the inventor
of machines, are given to men, with which they can dig them out.[35]
Yet from this we do not conclude that all men are wealthy. First, they
must gird themselves for work, and that wealth which has been
hidden in the darkness must be excavated with great labor. It does
not offer itself up to the idle and indolent,

lio 35)   nor indeed to all who seek it, since some we see toil to no avail. But, if
we should discover only a few who are guided by reason in the
concerns of their daily life, there is no wonder that concerning this
law, which is not so easily apprehended, there is such a great variety
of opinions among mortals, since but rarely do men probe deeply
into themselves to discover there the cause of their life, its proper
mode, and purpose. Most men are but little concerned about their
duty, for they are guided not so much by reason as by either the
example of others or the practices of their country and the custom of
the place [where they live], or, finally, by the authority of those they
judge to be good and prudent. They seek no other rule of life or
conduct, but are content with that derivative rule which the conduct
of others, their opinions and advice, readily suggest to the thought-

[35]*Good rich veins of gold and silver.* This seems an allusion to Job 28:1–28, and
especially verses 1–3: "Surely there is a vein for the silver, and a place for gold where
they fine it. Iron is taken out of the earth, and brass is molten out of stone. He setteth
an end to darkness, and searcheth out all perfection: the stones of darkness, and the
shadow of death."

(folio 36) non esse cognoscibilem quia pauci admodum sunt qui nec vitiis corrupti nec per[1] incuriam negligentes, lumine illo recte utuntur.

III. An lex naturae per traditionem nobis innotescat? Negatur[.][2]

[1]*per* inserted by Locke in B. [2]Number and title added by Locke in B.

less, without any deep reflection or study. From this it does not follow that,

(folio 36) since those are very few in number who make proper use of that light and are neither corrupted by vices nor indifferent and careless, the law of nature cannot be known by the light of nature.

III. Does the Law of nature become known to us by tradition? It does not.

(folio 37) ### IV. An Lex Naturae hominum animis inscribatur? Negatur[.]¹

Quum dari legem naturae, eamque legem non traditione sed lumine naturae esse cognoscibilem superius probavimus, quid sit illud lumen naturae dubitari potest, quod ut lux solis, dum res caeteras radiis suis nobis ostentat, ignoratur tamen ipsa, et natura
5 illius in occulto latet. Quum vero nihil homini cognoscatur, cujus cognitionis principium aut animae in ipsis natalibus non imprimatur, aut ab extra per sensus intret, hujus cognitionis primordia investigare operae pretium videtur, et quaerere an hominum nascentium animae sint rasae tantum tabulae, observatione et ratiocinio
10 postmodum informandae, an leges naturae officii sui indices² connatas sibique inscriptas habeant[.] Dum³ autem quaerimus an lex naturae hominum animis inscribatur, id volumus, scilicet an dentur aliquae propositiones practicae menti connatae, et quasi insculptae, ut tam naturales sint animae et ei intimae, quam ipsae facultates[,]
15 voluntas scilicet et intellectus, et sine studio omni, aut ratiocinatione[,] immutabiles semperque patentes nobis innotescant. verum hujusmodi⁴ nullam dari legis naturae in pectoribus nostris inscriptionem sequentia suadent argumenta.

---

¹Title in B's hand; numeral in Locke's (?) in B. ²*officii sui indices* Locke's correction for *et officio suo convenientes* B. ³*Dum . . . innotescant* added by Locke on verso of fol. 36 in B. ⁴*autem* deleted after *hujusmodi* B.

(folio 38)   1°¹ gratis tantum dictum est et a nemine hactenus probatum etiamsi in² eo laborarunt multi³ scilicet nascentium⁴ hominum an-

lio 37) IV. Is the Law of Nature inscribed in
the minds of men? It is not.

Since we have proved above that there exists a law of nature, and
that this law can be known, not by tradition, but by the light of
nature, one can wonder what this light of nature is, which, like the
light of the sun, while making everything else visible to us by its rays,
is not itself known to us, and its nature remains obscure and hidden.[36] Since, indeed, nothing can possibly be known to man, which,
as it first comes to be known, is not either imprinted in the soul at its
very birth, or does not enter through the senses from without, it
seems worth our labor to seek the origins of this knowledge, and to
inquire whether the minds of men at birth are simply clean slates to
be filled later by observation and reasoning, or whether they have
inborn and inscribed in them the laws of nature as guides to their
duty. Yet, inasmuch as we are inquiring whether the law of nature is
inscribed in the minds of men, it is our purpose to discover whether
there exist some practical propositions innate to the mind and, as it
were, graven upon it, so that they are as natural to the soul and as
integral to it as its very faculties, the will and intellect, that is, and
whether they become known to us without any effort or reasoning
immutable and forever obvious. However, the following arguments
persuade [us] that there exists no such law of nature inscribed in our
hearts.

lio 38)   1°, That the minds of men at birth are something more than clean
slates capable of receiving any impressions whatsoever, yet bearing

[36]*its nature remains obscure and hidden*. Comparable is the situation presented at the
opening of the *Essay*, ed. Nidditch, I 1, p. 43: "The Understanding, like the Eye,
whilst it makes us see, and perceive all other Things, takes no notice of itself."

imas aliquid esse praeter rasas tabulas quorumlibet characterum
capaces, nullos tamen a natura inscriptos sibi gerentes.

5   2⁰⁵ Si lex haec⁶ naturae hominum animis naturaliter tota simul in
ipsis natalibus imprimatur, quomodo evenit quod homines ad unum
omnes qui suas secum habeant animas, lege hac instructas, de ea
statim sine haesitatione omni non consentiunt ad obsequium parati?
cum circa hanc legem tam in diversum abeant, cum alibi hoc, alibi
10 illud, dictatum naturae et rectae rationis praedicatur, idem apud hos
honestum quod apud alios turpe, cum legem naturae hi aliam, hi
nullam, omnes obscuram agnoscunt. hic (quod a nonnullis fieri scio)
siquis responderet legem hanc a natura pectoribus nostris inscriptam lapsu primi hominis aut partim obliterari, aut prorsus et in
15 universum deleri

---

¹Numeral added by Locke in margin of B. ²*in* added by Locke in B. ³*laborarunt multi*
Locke's correction for *laborat acutissimus Caresius [Cartesius]* B. ⁴*nascentium* vL; *noscen-*
tium B. ⁵Numeral added by Locke in margin of B. ⁶*haec* vL; *hac* B.

no impressions inscribed [in them] by nature has been urged without evidence and been proven by none, although many have labored to do so.[37]

2°, If this law of nature were naturally impressed entire on the minds of men immediately at birth, how does it happen that all men who are in the possession of souls furnished with this law do not immediately agree about this law to a man, without any hesitation, [and are] ready to obey it? When it comes to this law, men depart from one another in so many different directions; in one place one thing, in another something else, is declared to be a dictate of nature and of right reason; and what is held to be virtuous among some is vicious among others. Some recognize a different law of nature, others none, all recognize that it is obscure. Here it would not do away with all doubt were someone to respond to these [objections]— (as I know some do)—by claiming that this law, which has been inscribed by nature in our hearts, was either partially effaced by the fall of the first man or utterly and everywhere destroyed[38]

---

[37]Originally Locke had written for "for many had labored to do so"—*laborat acutissimus Car[t]esius*. He would seem to have in mind especially Descartes's demonstration of the existence of God in *Meditations* III and V (LL 601a [1658]), to which he returns in Question V, fol. 57, for which see n. 53, below. In a fragment of a letter to Mersenne (16 June 1641), Descartes clarifies his analysis of ideas against the spate of objections that had been urged against them (by Hobbes and others), and he repeats the distinctions of his third *Meditation* (in *Oeuvres de Descartes*, ed. Charles Adam and Paul Tannery, new ed. [Paris, 1971], 7:37–38): *Ex his autem ideis aliae innatae, aliae adventitiae, aliae a me ipso factae mihi videntur* ("Of these ideas some seem to be innate, others to be derived from a source outside myself, others to be created by me myself"). Cf. *quaedam sunt adventitiae, aliae factae vel factitiae, et aliae innatae* ("some ideas are derived from external sources [example: our idea of the sun]; others created or factive [example: the astronomical conception of the sun]; others innate [examples: 'the idea of God, Mind, Body, Triangle, and generally all those ideas that have as their objects Essences which are True, Immutable, and Eternal'])" in ibid., 3:383.

[38]Von Leyden refers to Saint Augustine, "and the more pessimistic and severe Fall-doctrines of Calvin (*Institutes*, ii. 1. 8–9), Luther, and the Jansenists" (*John Locke: Essays*, p. 139, n. 2). There is a trace of a conception that man's God-given reason was dimmed after the fall in Saint Augustine, *City of God* XXII 24; this passage constitutes a panegyric on the "spark of reason still remaining in man" and does not concern our knowledge of the law of nature. The reference to Calvin, however, comes closer to the kind of thought Locke had in mind, especially in Calvin's passing reference to those thinkers for whom "original sin is a lack of original justice"; *Institutes* II 1.8; cf. II 1.9, where Calvin refers to his own conception. Locke had two copies of the *Institutio Christianae religionis* (LL 570 and 571). The notion that "the light which sprung from

(folio 39) (quod sane argumentum maximae mortalium parti penitus igno-
tum, qui de primo homine aut illius lapsu ne semel quidem cogitave-
rint) hujusmodi responsum praeterquam quod ad Philosophos
minus pertineat, nodum minime solveret, nec dubium eximeret,
5 dum enim hanc legem in cordibus hominum primitus inscriptam,
deletam asserunt, alterum horum affirment necesse est, scilicet
legem hanc naturae aut partim amissam, aliqua nempe illius
praecepta prorsus intercidisse; aut omnia. si aliqua hujus legis praecepta omnino deleta sunt ex hominum pectoribus; quae inscripta
10 remanent, aut eadem sunt in omnibus, aut diversa, si eadem dicant
tum de his cognitu facilibus inter se facile consentirent omnes qui
ubique sunt homines quod minime factum videmus, si diversa esse
quae in hominum animis relicta sunt naturae decreta asserant, et
inter se differre nativas has

(folio 40) inscriptiones, rogo hic, quaenam sit hujus differentiae causa, cum
natura in operibus suis ubique eadem sit et uniformis? deinde an

lio 39) (which argument is completely unknown to the greatest part of mankind, who have never once given a thought to the first man or to his fall). Beyond the fact that a response of this kind hardly pertains to Philosophers, it would hardly undo the knot at all, nor would it remove all doubt. For, inasmuch as they affirm that this law, which was originally inscribed in men's hearts, was destroyed, they must maintain one of two things: either this law of nature has been lost in part—which is to say that some of its precepts have utterly perished—or that all its precepts have been lost. If some of the precepts of this law have been erased completely from the hearts of men, those that remain inscribed there are either the same in all men or different. Should they say they are the same, then all men everywhere would easily agree among themselves concerning these easily known precepts—something we hardly see happen at all. Should they claim that the decrees of nature which have remained in the minds of men are different, and that these native inscriptions disagree among themselves,

lio 40) I now ask: What is the cause of this difference, for in her working nature is the same and uniform?[39] Then, [I ask], does it not seem

---

this law has partially be darkened in that grave collapse of human nature which followed Adam's fall" was a part of Robert Sanderson's treatment of the theory of natural law in his Oxford lectures on the obligation of conscience (1647) *De obligatione Conscientiae* (London, 1661) IV 24, p. 138 (LL 2548). *Ex hac lege, ortum lumen, in gravi illa humana ruina, quae lapsum Adae insecuta est, admodum obscuratum est: unde crassae illae erroris et ignorantiae tenebrae, in quibus dum hic vivimus omnes ejus posteri assidue versamur. . . . Sed voluit Deus quasdam propositiones et principia practica, quas* κοινὰς ἐννοίας, προλήψεις φυσικὰς *vocant Philosophi,* ἐγκεκρυμμένον ἡμῖν σπινθῆρα . . . *quasi conservatam ex tanto incendio inter medios cineres et favillas ignis divini scintillulam, in nobis remanere* ("The light that has arisen from this law [of nature] has now been dimmed in that ruin of mankind which followed upon the fall of Adam. From that fall came that darkness of error and ignorance in which all of us who are his descendants are deeply involved as long as we live here [in this world]. But God wanted certain propositions and principles of action to remain in us, which philosophers call 'common notions' and 'natural conceptions'—'a spark hidden within us'—as if a small spark of divine fire preserved in the midst of the ashes and embers of so great a conflagration").

[39]*In operibus suis eadem sit et uniformis*, and consequently any law of nature must be the same at all times and among all peoples; cf. Aristotle, *Nicomachean Ethics* V 7 (n.

non absurdum videtur asserere hominum mentes inter se principiis ipsis differre, quo etiam pacto cognosci poterat lex naturae et certa
5 recti et honesti regula, si concedatur semel, in diversis hominibus diversa et alia esse dictata naturae et actionum principia? Quod si legem hanc primitus inscriptam, prorsus deletam asserunt? ubi tandem erit lex illa naturae de qua quaerimus, nulla sane erit hoc concesso, nisi alium[1] praeter inscriptionem reperiamus[2] cognos-
10 cendi modum.

3[3] si lex haec naturae hominum mentibus inscribatur, qui fit quod pueruli juniores, Indocti, et barbarae illae nationes, qui sine institutis, sine legibus, sine eruditione omni secundum naturam vivere dicuntur, hanc non optime omnium cognoscant callentque
15 legem? qui ab aventitiis

[1]*alium* vL; *aliam* B. [2]*reperiamus* Locke's correction for *inveniamus* B. [3]Numeral added by Locke in margin of B.

(folio 41) liberimi sunt notionibus, quae alio animos avocare possint, qui mutuatitias aliunde non imbibunt opiniones, quae dictata naturae aut pervertere, aut obliterare, aut delere possunt? cum non alios habeant praeceptores praeter seipsos, nec aliud sequuntur quam natu-
5 ram. si lex naturae pectoribus hominum inscriberetur, inter hos homines illam sine lituris sine mendis repertam iri credendum esset; verum quam longe horum hominum mores a virtute distent, quam alieni sunt ab omni humanitate, dum nullibi tam incerta fides, tanta perfidia, tam immanis crudelitas, dum caesis hominibus cognato
10 sanguine et diis et genio suo simul sacrificant, facile patebit consulenti et veteris et novi orbis historias et peregrinantium itineraria,

absurd to maintain that the minds of men differ among themselves in their very principles? And then, how could the law of nature and the fixed rule of rectitude and virtue be known, once it were granted that in different men the dictates of nature and the principles of action are different and divergent? But, if they claim that this law was originally inscribed and then completely destroyed, where, I ask, will that law of nature which is the object of our dispute [prove to] be? If this is granted, there will be no law [of nature], unless we should discover some means of knowledge other than inscription.

3°, If this law of nature were inscribed in men's minds, how does it come about that the very young, the Uneducated, and those barbarian nations, which are said to live according to nature, without institutions, without laws, without any learning or culture, do not know this law better than any and are not most expert in it?[40]

lio 41) [These are peoples] who are freest of the kinds of foreign notions that can call the mind away to other places, who do not receive from elsewhere derivative opinions which can either pervert, or obliterate, or destroy the dictates of nature. For they have no tutors other than themselves and no guide other than nature. If the law of nature were inscribed upon the hearts of men, one would be obliged to believe that it would be discovered among these peoples without a blot or flaw. Yet how far removed are the morals of these men from virtue, how alien are they to any [sense of] humanity! Nowhere is there such fickle faith, so much perfidy, such monstrous cruelty; and, by murdering men and shedding kindred blood, they sacrifice both to their gods and to their own "genius." [This] will easily become plain to whoever consults the histories of the old and new world and the narratives of travelers.[41] Nor can one believe that the

---

14, above); *Rhetoric* I 13.1373bff; Cicero, *Republic* III 22.33, where Cicero calls the law of nature constant, eternal, and infused in men everywhere (cf. n. 6, above); and *Tusculans* I 30; Justinian, *Institutes* I 2.11.

[40]A question posed again in the *Essay* to reveal the absurdity of the belief in innate principles in the mind (*Essay*, ed. Nidditch, I 2.5–24, pp. 49–63).

[41]Locke's vast collection of books of travels would yield abundant examples of the atrocities he touches on here. For these, see Appendix V to Harrison and Laslett, *The*

nec quis credet inter barbaras hasce et rudes[1] gentes, cognosci maxime

[1] *rudes* Locke's correction for *nudas* B.

(folio 42) et observari legem naturae, quum inter plurimas harum, pietatis, mansuetudinis, fidei, castitatis et reliquarum virtutum appareat nec vola nec vestigium, sed inter rapinas, furta, stupra, et homicidia misere vitam transigunt, lex igitur naturae hominum pectoribus
5 inscribi non videtur, cum illi, qui non alium habent ducem praeter ipsam naturam, in quibus dictata naturae a positivis morum institutis minime corrumpuntur, ita vivunt omnis legis ignari quasi nulla omnino recti et honesti habenda esset ratio.

Fateor ego inter moratiores populos, et eruditione et morum
10 institutis perpolitos, dari, aliquas certas indubitasque de moribus opiniones, quae licet pro lege naturae agnoscunt, et pectoribus suis a natura inscriptas[1] credant, vix tamen puto a natura acceptas sed aliunde promanasse, quae licet sint fortasse legis naturae aliqua praecepta, non tamen a natura edocti sunt, sed ab hominibus, hae
15 enim opiniones de recto et honesto quae tam

[1] *inscriptas* vL.; *inscriptos* B.

(folio 43) arcte amplectimur hujusmodi plerumque sunt, quae in tenera adhuc aetatula antequam de iis quicquam judicare adhuc possimus, vel observare quomodo se insinuent, animis nostris parum cautis, infunduntur, instillanturque a parentibus vel praeceptoribus nostris,
5 aliisque, quibuscum versamur, qui dum eadem credunt ad vitam bene efformandam conferre, ipsi etiam eodem forsan modo eadem

law of nature is best known and most observed among these barbarous and rude peoples,

io 42) for among most of these there appears not even the slightest trace of
piety, gentleness, good faith, chastity, and the other virtues, but they
spend their lives wretchedly in rapine, theft, debauchery, and murder. The law of nature, therefore, does not appear to be inscribed in
the hearts of men, since those who have no other guide than nature
herself, among whom the dictates of nature are least corrupted by
positive regulations concerning morals, live ignorant of any law, as if
they needed to take no account at all of what is right and virtuous.

I confess that among more civilized peoples, who have been re-
fined by education and regulations for their conduct, there exist
certain definite and unquestioned opinions concerning morals,
which, I allow, they recognize as the law of nature and believe to be
inscribed in their hearts by nature. Yet I hardly think that these
opinions are derived from nature, but they spring from some other
source. They could possibly be, I grant, some of the precepts of the
law of nature, yet men are not instructed by nature, but by men.
Indeed, these opinions concerning what is right and virtuous which
we embrace so firmly

io 43) are, for the most part, the kind which are infused into our minds, at
an age when our minds are little on their guard, when we are still of
a tender age, before we can yet form a judgment concerning them or
notice how they insinuate themselves. They are instilled by our
parents or teachers and by others with whom we associate, who,
since they believe that these very opinions contribute to the proper
formation of a life, are themselves, possibly because they have been
themselves taught these same opinions in the same manner, in-

---

Library of John Locke, pp. 307–308. As for sacrifices to one's *genius*, Locke would seem
to have in mind the Roman practice of offering sacrifice to one's personal spirit or
tutelary "genius" (cf. Plautus, *Captivi* 290).

edocti, proni sunt his opinionibus recentes adhuc puerulorum animos imbuere, quas necessarias putant ad bene beateque vivendum,
in hac enim re maxime cauti sunt et seduli qui putant his quae primo
10 jacta sunt morum fundamentis totam futurae vitae spem niti, et hoc
demum modo cum opiniones hae animis nostris parum attentis sine
observatione nostra irrepserint, in pectoribus nostris radices agen-
tes, nobis interim aut quomodo aut quando ignorantibus, suamque
etiam confirmant authoritatem communi hominum quibuscum
15 nobis

(folio 44) consuetudo est consensu et laude, illico concludendum putamus,
cum non aliam illarum observemus originem, hasce opiniones a
deo[1] et natura pectoribus nostris inscriptas, et dum eas quotidiano
usu vitae regulas constituimus si has dubitaremus esse legem natu-
5 rae, et futurae vitae incerti essemus, et paeniteret[2] anteactae, cum
judicare necesse esset si haec non sit lex naturae quam hactenus
observavimus, nos male et sine ratione adhuc vixisse, hanc igitur ob
rationem, has primae juventutis opiniones ab aliis infusas quam
arctissime amplectimur, pluris aestimamus, credimus obstinate, nec
10 in dubium vocari a quoquam patimur, et dum haec principia esse
praedicamus, de iis nosmet ipsos nec dubitare, nec contra negan-
tem, (principia enim credimus), disputare permittimus, ex his igitur
patet, multa esse posse quae quis credat a natura menti suae inscripta, quae tamen aliunde mutuantur

---

[1]*a deo* Locke's correction for *adeo* B. [2]*paeniteret* vL.; *paeniterit* B.

clined to instill those opinions they think necessary to a happy and blessed life into the yet inexperienced minds of the very young. Indeed, those who believe that all hope for a future life[42] rests on those foundations that are first laid down are most careful and industrious in this matter. And so, when these opinions have slipped into our minds in this way, when we are but little attentive and without our noticing it, they take root in our hearts, while we, at the time, know neither how nor when they do so. And they also strengthen their authority by the common customs, agreement, and praise of those men with whom we associate.

(folio 44) From this we think we must conclude, that, since we observe no other origin for them, these opinions are inscribed in our hearts by god and nature. And inasmuch as we establish these as rules in the daily course of our life, were we to doubt that these constitute the law of nature, we would be unsure both of our future life and repent of our past, since, if this law, which we have always followed, were not a law of nature, it would be necessary to conclude that until now we have lived badly and without fixed principle. For this reason, therefore, we embrace with all our might those opinions of our earliest youth which have been instilled in us by others, set a high value on them, stubbornly believe in them; nor do we suffer anyone to call them into question, and, since we call these "principles," we do not permit ourselves to question them, or others to challenge them, for we believe they are "principles."[43] From this, then, it is obvious that there are many things which one might believe to be inscribed in his mind by nature, but which, nevertheless, have their origin in another source.

[42]Given the pagan cast of Locke's Latin, it is not quite certain that by *futurae vitae spem* Locke means hope for the afterlife rather than one's life in the future; there is the same ambiguity in fol. 44, line 5.

[43]*Principia*. Locke develops this reflection in the *Essay* (ed. Nidditch, I 3.25, p. 82): "it is no wonder that grown *Men*, either perplexed in the necessary affairs of life, or hot in the pursuit of pleasures, should *not* seriously sit down to *examine their own tenets*; especially when one of the Principles is that Principles ought not to be questioned." This entire passage from the *Essay* (I 3.20–27) develops out of the questioning of innate principles of morality in the *Questions*.

(folio 45) originem, nec ideo sequi quod quicquid proni credimus et pro principio amplectimur, cujus tamen fontem[1] ignoramus id esse legem naturae a natura pectoribus nostris inscriptam.

4o[2] si lex haec[3] naturae pectoribus nostris inscriberetur, cur stulti
5 et mente capti nullam hujus legis habent cognitionem cum dicatur immediate ipsis mentibus imprimi quae minime pendent ex constitutione et structura organorum corporis quam solam esse differentiam inter Sapientes insipientesque in confesso est.

5o si lex naturae pectoribus nostris inscribatur concludendum
10 foret speculativa principia aeque inscribi ac practica, quod tamen vix probandum videtur, si enim primum illud et celeberimum scientiarum principium excutere velimus, impossibile scilicet est idem simul esse et non esse, facile constabit axioma illud pectoribus nostris a natura non inscribi nec a quoquam pro concesso haberi

---

[1]*fontem* vL; *fonten* B. [2]Numeral added by Locke in margin of B. [3]*haec* vL; *hac* B.

(folio 46) priusquam aut ab alio didicerit aut inductione et particularium rerum observatione, quae legitima est axiomatum stabiliendorum methodus, sibimet ipsi probaverit, nulla igitur mihi aut practica aut speculativa principia hominum animis a natura inscribi videntur.

ilio 45) Nor does it follow from this that whatever we are inclined to believe and embrace as a principle, but whose source we do not know, is a law of nature, inscribed in our hearts by nature.

4°, Were this law of nature inscribed in our hearts, why do fools and madmen have no knowledge of this law? For it is said to be impressed immediately upon our very minds, which depend least on the constitution and structure of the organs of the body, which is the only confessed difference between the Wise and ignorant.[44]

5°, If the law of nature were inscribed in our hearts, it would be necessary to conclude that speculative principles are inscribed there as well as practical principles, which seems hardly capable of proof. For if we care to examine the first and most celebrated principle of the sciences, that it is impossible for one and the same thing at once to be and not to be, it will be easily ascertained that this axiom is not inscribed in our hearts by nature; nor will it be considered by anyone as agreed to

ilio 46) before he has either learned it from someone else, or proved it for himself by induction and the observation of particulars, which is the legitimate method for establishing axioms. Therefore, it appears to me that no principles, either practical or speculative, are inscribed in the souls of men by nature.

[44]Here Locke must be used to translate Locke. A passage from the *Essay* (ed. Nidditch, I 2.27, p. 64) helps clarify the thought expressed here with a certain compression and (in Latin) ambiguity of reference: "It might very well be expected, that these Principles [innate practical principles] should be perfectly known to Naturels; which being stamped immediately on the Soul (as these Men suppose) can have no dependence on the Constitutions, or Organs of the Body, the only confessed difference between them and others." That is, it is the mind that distinguishes the simple-minded from the intelligent, yet, according to the theory of innate principles of morality, the minds of all humans are "stamped" at birth with these principles. As a consequence all of us, retarded or not, should recognize them, although we might differ in our physical characteristics.

(folio 47) V. An Ratio[1] per res a sensibus haustas pervenire[2] potest
in cognitionem[3] legis naturae? Affirmatur.[4]

Legem naturae lumine naturae esse cognoscibilem supra probavimus. cum[5] vero lumen illud naturae quod unicum[6] nos vitae
hujus iter ingressuros dirigit, quodque per varios officiorum anfrac-
tus devitatis hinc vitiorum salebris, illinc errorum deviis[7] ad id vir-
5 tutis faelicitatisque fastigium nos deducit quo et vocant dii et tendit
natura. cum inquam lumen illud in obscuro lateat, et difficilius
longe cognitu[8] videtur quid sit, quam quo dirigat,[9] operae pretium
videtur has etiam excutere tenebras, et in sole ipso non caecutire,
decet sane non tantum brutorum more ad vitae usum luce frui, et ad
10 dirigendos gressus adhibere, sed quid lumen illud sit, quae ejus
natura et ratio, altiore indagine investigare. Quandoquidem vero
lumen hoc naturae (ut alibi ostensum est) nec traditio sit nec internum aliquod practicum principium mentibus nostris a natura inscriptum,

[1]*sive Facultas discursiva* crossed out after *Ratio* in A. [2]*pervenire* B; *devenire* A. [3]*cognitionem* B; *Cognitionem* A. [4]Title and numeral in Locke's hand in B. [5]*cum* A; *Cum* B. [6]*per*
deleted after *unicum* B; in A. [7]*deviis . . . tendit* added by Locke on fol. 46ᵛ in B; in A (line
skipped by B). [8]*cognitu . . . has* added by Locke on fol. 46ᵛ in B; in A (line skipped by
B). [9]*dirigat* A; *dirrigat* B.

(folio 48) nihil remanet quod lumen naturae dici possit praeter rationem et
sensum, quae solum duae facultates hominum mentes instruere et
erudire videntur, et id praestare quod luminis propium est, scilicet
ut res aliter ignotae prorsus, et in tenebris latentes, animo obversen-
5 tur, et cognosci, et quasi conspici possint. Quae dum mutuas sibi
invicem tradunt operas, dum sensus rerum particularium sensibi-

io 47) V. Can Reason[45] arrive at a knowledge of the law
of nature through sense experience? It can.

We have proved above that the law of nature is knowable by the
light of nature. Since, in truth, this light of nature is the sole thing
that directs us as we are about to enter the path of this life and that
guides us, when we have avoided here the rough stretches of vice
and there the maze of error, through the various turns of our duties
to that summit of virtue and happiness to which both the gods
beckon [us] and our nature tends—since, I say, this light lies hidden
in the dark, and it seems far more difficult to know what it is than the
direction it points to, it seems worth our while to dispel these shadows too, and not to stand blindly in the very [light of the] sun.
Indeed, it is fitting, not only to use this light as do animals for the
necessities of life and to employ it to direct our steps, but to investigate also by a deeper inquiry what this light is and [to discover] its
nature and its principle. Now inasmuch as this light of nature is not
tradition (as has been shown elsewhere),[46] nor any inner principle of
action inscribed in our minds by nature,[47]

io 48) there remains nothing that can be called the light of nature except
reason and sense. These two faculties alone appear to instruct and
improve men's minds and to exhibit the property of light: that is,
they make things which are otherwise entirely unknown and hidden
in shadows observable to the mind and capable of being known and,
as it were, visible to sight. So long as reason and the senses serve one
another in their mutual operations, so long as sense furnishes rea-

---

[45][or the discursive faculty] deleted in A. In his *Essay* Locke joins reason with the
discursive faculty (ed. Nidditch, I 1. 15, p. 55). The reason for the deleted gloss, if not
the deletion, is clear in the sequel (fol. 49–50), where Locke distinguishes between
ratio as a set of principles already discovered and an activity of mind as the mind
discovers these principles; cf. the *Essay*, ed. Nidditch, I 2. 10, p. 52: "For all reasoning
is search and casting about, and requires Pains and Application."

[46]In Question II, fol. 23, and 28–31.

[47]In Question II, fol. 23 and 25, and more fully in Question IV.

lium ideas rationi administrat, et suggerit discursus materiam, ratio
e contra, sensum dirigit, et ab eo haustas rerum imagines inter se
componit, alias inde format[1] novas deducit, nihil tam obscurum est,
10 tam reconditum,[2] tam ab omni sensu remotum, quod his adjutus
facultatibus, cogitando et ratiocinando assequi non possit omnium
capax animus. quod si alterutram tollas altera

[1]*format* Locke's correction in B; *formit*(?) A. [2]*reconditum* A; *recognitum* B.

(folio 49) certe frustra est, sine ratione enim sensibus instructi, ad brutorum
naturam vix assurgimus, cum sus, et simia, et plura inter quad-
rupedes animalia sensuum acumine homines longe superent.[1] sine
sensuum autem ope, et ministerio, nihil magis praestare potest
5 ratio,[2] quam clausis fenestris in tenebris operarius, nisi illic trans-
eant rerum ideae, nulla erit ratiocinandi materia, nec plus possit ad
extruendam cognitionem animus, quam ad aedificanda domicilia
architectus cui desunt saxa[,] arbores, arena, et reliqua aedificiorum
materia. Per rationem hic intelligimus, non practica aliqua prin-
10 cipia, vel propositiones quasvis in animo repositas, quibus dum vitae
nostrae actiones apte respondeant,[3] dicuntur conformes rectae rationi, hujusmodi enim recta ratio est ipsa lex naturae jam cognita,
non modus vel lumen illud naturae quo cognoscitur, et est

[1]*superent* B; *superant* A. [2]*ratio* inserted by Locke in B; in A. [3]*respondeant* A, B;
respondent vL.

son with the ideas[48] of particular sensible things and supplies the material for its discourse, [and] reason, for its part, directs sense, and arranges and orders the images of things derived from the senses, and forms [and] derives from this source other new images, there is nothing so obscure, so hidden, so remote from all possible sense experience, that the mind, in its infinite capacity and with the aid of these faculties, cannot reach by thought and reasoning. But take one of these away, and the other

lio 49) is surely useless. Indeed, if we are provided with senses but not with reason, we hardly rise to the level of brutes, since the pig, the ape, and many of the four-footed animals far surpass man in the keenness of their senses. Yet without the help of the senses and their service, reason can produce nothing more than can a workman in the dark behind closed shutters.[49] Unless the ideas of things penetrate [the mind] from the outside, there will be no matter for reasoning, nor could the mind erect a structure of knowledge any more than could an architect erect buildings, if he had no stones, timber, sand, and other building materials. By reason we here understand, not some principles of action, nor any propositions laid up in the mind, which, so long as the actions of our life closely correspond to them, are said to conform to right reason; for right reason so understood is the law of nature itself, as it has already become known, not the means, nor that light of nature, by which it becomes known;

[48]*ideas.* Not in the larger definition of the *Essay* ("whatsoever is the object of the Understanding when a Man thinks") (ed. Nidditch, I 1. 8, p. 47), but more narrowly the "images of things." Thus, the visual is primary in this early formulation of an empiricist theory of ideas; cf. n. 49.

[49]Compare the *Essay* (ed. Nidditch, II 11. 17, pp. 162–63): "I pretend not to teach, but to enquire; and therefore cannot but confess here again, That external and internal sensation, are the only passages that I can find, of knowledge, to the Understanding. These alone, as far as I can discover, are the Windows by which light is let into this *dark Room.* For, methinks, the *Understanding* is not much unlike a Closet wholly shut from light, with only some little openings left, to let external visible Resemblances, or *Ideas* of things without; would the Pictures coming into such a dark Room but stay there, and lie so orderly as to be found upon occasion, it would very much resemble the Understanding of a Man, in reference to all Objects of sight, and the *Ideas* of them." Cf. ibid., I 2. 15, p. 55.

(folio 50) tantum objectum rationis, non ratio ipsa, hujusmodi scilicet veritates quas ratio quaerit,[1] et investigat ad vitam dirigendam moresque efformandos necessarias. Ratio autem hic sumitur pro facultate animae discursiva quae a notis ad ignota progreditur, et unum ex
5 alio certa et legitima propositionum consecutione deducit. Haec est illa ratio cujus ope gens humana in cognitionem legis naturae pervenit. fundamentum autem cui innititur[2] tota illa cognitio, quam ratio in altum extruit et ad caelum usque attolit, sunt objecta sensuum; sensus enim omnium primi suggerunt, et ad secretos animi
10 recessus intromittunt totam et primariam discursus materiem. ex cognitis enim et concessis semper procedit omnis argumentatio, nec sine posita[3] et intellecta aliqua veritate magis discurrere vel ratiocinari potest animus; quam agillimum quodvis, e quadrupedibus animal[4]

[1]*ratio quaerit* A; *quaerit ratio* B. [2]*innititur* vL.; *innitur* A, B. [3]*posita* B; *possita* A. [4]*animal* added by Locke in B; in A.

(folio 51) sese movere, vel e loco in locum progredi, sine stabili aliquo vestigiorum fulcimento. Mira sunt fateor quae in scientiis mathematicis, invenit et investigat ratio, sed quae omnia de linea pendent, superficei inaedificantur et corpus habent pro fundamento cui in-
5 nitantur, haec enim operationum suarum objecta, et alia insuper communia principia et axiomata sibi dari postulat non invenit, nec probat Mathesis. eadem plane in aliis etiam disciplinis tradendis tractandisque ratio utitur methodo, in quibus ornandis excolendisque, et si abscondita, sublimia, et digna, quae et ratio ipsa miretur
10 inventa, proferatque prodatque; nulla tamen est si singulas percurrere velis scientias speculativas, in qua non aliquid semper supponitur, et pro concesso habetur, et a sensibus aliquo modo mutuo accipitur. omnis enim[1]

[1]*enim* A; omitted in B.

(folio 52) conceptus animi uti et corporis fit semper ex aliqua praeexistente materia, nec minus in moralibus et practicis disciplinis[1] eodem

lio 50) and it is only the object of reason, not reason itself. That is, [it consists of] such truths as reason seeks and investigates as necessary to the direction of life and the development of moral character. Here, however, the word "reason" is used for the discursive faculty of the soul which progresses from the known to the unknown, and deduces one thing from another by the certain and valid consequences of propositions. It is this reason by whose help the human race arrives at a knowledge of the law of nature. Yet the foundations on which all of this knowledge, which reason raises on high and lifts up to heaven, rests are the objects of the senses. For before anything else, the senses furnish the entire and primary matter for discourse and introduce it into the hidden recesses of the mind. All argumentation always proceeds from what is known and granted, nor can the mind discourse or reason without some established and understood truth any more than can a four-footed animal, be it ever so nimble,

lio 51) move itself or progress from place to place, without some stable support for its steps. I confess that the things reason discovers and investigates in the mathematical sciences are marvelous, but they all depend on a line, are constructed on a plane surface, and have body as the foundation on which they rest. Indeed, Mathematics does not discover or prove these objects of its operations nor other common principles and axioms in addition; it takes them as given. Clearly, reason makes use of the same method in the transmission and treatment of other disciplines as well. In embellishing and refining these, it brings forth and makes known discoveries—even those which are hidden away, sublime, and the noble objects at which reason itself marvels, once they have been discovered. Yet, if one were to examine the theoretical sciences one by one, there is none in which there is not something which stands always as a premise and is taken as given and which is not somehow received from the senses in some derivative manner.

lio 52) Indeed, every conception of the mind, as of the body, always comes from some preexistent matter, and reason proceeds in exactly the

modo progreditur, et eadem sibi concedi postulat ratio.

Ut vero cognoscatur quomodo sensus et ratio dum sibi mutuo
5 opitulentur, nos deducere possunt in cognitionem legis naturae,
praemittenda sunt aliqua quae ad legis cujusvis cognitionem necessario supponuntur.

1o[2] Igitur, ut se lege teneri quisquam cognoscat, scire prius oportet, esse legislatorem, superiorem, scilicet aliquam potestatem cui
10 jure subiicitur.

2o[3] Scire etiam oportet esse aliquam superioris illius potestatis
voluntatem circa res a nobis agendas, hoc est legislatorem illum
quicunque is demum fuerit, velle nos hoc agere, illud vero omittere
et exigere a nobis, ut vitae nostrae mores suae volun-

---

[1]*disciplinis* B; *disciplis* A. [2]New paragraph in A; not in B; *Igitur* A; *igitur* B. [3]New
paragraph in A; not in B; *Scire* A; *scire* B.

(folio 53) tati sint conformes; ut vero haec duo supposita ad legis naturae
cognitionem necessaria nobis innotescant,[1] quid sensus confert,
quid ratio in sequentibus patebit.

1o Igitur[2] dicimus ex sensu patere[3] esse in rerum natura res
5 sensibiles hoc est revera existere corpora, et eorum affectiones scilicet levitatem[,] gravitatem, calorem[,] frigus, colores et caeteras[4]
qualitates sensui obvias, quae omnes aliquo modo ad motum referri
possint. esse mundum hunc visibilem mira arte et ordine construc-
tum, cujus etiam pars nos sumus genus humanum, videmus enim
10 perpetuo certoque cursu circum rotari sydera,[5] volvi in mare flu-
mina, et se certo ordine sequi anni et tempestatum vicissitudines.
haec[6] et infinita pene plura docet sensus.

2do Dicimus cum mens a sensibus[7] acceptam hujus mundi machi-

same way in the moral and practical disciplines, demanding that the same things be granted to it.

Now, in order to discover how sense and reason, when they mutually assist each other, can lead us to a knowledge of the law of nature, some premises must first be set forth, which are necessary to the knowledge of any law whatsoever:[50]

1°, Thus, for anyone to know that he is bound by law, he must first know that there is a legislator, a superior; that is, some power to which he is rightfully subject.

2°, We must also know that there is some will of that superior power as regards the things we must do; that is, that that legislator, whoever he may prove to be, wills us to do this, or to refrain from that, and demands of us that the conduct of our life be in agreement with his will.

lio 53)   Now, to make these two premises which are necessary to a knowledge of the law of nature known to us, it will become clear in what follows what sense and what reason contribute [to a knowledge of these premises].

1°, We say, therefore, that it is evident from sense that there are in the physical world sensible things; that is, in effect, that bodies exist and their states: lightness, heaviness, heat, cold, colors, and the other qualities obvious to sense, all of which can in some way be referred to motion. [It is evident from sense] that this visible world exists, framed with wonderful art and order, of which we too, the human race, are a part; for we see the stars revolve about us in their constant and fixed course, the rivers roll into the sea, and the procession of the year and the seasons following one upon another in a fixed order. These and virtually an infinite number of other things sense teaches us.

2°, We say that once the mind has carefully and exactly weighed

---

[50]These two premises are articulated by Suarez, *De Legibus ac Deo Legislatore*, I 2, pp. 40–42, and II 5, pp. 78–79; cf. Locke, *Essay* (ed. Nidditch, I 4. 8, p. 87): "Without a Notion of a Law-Maker, it is impossible to have a Notion of a Law, and an Obligation to observe it."

nam secum accuratius[8] perpenderit, et rerum sensibilium speciem,
15 ordinem

[1]*innotescant* A; *intotescant* B. [2]New paragraph in A; not in B. [3]*ex sensu patere* A; *patere ex sensu* B. [4]*levitatem gravitatem, calorem* . . . *et caeteras* Locke's correction for *levitas gravitas, calor* . . . *et caetera* B; *levitas* . . . *caeterae* A. [5]*sydera* A; *sidera* B. [6]A new paragraph here; *haec* A; *Haec* B. [7]*a sensibus* omitted in B. [8]*accuratius* A; *acuratius* B.

(folio 54) ornatum et motum contemplaverit, inde progreditur ad eorum
originem, inquirendum,[1] quae causa, quis author fuerit tam egregii
operis; cum certo constet id casu et fortuito in tam justam tam
undique perfectam, affabreque factam compagem coalescere non
5 potuisse: unde certe colligitur oportere esse potentem, sapientemque harum rerum omnium opificem qui totum hunc fecit fabricavit-
que mundum, et nos homines non infimam in eo partem: cum
autem inanimatorum brutorumve[2] caetera turba efficere non possint hominem seipsis longe perfectiorem; nec se ipsum homo. nos
10 enim nobismet ipsis originem nostram non debere vel inde constat,
non solum quod sui ipsius causa nihil[3] sit, nam id axioma non
prohibet quo minus credamus aliquid esse quod non est ab alio[4] si
deum[5] agnoscere velimus, sed etiam quod homo eas omnes in se
non invenit perfectiones quas animo concipere potest.

[1]*inquirendum* A; *inquirendam* B. [2]*brutorumve* A; *brutorumque* B. [3]*causa nihil* A; *nihil causa* B. [4]*quod non est* added by Locke in B; *aliquid non esse ab alio* A. [5]*deum* A; *Deum* B.

(folio 55) (nam ut omittam omnium rerum perfectam cognitionem et in res
naturales majorem potentiam) si homo sui ipsius author esset, qui
sibi dare poterat essentiam[,] qui se produceret in rerum naturam,
daret etiam sibi suae existentiae durationem sempiternam; cum
5 concipi non potest, aliquid sibi adeo infensum adeo inimicum fore,

the machine of this world, which has been received from the senses, and contemplated the appearance, order,

olio 54) the array, and motion of sensible things, it progresses from this point to investigate the origin of these things; what was the cause, who the author of so extraordinary a work. For it is certain that it could not have been formed by chance and accident into a frame so fitting, so perfect everywhere and wrought with such skill. From this [observation] it is a certain inference that there must exist some powerful and wise creator of all these things, who made and constructed this whole world, and us men who are not the least part of it. For, indeed, all the multitude of inanimate beings or animals other than man cannot produce man, who is far more perfect than they; nor can man produce himself. Assuredly, it is established from this that we do not owe our origin to ourselves, not only because nothing might be the cause of itself—for, if we are willing to acknowledge god, this axiom[51] does not prevent us from believing that there exists something which does not come from something else—but also because man does not find in himself all those perfections of which his mind can conceive.

olio 55) For, if man were creator of himself, someone who could give himself being, who could bring himself into the world, he would also have granted himself an eternal duration for his existence (not to mention a perfect knowledge of all things and a greater power over natural things). For it is impossible to imagine anything so hostile

[51]The difficulty with this scholastic axiom *sui ipsius nihil causa* is that it must be suspended by its one great exception, the case of God, who is, by definition, *principium sui* (cf. Thomas Aquinas, *Summa Theologiae* Ia 2ae Q. 16, art. 1). Thus, God is defined by Spinoza as the cause of himself—*causa sui, Ethics* I 1, Definition 1: *Per causam sui intelligo id, cuius essentia involvit existentiam, sive id, cuius natura non potest concipi nisi existens* ("I understand a cause of itself as that whose essence involves its existence, or that whose nature cannot be conceived except as existing"). Spinoza, *Opera*, ed. Carl Gebhardt (Heidelberg: Carl Winter, 1972), 2:45.

quod cum sibi tribuere poterat existentiam, non simul eandem con-
servaret, vel peracto brevis aetatulae curriculo eam libenter amittere
vellet, sine qua reliqua omnia, chara, utilia, jucunda, beata, reteneri
non possunt, et frustra quaeruntur; cum certe minoris vel saltem
10 ejusdem sit potentiae conservare ac constituere, et qui quovis momento aliquid incipere jussit id ne[1] quovis momento desinat, efficere possit. his ita positis necessario sequitur alium esse praeter nos
potentiorem aliquem[2] et sapientiorem authorem

[1]*ne* Locke's correction of *in* B; *ne* A. [2]*aliquem* A; omitted in B.

(folio 56) qui pro libitu suo nos producere, conservare ac tollere[1] potest. his ita
a sensuum testimonio deductis, dictat ratio aliquam esse superiorem
potestatem cui merito subiicimur, deus[2] scilicet qui in nos justum
habet et ineluctabile imperium, qui prout sibi visum fuerit, nos
5 erigere potest, vel prosternere, eodem nutu, faelices vel miseros
reddere: qui cum animam ipse creavit, corpusque mira arte contex-
uit, utriusque facultates, vires, et secretam fabricam,[3] naturamque
probe perspectam habet,[4] illam aerumnis vel gaudio, hoc dolore vel
voluptate implere et exagitare potest. et utrumque simul ad sum-
10 mam beatitudinem attollere[5] vel miseriam poenamque detrudere.
unde liquido apparet rationem sensu monstrante viam nos deducere posse in cognitionem legislatoris sive superioris alicujus potestatis cui necessario subiicimur, quod primum

[1]*tollere* B; *tolere* A. [2]*deus* A; *Deus* B. [3]*et secretam* Locke's correction for *secretamque* B;
secretamque fabricam et naturam A. [4]*habet* B; *habeat* A. [5]*attollere* A; *tollere* B.

(folio 57) erat requisitum ad cognitionem alicujus legis.
      Fateor[1] quidem[2] alios numen esse et mundo huic praesidere ex
conscientiae testimonio probare agressos, alios ex idea illa dei quae

and inimical to itself which, though it could grant itself existence, would not at the same time preserve it, or which would be willing to readily abandon it once the course of its brief life had been spent; without life, all other things, dear, useful, pleasant, blessed, cannot be preserved and are sought in vain. Surely it requires a lesser or at least the same power to preserve a thing—and, whoever has commanded a thing to come into being at any instant, can prevent its cessation at any instant. Once these [conclusions] have been established in this manner, it necessarily follows that there exists some creator other than ourselves, more powerful and wiser,

olio 56) who at his pleasure can bring us into being, preserve, and destroy us. Once these [conclusions] have been deduced in this manner from the testimony of the senses, reason dictates that there is some superior authority to which we are rightly subject, god, that is, who holds over us a just and ineluctable power, who, as he thinks proper, can lift us up or throw us down, [and], with the same powerful command, make us happy or wretched; who, since he himself has created the soul, and wrought the fabric of the body with wonderful art, has an intimate view of the faculties and powers of both, their hidden fabric and nature; the soul he can fill and disturb with anxieties and delight, the body with pain or pleasure; and he can instantly raise either of them to the heights of blessedness or thrust them down into wretchedness and punishment. From this it is perfectly clear that reason, with sense to show the way, can lead us to a knowledge of a legislator, or some superior power, to whom we are necessarily subject, which was the first

folio 57) requirement for the knowledge of any law.

I acknowledge, however, that others have set out to prove from the witness of conscience that there is a divine power and that it presides over this world,[52] [and] others, from that idea of god which

---

[52]Von Leyden helpfully cites Calvin and the Cambridge Platonist Henry More as proponents of the argument proving the existence of God from human conscience. The argument occurs in Calvin's *Institutiones Christianae* I 3; and without elaboration

nobis innata videtur, quae utraque argumentandi methodus si
5 deum esse[3] certo probet, et si (quod rem accuratius intuenti forsan
apparebit) vim suam omnem utriusque argumenta a nativis nostris
facultatibus sensu scilicet et ratione circa res sensibiles operantibus
et inde deductis argumentorum momentis non mutuentur. sufficit
tamen ad confirmandam argumenti nostri veritatem, posse homi-
10 nem sensu simul et ratione utentem[4] pervenire in cognitionem
summi alicujus numinis, uti supra ostensum est, ut omittam in
praesens merito dubitari posse, utrum idea illa dei omnibus hominibus a natura insit, cum si qua peregrinantibus adhibenda fides,
aliquas esse in orbe

[1]New paragraph in A; not in B. [2]*quidem* A; *equidem* B. [3]*si deum esse* deleted after
utraque, then added by Locke in B; in A. [4]Our correction for *utens* A, B.

(folio 58) terrarum gentes, quae nullum omnino agnoscunt numen[1] uti tes-
tantur eorum itineraria. cum nulla ubique sit gens tam barbara, tam
ab omni humanitate[2] remota, quae sensuum usu non gaudeat, quae
rationis privilegio et argumentandi facultate belluas non superat,
5 licet forsan facultates illas[3] nativas parum excoluerit adhibita discip-
lina, et adeo omnes ubique homines sufficienter a natura instructi
sunt ad deum in operibus suis investigandum, si nativis hisce facultatibus uti non negligant;[4] et quo ducat natura sequi non dedignen-
tur. patet igitur posse homines a rebus sensibilibus colligere superi-
10 orem esse aliquem potentem sapientemque[5] qui in homines ipsos

seems innate to us.[53] If either of these methods of arguing should prove certainly that god exists, and if (as will perhaps be apparent to one who examines the matter with some care), the arguments of neither method derive their entire force from our native faculties, sense, that is, and reason working on sensible things, and from the stages of arguments deduced from sensible things, it is sufficient, nevertheless, to confirm the truth of our argument that man can, by making use of sense and reason together, arrive at a knowledge of some supreme power, as has been shown above. I will not mention at present that it can be doubted with reason whether that idea of god exists in all men by nature, for if any credence is to be given to travelers, there exist some races

lio 58) in the world who recognize no divine power at all, as the accounts of their travels testify.[54] But there exists nowhere a race so barbarous, so far removed from all humanity, that it does not take joy in the use of the senses [and] is not superior to brute beasts in the privilege of reasoning and the faculty of argumentation; [even] granted perhaps that they cultivate but slightly these native faculties with the application of discipline. And for this reason all men, wherever they are, are adequately provided by nature for the investigation of god in his works, if they do not neglect to make use of these faculties and do not disdain to follow nature's guidance. It is obvious, therefore, that men can infer from sensible things that there exists some powerful

in Henry More's *An Antidote against Atheism* (1653, which Locke had in the edition of 1655, LL 2047a). The text Locke knew can be consulted in Henry More, *Opera Omnia*, ed. Serge Hutin (Georg Olms, 1966), bk. I, chap. 10, secs. 1–5, pp. 46–47.

[53]The most immediate argument for the existence of God from innate ideas is that of Descartes in *Meditations* V (to be consulted in *Oeuvres de Descartes*, ed. Adam and Tannery, 7:65–71; cf. LL 601a and 602). It is also urged by Henry More (n. 52, above), vol. II.2, pp. 36–46.

[54]Locke gives several examples in the *Essay*, ed. Nidditch, I 4. 8, pp. 87–88. But the most striking example known to him as he wrote the *Questions* might be that of Jean de Léry, who described the amazement of the Brazilian Tapinamba (Locke's Tououpi-nambos) at the Calvinist Léry's discourses on God and his creation, *Histoire d'un voyage fait en Bresil* (La Rochelle, 1578 [LL 1578]), chap. XVI, pp. 230–61). Significant, too, is the entry Locke made in his *Lemmata Ethica*, before writing the *Questions*, under the heading *Atheismus* (from 1659, Bodl. Locke MS d.10, p. 3).

jus habet et imperium. quis enim negabit lutum figuli voluntati esse
subjectum, testamque eadem manu qua formata est

[1]*agnoscunt numen* A; *numen agnoscant* B. [2]*omni humanitate* A; *humanitate omni* B.
[3]*facultates illas* Locke's correction for *facultatem illas* B; *facultatem illas* A. [4]*negligant* B;
neglicant A. [5]*sapientemque* A; omitted in B.

(folio 59) posse comminui.

2⁰ Igitur cum ex sensuum testimonio concludendum sit, esse
aliquem harum rerum omnium opificem quem non solum potentem sed sapientem agnoscere necesse sit, sequitur inde, illum non
5 frustra et temere fecisse hunc mundum, repugnat enim tantae sapientiae nullo destinato fine operari. neque enim credere potest
homo cum se sentiat mentem habere agilem capacem ad omnia
promptam et versatilem ratione et cognitione ornatam, corpus insuper agile et pro animae imperio huc illuc mobile. haec omnia ad
10 agendum parata sibi a sapientissimo authore dari, ut nihil agat, his
se[1] facultatibus omnibus instrui ut eo splendidius otietur, et tor-
pescat: unde liquido constat, deum velle illum aliquid agere. quod
secundum erat requisitum ad legis cujusvis cognitionem, scilicet
voluntas superioris potestatis

[1]*se* A; omitted in B.

(folio 60) circa res a nobis agendas[,] hoc est velle illum nos aliquid agere. quid
vero illud sit quod nobis agendum est, partim ex fine rerum omnium
quae cum a beneplacito divino suam mutuentur originem, et opera
sint authoris summe perfecti et sapientis non videntur ab eo ad
5 alium[1] destinari finem, quam ad sui ipsius gloriam, ad quam omnia
referri debent, partim etiam officii nostri rationem certamque regulam colligere possumus ex hominis ipsius constitutione, et faculta-

and wise being who has jurisdiction and power over men themselves. Who, indeed, will say, that clay is not subject to the potter's
will and that the pot cannot be destroyed by the same hand that
shaped it.[55]

lio 59)   2º, Therefore, since it is necessary to conclude from the testimony
of the senses that there exists some creator of all these things, whom
it is necessary to recognize not only as powerful but also as wise, it
follows from this that he has not made this world at random and to
no purpose, since it is repugnant for a wisdom so great to work with
no end set out before it. Nor, indeed, since he perceives that he
possesses a mind which is quick, receptive, ready for everything, and
versatile, adorned with reason and knowledge, and a body too which
is agile and can move to one place or another as the mind commands, can man believe that all of these things have been given to
him by a most wise creator, ready for use, so that he can do nothing;
that he is provided with all of these faculties so that with all the more
brilliance he can remain idle and languish? From this is perfectly
clear that god wills him to do something—which was the second
requirement for a knowledge of any law, that is, the will of a superior
power

lio 60)   concerning what we must do; that is, that he wills us to do something. What it is we must do we can infer in part from the end and
purpose of all things which, since they derive their origin from a
divine decree and are the works of a most perfect and wise creator,
do not seem to be destined by him to any other end than to his own
glory, to which all things ought to be directed. In part too, [we can
infer] the principle of our duty and its certain rule from the constitution of man himself and the equipment of the human faculties, since

[55]Cf. Romans 9:21 ("Hath not the potter power over the clay, of the same lump to
make one vessel unto honour, and another into dishonour?"), Isaiah 64:8, and Jeremiah 18:6.

tum humanarum apparatu, cum enim nec temere factus sit homo,
nec in nihilum his donatus facultatibus quae exerceri et possunt et
10 debent, id videtur opus hominis, ad quod naturaliter agendum
instructus est, id est, cum in se sensus, et rationem reperit pronum se
et paratum sentit, ad dei[2] opera, ejusque in iis sapientiam poten-
tiamque contemplandam, et laudem deinde honorem et gloriam
tanto tamque benefico authore

[1]*alium* B; *allium* A. [2]*dei* A; *Dei* B.

(folio 61) dignissimam tribuendam reddendamque. deinde[1] ad vitae conjunc-
tionem cum aliis hominibus conciliandam et conservandam, non
solum vitae[2] usu et necessitate impelli, sed ad societatem ineundam
propensione quadam naturae incitari eamque tuendam sermonis
5 beneficio et linguae commercio instrui, quantum vero ad se ipsum[3]
conservandum obligetur cum ad eam officii partem interno instinctu nimium quam impellatur, nemoque repertus sit qui se negligit se ipsum abdicet, et in hanc rem omnes forte magis[4] attenti sint,
quam oportet non opus est ut hic moneam, sed de his tribus quae
10 omne hominum erga deum,[5] vicinum et seipsum complectuntur
officium alibi[6] forte[7] singillatim disserendi erit locus.

VI. An ex inclinatione hominum naturali potest cognosci lex Naturae? Negatur.[8]

[1]*deinde* A; *Deinde* B. [2]*vitae* added by Locke in B; not in A. [3]*se ipsum* A; *seipsam* B.
[4]*magis* added by Locke in B; *forte attentiores sint* A. [5]*deum* A; *Deum* B. [6]*alibi* B; *allibi* A.
[7]*forte* added by Locke in B; not in A. [8]Title and numeral in Locke's hand in B. Title in
A: *An firma animi persuasio probat legem naturae.*

man is not made by accident, nor has he been given these faculties, which both can and ought to be exercised, to do nothing. It seems that the function of man is what he is naturally equipped to do; that is, since he discovers in himself sense and reason, and perceives himself inclined and ready to perform the works of god, as he ought, and to contemplate his power and wisdom in these works, and then to offer and render him the laud, honor, and glory most worthy of so great and so beneficent a creator.

)lio 61) Then, [he perceives that he is] impelled to form and preserve a union of his life with other men, not only by the needs and necessities of life, but [he perceives also that] he is driven by a certain natural propensity to enter society and is fitted to preserve it by the gift of speech and the commerce of language. And, indeed, there is no need for me to stress here to what degree he is obliged to preserve himself, since he is impelled to this part of his duty, and more than impelled, by an inner instinct, and no man has been found who is careless of himself, or capable of disowning himself. In this matter all men are perhaps more attentive than they ought to be. But concerning these three things which comprehend all of men's duty toward god, his neighbor, and himself, perhaps there will be a place elsewhere to discuss each in its turn.

VI. Can the law of Nature be known from the natural inclination of mankind? It cannot. [MS B.] Does the firm persuasion of the mind prove the law of nature? [MS A.]

7 An lex naa cognosci potest ex. 62
Hominum consensu.? Neg

Vox populi, vox Dei, quam incerta quam
fallax sit hoc regula malorum ferax
quanto; nos certe infelici nimis documento didicimus, adeo ut si huic banderae
~~corde tomus esse toium~~ quid enim est tam
nefarium, tam impium, tam contra
jus omne falsa quod non aliquando
suadetur populi insanientis congressus,
sive potius conjuratio? hinc spoliata
deorum templa, confirmatam audaciam
et turpitudinem, violatas leges everga
regna accepimus; at certe si hoc sit
vox Dei, contraria plane est, primo
illi Fiat, quo exornatam hanc compagem
creavit, et e nihilo eduxit, nec unquam
sic homines alloquitur Deus, nisi cum
omnia iterum misera et in chaos redigere velit; frustra ~~etiam~~ igitur in hominum consensu quaeremus rationis dictata aut decreta naa. Consensus autem
hominum diversimode considerari

Vox populi vox dei, quam incerta quam fallax
sit haec regula, et malorum ferax, quanto partium
studio, quam atroci consilio in vulgus jactatam
sit hoc mali ominis proverbium, nos certe nisi foelici
nimis documento didicimus, adeo ut si huic voci
tanquam legi divinae praeconi auscultare volimus
vix aliquem tandem crederemus esse deum

VII. An lex naturae cognosci potest ex hominum consensu? Negatur.[1]

Vox[2] populi vox dei, quam incerta quam fallax sit haec regula, et malorum ferax;[3] quanto partium studio, quam atroci consilio in vulgus jactatum[4] sit hoc mali ominis[5] proverbium, nos certe in-faelici[6] nimis documento didicimus, adeo ut si huic voci tanquam
5 legis divinae[7] praeconi auscultare velimus[,] vix aliquem tandem crederemus esse deum. quid enim est tam nefarium, tam impium, tam contra jus omne, fasque, quod non aliquando suaderet multi-tudinis[8] insanientis consensus, sive potius conjuratio? hinc spoliata

ılio 62) VII. Can the law of nature be known from the
consensus[56] of mankind? It cannot.

"The voice of the people is the voice of god."[57] We have learned
from experience that is all too unfortunate, how uncertain and how
deceptive this rule is, how productive it is of evils, [and] with what
great partisan zeal and grim designs this maxim of ill omen has been
hurled at the lowest classes, so much so that were we willing to
harken to this voice as if it were the herald of divine law, we should
finally hardly believe in the existence of any god at all. What is there
so evil, so impious, so contrary to every law, civil and divine, that at
some time the consent, or rather the conspiracy to which the multi-

---

[56]*consensus* I translate by "consensus" and "agreement" rather than a term like
"General Consent," which is the term Locke chose in the *Essay*, for reasons I give in
my Translator's Introduction, sec. 5.

[57]*Vox populi vox dei*. The proverb can be traced back to Alcuin and a letter to
Charlemagne of 798 (in *Monumenta Germaniae Historica*, vol. 4 [Berlin 1895], p. 199).
Alcuin treats it as already proverbial and with caution. But in the theory of natural
law it came to figure as an instance of the axiom that a universal effect requires a
universal cause. Culverwel, in his treatment of the "consent of Nations," *Discourse*,
(chap. 10, p. 81), evoked the proverb with cautious approval: "As face answers face,
so does the heart of one man the heart of another, even the heart of an Athenian, the
heart of an Indian." Culverwel cites Hugo Grotius's a posteriori argument for the law
of nature that a universal effect requires a universal cause: *universalis effectus universalem requirit causam* (p. 78). The reference is to *De Jure Belli ac Pacis* (1625) I 1.sec. 12;
cf. p. 14 of his *Prolegomena*. Hooker, too, adduces the proverb to demonstrate the
existence of a law of nature in his *Ecclesiastical Polity* I 8. 3.3: "The general and
perpetual voice of men is as the sentence of God himself. For that which all men at all
times have learned, Nature herself must needs have taught." But Locke is not as
approving. In his *Conduct of the Understanding* (*The Works of John Locke* [London, 1801],
3:226) he demurs: "But however 'vox populi vox Dei' has prevailed as a maxim; yet I
do not remember where ever God delivered his oracles by the multitude; or nature,
truths by the herd." Sir Thomas Browne entertained the same contempt for the
proverb in his *Pseudodoxia Epidemica*, ed. Robin Robbins (Oxford: Clarendon Press,
1981) I, chap. 3, p. 18. (The work was first published in 1646.)

deorum templa, confirmatam audaciam et turpitudinem, violatas
10 leges, eversa regna accepimus; et certe si haec sit vox dei,[9] contraria
plane est, primo illi Fiat, quo ornatam hanc compagem creavit, et e
nihilo[10] eduxit, nec unquam sic homines alloquitur[11] deus,[12] nisi
cum omnia iterum miscere et in chaos redigere velit; frustra igitur[13]
in hominum consensu quaereremus rationis dictata aut decreta na-
15 turae. consensus[14] autem hominum diversimode considerari

[1]Title and numeral in Locke's hand in B. [2]*Vox . . . deum* recopied by Locke on fol.
61ᵛ in B (B had skipped two lines of A). [3]*plena* after *ferax* A. [4]*jactatum* Locke's
correction for *jactata* B; *jactata* A; *non ita pridem* inserted above *jactata* A; omitted in B.
[5]*ominis* B; *omnis* A. [6]*infaelici* B; *nifaelici* A. [7]*divinae* B; *diviniae* A. [8]*multitudinis* Locke's
correction for *populi* B; *populi* A. [9]*dei* A; *Dei* B. [10]*nihilo* Locke's correction for *chao* B;
chao A. [11]*alloquitur* B; *aloquitur* A. [12]*deus* A; *Deus* B. [13]*igitur* Locke's correction for
iterum B; *igitur* A. [14]*consensus* A; *Consensus* B.

(folio 63) potest, 1° enim dividi potest in consensum positivum, et naturalem:
positivum eum vocamus, qui[1] ex pacto fit, vel tacito, suadente scilicet communi hominum necessitate, et commodo; qualis est legatorum liber commeatus, mercatura libera,[2] et id genus alia, vel ex-
5 presso,[3] ut inter finitimas gentes terminorum constituti limites,
certas merces emendi et importandi prohibitio, et alia plurima, qui
uterque[4] consensus cum[5] totus ex pacto pendeat, nec ex principio
quovis naturae fluat, legem[6] naturae minime probat. nam verbi
gratia consensum illum de legatis recipiendis qui apud omnes pene
10 gentes obtinuit positivum esse nec inferre legem naturae inde constat quod ex[7] lege naturae omnes homines inter se amici sint,[8] et
communi necessitudine[9] conjuncti, nisi, quod aliqui volunt, in statu
naturae commune sit bellum, et hominibus inter ipsos perpetuum et

tude in its madness, has not persuaded [men to]? We know that by the urgings of this voice the temples of the gods have been despoiled, audacity and viciousness strengthened, laws trampled, and kingdoms overthrown. And, surely, were this the voice of god, it is clearly contrary to that original Fiat by which he created and adorned the fabric [of this world] and brought it into being out of nothing.[58] Nor does god ever address men in this manner except when he wishes to cast all things into confusion once again and return them to chaos. Therefore, we seek in vain for the dictates of reason or the decrees of nature in the consensus of mankind.

Now the consensus of mankind can be considered in different ways:

)lio 63)   1º, It can be divided into a positive consensus and a natural consensus. We call a positive consensus one which issues from a compact, either tacit, as when some common human necessity or advantage draws men to it, such as the free movement of ambassadors, a free market, and other things of this kind; or expressed, as the establishment of boundaries among neighboring nations, the embargo against buying or importing certain goods, and many other agreements of this kind. Neither of these kinds of agreements proves the existence of a law of nature at all, since they both depend entirely on a compact, and issue from no principle of nature whatsoever. For, to give one example, it is clear that the common agreement on the treatment of envoys which has obtained among almost all nations is a positive agreement and does not imply a law of nature, for the reason that by the law of nature all men should be friends to one another and joined together by a common necessity, unless it is the case, as some will have it, that in the state of nature war is common, and there exists among men a perpetual, mutual, and internecine enmity.[59] Whichever alternative you settle on,

[58]Cf. Genesis 1:3.

[59]Cf. Hobbes, *Leviathan* I 13, p. 62: "Hereby, it is manifest, that during the time when men live without a common power to keep them all in awe, they are in a condition which is called war; and such a war, as is of every man, against everyman"; cf. *De Cive* (1647) in *Opera Latine*, ed. Molesworth, 2:15.

internecinum odium, sive autem hoc, sive illud statueris; sive homi-
15 nes infensos inter se, sive amicos esse velis, nulla tamen ex lege
naturae dari potest ratio, cur legati apud exteros populos, quam
privati cujus-

[1]*qui* Locke's correction for *quae* B; *quae* A. [2]*libera* added by Locke in B; in A. [3]*vel expresso* added by Locke in B; in A. [4]*uterque* added by Locke in B; not in A. [5]*cum* B; *quum* A. [6]*legem.... quod* added by Locke on fol. 62ᵛ in B; not in A. *legem naturae minime probare possit* struck out in A. [7]*Cum enim* struck out before *ex* B; *Cum enim* A. [8]*sint* Locke's correction for *sunt* B; *sunt* A. [9]*necessitudine* A; *necessitate* B.

(folio 64) piam tutior sit commeatus, aut potior conditio; nisi ex tacito hominum id fieret[1] pacto, ex necessitate orto; ut scilicet res per injuriam
ablatas unius potius[2] postulationibus, quam multorum aperta vi
repetere possint; cum sane lex naturae privatum quemvis aeque ac
5 legatum sine causa laedere aut violare omnino prohibeat; fateor
equidem supposito hujusmodi pacto, majus est legatorum quam
privati cujuspiam violati crimen, cum duplex sit reatus,[3] facta scilicet
injuria et laesa fides, quod igitur sanctior sit apud homines legatus
quam alter quispiam, id non ex lege naturae sancitum sit,[4] cum lex
10 illa homines inter se odio flagrantes, in hostiles civitates divisos, nec
supponit, nec permittit; nec sane consensus ille positivus[5] dictus in
aliis rebus tantus est ut[6] ad omnes pertineat[7] populos, quod enim
forte inter finitimas hasce et vicinas Europae gentes pro rato et ab

[1]*hominum id fieret* A; *id fieret hominum* B. [2]*potius* Locke's correction for *potitus* B; *potitus* A. [3]*reatus* Locke's correction for *ratus* B; *ratus* A. [4]*sit* A; *est* B. [5]*positivus* B; *possitivus* A. [6]*in ... ut* added by Locke in B; not in A. [7]*pertineat* Locke's correction for *pertinet* B; *pertinet* A.

(folio 65) omnibus comprobato habetur, alii et Asiae et Americae populi
longo terrarum tractu sejuncti, nec moribus nostris aut opinionibus
assueti, negligunt prorsus et nihili aestimant, nec iisdem legibus se
teneri arbitrantur. Hic igitur totus ex pacto consensus legem natu-
5 rae non probat, sed potius jus gentium dicendus est, quod lex naturae non jussit, sed communis utilitas persuasit hominibus.
    2° Consensus naturalis, in quem scilicet homines feruntur in-
stinctu quodam naturae sine alicujus foederis interventu, triplex

whether you will have men as friends or enemies to one another, in either case, no principle can be adduced from the law of nature to explain why ambassadors to foreign peoples have a safer passage or better treatment than any private citizen,

io 64) unless this were to originate in a tacit compact of men, which has arisen from a necessity, that men can, for example, by the representations of a single individual, rather than the open force of many, reclaim possessions which have been wrongfully taken from them. Yet it is clearly the case that the law of nature prohibits altogether injuring or doing violence without cause to any private citizen or envoy alike. I admit, however, that, on the assumption of a pact of this kind, a crime against an envoy is greater than a crime against any private citizen, since the offense is double; that is, the wrong done and the breaking of a promise. The fact that among mankind an envoy is more sacrosanct than any single individual is not something sanctioned by the law of nature, because that law neither supposes nor permits men to be inflamed by mutual enmity, or to be divided into hostile states. Nor in fact is that agreement we have termed positive so all embracing in other matters that it pertains to all peoples. Although it is an agreement which is perhaps considered as right and universally established among these related and neighboring nations of Europe,

io 65) there are other peoples both of Asia and America, separated by great expanses of space, and familiar with neither our manners nor opinions, who pay it no heed and attribute no value to it, nor do they consider themselves to be subject to these same laws. Therefore, this entire consensus deriving from compact does not prove the law of nature, but it is better described as the law of nations [*jus gentium*], because it has not been enjoined by the law of nature but urged on mankind by their common advantage.

2°, Natural consensus, that is, an agreement to which men are brought by a kind of natural instinct without the intervention of any

esse potest. 1° Morum sive actionum, ea scilicet convenientia, quae
10 in hominum moribus et communis vitae usu reperitur.

2° Opinionum, quibus homines varium praebent[1] assensum aliis
firmum et constantem aliis tenuem[2] et instabilem[.]

3° Principiorum, quae hujusmodi plane sunt ut facilem a quovis
homine mentis suae compote extorqueant assensum, nec quivis
15 unquam sanus repertus est qui de eorum veritate intellectis[3] ter-
minis dubitare possit ⟨quae[4] omnia

---

[1]*praebent* Locke's correction for *praebet* B; *praebet* A. [2]*flexumque* deleted after *tenuem*
B; in A. *et instabilem* Locke's addition in B. [3]*intellectis* Locke's correction for *auditis* B;
auditis A. [4]*quae . . . identica* struck out by Locke in B; in A.

(folio 66) principia communi ita consensu comprobata mihi videntur hujusmodi esse quae manifestam in se continent repugnantiam quale
est illud idem non potest esse et non esse aut[1] plane identica.⟩

1° Igitur de morum consensu dicimus, eum minime probare
5 legem naturae, actum enim esset de morum rectitudine, et hones-
tate, si ex hominum vita jus fasque aestimandum esset, quae turpitudo[2] non modo licita, sed etiam necessaria non esset? si legem
nobis darent majoris partis exempla? in quam nos infamiam, ne-
quitiam, et omne genus flagitiorum deduceret lex naturae, si illic[3]
10 eundum esset, quo a pluribus itur? quotusquisque enim est inter
moratiores[4] populos, certis sub legibus, quas omnes agnoscunt, et
quibus se teneri fatentur enutritos, qui moribus suis vitia non com-
probat, et malo exemplo alios saepissime errare non docet? cujus
frequentes numerari non possunt lapsus? adeo jam omne genus
15 malorum inter homines excrevit, et per universum orbem se diffu-
dit, rebusque[5] omnibus se imiscuit[,]

---

[1]*aut. . . . identica* added by Locke in B; not in A. [2]*turpitudo* Locke's correction for
turpitudine B; *turpitudine* A. [3]*illic* A; *illuc* B. [4]*moratiores* added by Locke in B; in A.
[5]*rebusque* Locke's correction for *et rebus* B; *et rebus* A.

compact, can be threefold: first, [consensus] of conduct or actions, that is, that accord which is discovered in men's conduct and the experience of daily life; second, of opinions, to which men offer varying degrees of assent—to some firm and constant, to others weak and unstable; third, of principles, such as are sufficiently clear that they exact the ready assent of any man of sane mind, nor has any sane person ever been found who could doubt their truth, once their terms have been understood.

(io 66)   ⟨All of the principles which are established by this kind of common agreement seem to me to be of the sort that contain within themselves some obvious contradiction, such as the well-known example that it is impossible for the same thing to be and not to be, or propositions that are clearly tautologous.⟩[60]

1°, We say therefore of the consensus of conduct that [of the three kinds of natural consensus], it least proves the existence of the law of nature. The case concerning right conduct and virtue would be settled, if moral and religious duty were to be judged on the basis of men's lives. What form of viciousness would be not only permitted, but necessary, if the example of the majority were to give us law? Into what shame, iniquity, and into what a variety of crimes would the law of nature lead us, if we were to follow the path taken by the majority? How many are there in the more civilized nations, living under fixed laws, which all recognize, and under which they acknowledge themselves to have been raised and to be ruled, who do not sanction their vices by their own conduct, and who do not on innumerable occasions teach others to err by their own bad example, whose frequent lapses cannot be counted? Now every variety of evil has grown so rank among mankind, and spread itself throughout the entire world, insinuated itself in all things;

[60]Locke deleted this passage in MS B. This speculative principle—"'Tis impossible for the same thing to be, and not to be"—is addressed in the *Essay*, ed. Nidditch, I 2.4, p. 49, as an example of a maxim that, for the theorists of innate ideas, commands "universal consent." What Locke shows is that this consent cannot possibly be regarded as universal.

(folio 67) tanta jam olim fuit hominum in moribus corrumpendis solertia; et
vitiorum tanta varietas, ut posteris quod reperiri possit quod super-
addi nihil relictum sit. nec possibile est quemquam jam nullo exemplo crimen quodvis admittere, adeo ut qui ad hunc actionum
5 humanarum consensum, morum rectitudinem exigere velit; et inde
legem naturae colligere. nihilo plus agit, quam si det operam, ut
cum ratione insaniat. Nemo igitur ex hac pessima hominum concordia legem naturae astruere conatus est, dici sane potest non ex
hominum moribus, sed sententiis colligendam esse legem naturae;
10 non vitas hominum sed animas scrutari[1] debemus; illic enim inscribi
naturae decreta, illic latere morum regulas, et principia illa, quae
mores corrumpere non possunt: quaeque cum in omnibus eadem
sint, alium authorem habere non possunt praeter deum[2] et naturam; et hinc esse, quod[3] illam legem internam, quam negant saepe

[1]*scrutari* Locke's correction for *scrutare* B; *scrutare* A. [2]*deum* A; *Deum* B. [3]*quod* Locke's
correction for *ut* B; *ut* A.

(folio 68) vitia, fateatur hominum conscientia, et illi ipsi qui perverse agunt,
recte sentiant. transeamus igitur ad consensum illum quem[1] in hominum opinionibus repertum iri speramus.

2º Dicimus igitur 1º[2] non dari inter homines de rebus moralibus
5 universalem et communem consensum. 2º Si daretur constans et
unanimis omnium qui ubique sunt hominum de rebus agendis consensus, ex eo tamen colligi et certo cognosci non posse legem naturae.

1º Non datur inter homines de morum rectitudine communis
10 consensus. et hic priusquam ad singula descendero, breviter dicam,
nullum pene esse vitium, nullam legis naturae violationem, nullam
morum turpitudinem, quam non facile patebit mundi historias con-

lio 67) for so long now has there been such great genius among men in corrupting morals, and so great the variety of vice, that there is nothing left which can be discovered or added by posterity. Nor is it possible for someone to confess to any crime for which there has not already been some example. As a result, whoever wants to make moral rectitude conform to this consensus among men, and from this to derive the law of nature, has no more success than if he were to devote his energies to playing the part of the madman according to reason.[61] No one, therefore, has attempted to establish a law of nature on the basis of this, the worst kind of harmony and concord among men. Surely, it can be said rather that the law of nature should be derived not from men's conduct, but from their opinions. We should not examine men's lives, but their souls. Indeed, it is there that the decrees of nature are inscribed, that the rules of conduct lie hidden, and those principles [reside] which [bad] habits cannot corrupt. These, since they are the same in all men, can have no other author than god and nature, and this explains why men's conscience confesses to that inner law which their vices often deny,

lio 68) and why those very persons who act wrongly, yet think rightly. Let us then proceed to that consensus which we hope will be discovered in men's opinions:

2°, We say therefore: i. There does not exist among men a universal and common consensus concerning moral matters. ii. If there did exist a stable and unanimous consensus of all men everywhere concerning what they should do, it would be impossible even then to derive the law of nature from this or come to a certain knowledge of it.

1°, There exists among men no common consensus concerning right conduct. And now, before I descend to particulars, I will state in brief that there exists virtually no vice, no violation of the law of nature, no moral viciousness, which will not be quite evident to

[61]A quotation from Terence, *The Eunuch* I l. 17–18. The slave Parmeno is speaking to his master, the love-sick Phaedria: "If you fancy that you can manage all these uncertain matters [love], you will have no more success than if you resolved to rave with reason" (*nihilo plus agas / quam si des operam ut cum ratione insanias*).

sulenti, et hominum res gestas observanti, alicubi terrarum, non solum privatim admissam, sed publica authoritate,[3] et consuetudine
15 comprobatam. nec[4] aliquid tam sua natura turpe fuisse quin aut religione alicubi consecratum, aut virtutis loco, habitum, et laudibus cumulatum

[1]*quem* Locke's correction for *qui* B; *qui* A. [2]1º omitted in B; in A. [3]*authoritate* B; *autoritate* A. [4]*nec* A; *Nec* B.

(folio 69) fuerit; unde facile est scire, quaenam[1] fuit ea de re hominum sententia, cum hujusmodi rebus aut se deos[2] sancte colere aut se heroas fieri arbitrarentur, nam ut omittam varias populorum religiones, alias caeremoniis[3] ridiculas, alias ritibus impias, et cultu ipso
5 nefandas, quarum ipsam mentionem reliquae gentes perhorrescerent,[4] et sacros eorum ritus, cum ipsa naturae lege manifesto pugnantes novis sacrificiis expiandos crederent; ut haec inquam omittam; cum religionem[5] non tam lumine naturae, quam revelatione divina hominibus innotescere credendum sit, si singula virtutum et
10 vitiorum genera recensere velimus, quas[6] nemo dubitat esse ipsam legem naturae[7]: facile constabit nullum[8] esse de quo variae non sunt hominum opiniones, publica authoritate et consuetudine stabilitae,[9] adeo ut si hominum consensus habendus sit morum regula,[10] aut nulla erit lex

[1]*quaenam* B; *quae nam* A. [2]*deos* A; *Deos* B. [3]*caeremoniis* A; *ceremoniis* B. [4]*perhorrescerent* Locke's correction for *perhorrescunt* B; *perhorrescerent* A. [5]*religionem* Locke's correction for *religiones* B; *religiones* A. [6]*quas* Locke's correction for *quae* B; *quae* A. [7]*ipsam . . . naturae* Locke's correction for *partem legis naturae praecipuam* B; *partem . . . praecipuam* A. [8]*nullum* A; *nullam* B. [9]*stabilitae* Locke's correction for *stabilitas* B; *stabilitas* A. [10]*habendus* after *regula* B.

(folio 70) naturae, aut diversis in locis diversa, id hic honestum quod alibi turpe, et vitia ipsa transibunt in officia, quod nemo dixerit; dum enim homines ea quae obtinuit opinione ducti, hoc vel illud pro more gentis suae perpetrarunt, quod forte aliis nec sine ratione
5 inhonestum, et impium videretur, non se legem naturae violasse sed

anyone who consults the histories of the world and observes the human events [of his own time] as not only something allowed privately somewhere in the world, but also ratified by public authority and practice. Nor has there existed anything so disgraceful in its own nature that it has not in some place been sanctioned by religion or considered as a virtue and exalted with praise.

lio 69) This said, it is easy to know what men's thought has been concerning this matter, since by actions of this kind they thought they were worshipping and sacrificing to their gods or becoming "heroes"—I will not enter into the various religions of peoples, some ridiculous because of their ceremonies, others impious in the rites, and abominable in the very form of their worship—religions whose very name makes other races recoil with horror—and their sacred rites, which [these other races] thought were in open conflict with the law of nature itself and needed to be expiated by still fresh sacrifices. These things, I say, I will not enter into, since we ought to believe that religion becomes known to men not so much by the light of nature as by divine revelation. Should we survey, one by one, the kinds of virtues and vices, [virtues] which no one doubts constitute the law of nature itself, it will soon become evident that there exists no kind concerning which men's opinions do not vary and are not confirmed by public approval and practice. And so, were the consensus of mankind to be considered the rule of morals, there would either exist no law

lio 70) of nature, or this law would vary from place to place; one thing is considered virtuous in one place and vicious elsewhere; and vices themselves are transformed into duties—something no one will acknowledge. For men have judged themselves not to have violated, but to have observed, the law of nature, since they have been guided by the then dominant opinion [and] have performed one action or another in conformity with the custom of their race, actions which seem perhaps to others, and not without reason, vicious and im-

potius observasse putarunt, nulla senserunt conscientiae verbera, nec internum illud animi flagellum, quod ulcisci et exagitare solet criminis conscios, dum existimarent[1] id, quicquid fuerit, sibi non modo licere, sed etiam laudi fuisse, unde manifesto colligere licet, non solum qui hominum mores, sed quaenam etiam de moribus illis opinio fuerit.

Quid[2] de justitia, eximia illa lege naturae, et omnis societatis vinculo, sensisse homines putemus; cum accepimus ab authoribus[3] fide dignis totas gentes ex professo piratas fuisse,

---

[1]*existimarent* A; *existimarunt* B. [2]New paragraph at *Quid* A; not in B. [3]*authoribus* A; *autoribus* B.

(folio 71) et praedones, οὐ παράδοξον ἦν τοῖς παλαιοῖς λῃστεύην,[1] ἀλλ᾽ ἔνδο-ξον inquit in suo in Homerum scholio Didymus.[2] Apud veteres Aegyptios quod genus hominum constat et in artibus reperiendis solertes extitisse, et in cognitione rerum indaganda sagaces; furta omnia fuisse licita et impunita affirmat Aristo ab A. Gellio citatus. Apud Lacedaemonios[3] quoque sobrios illos ac acres viros, cujus rei non adeo ut Aegyptiis fides longinqua est, non pauci neque igno-biles scriptores, jus atque usum fuisse furandi dicunt, inquit idem[4] Gellius[.] et vero ipsi Romani qui universo orbi virtutum exempla exhibere perhibentur, qua ex re sibi honores, triumphos, gloriam, et immortalem[5] nominis sui memoriam conquisiverunt, nisi ex furto et latrociniis; quibus totum orbem terrarum devastarunt? quid aliud

pious. And they have felt none of the lashes of conscience, nor that internal goad of the heart, which usually wounds and torments those guilty of a crime, because they considered their action, whatever it was, not only permissible but even something praiseworthy. Whence one can plainly infer not only what the morals of mankind have been, but even what their opinion concerning these morals has been as well.

What should we think of men's opinions concerning justice, that sovereign law of nature and bond of all society? We have learned from authors worthy of confidence that entire nations have been, on their own admission, pirates

)lio 71) and brigands; "for the ancients, piracy was not something strange and unexpected, but something reputable," Didymus says in his comment on Homer.[62] Ariston, as quoted by Aulus Gellius, affirms: "Among the ancient Egyptians, a race of men well known as both ingenious in the discovery of arts and keen in pursuing the knowledge of nature, all acts of theft were permitted and went unpunished."[63] This same Gellius says that even among the Lacedemonians, those sober and fierce men, for whom our authority is not so remote as it is in the case of the Egyptians, no few and ignoble writers say that there was both a right and custom of theft.[64] And in truth, the Romans themselves, who are held up as having displayed examples of virtue for the entire world, how did they acquire for themselves honors, triumphs, glory, and an immortal memory for their own name, if not from robbery and rapine by which they laid

---

[62]Didymus's comment is on *Odyssey* III 71–74 and Nestor's question to Telemachus, who had just arrived on Pylos, if he was a pirate. Didymus's comment is preserved in codex 613 of the library of San Marco and appears in Aldus Manutius's edition of the scholia minora of 1528. It is Dindorf's *M*, *Scholia Graeca in Homeris Odysseam* (Oxford, 1855; reprint: Amsterdam, 1962), 1:125.

[63]This quotation and two others (cf. nn. 64 and 66, below) come from Aulus Gellius's treatment of thievery in *Attic Nights* XI 18. The first case, that of thievery among the Egyptians, comes from XI 18.16.

[64]*Attic Nights* XI 18.16.

apud illos tantis encomiis celebrata virtus illa, quid aliud inquam, quam, vis et injuria, nec

¹λησeύην A; ληστύeιν B. ²*inquit* . . . *Didymus* B; *inquit Didymus* A. ³*Lacedaemonios* A; *Lacaedemonios* B. ⁴*idem* B; *Idem* A. ⁵*immortalem* A; *immortalis* B.

(folio 72) adhuc exolevit inimica illa[1] justitiae opinio, cum plurimis adhuc populis spoliare[,] fallere, circumvenire, rapere, et vi et armis quantum possunt, possidere ea demum laus sit, et vera gloria, et inter artes imperatorias habeatur summa, justitiamque credunt, qualem[2]
5 sibi finxerunt, caecam esse, et gladio armatam. Fures inquit Cato privatorum furtorum in nervo atque in compedibus aetatem agunt, fures publici in auro atque in purpura.

Quid[3] de pudicitia et castitate, cum apud Assyrios foeminae nudo penitus corpore, et omnium oculis exposito conviviis interesse cum
10 laude consueverunt, dum apud alias gentes foeminas licet tectas in publicum prodire, aut faciem aperire, et ab ignotis conspici nefas sit; apud alias innuptis puellis stupra facere licet, ad nuptas solum castitatem pertinere arbitrantur, et a libidine mulieres solo matrimonio coerceri. alii sunt, qui genialem torum stupris consecrant, et
15 maritales taedas libidinis

¹*illa* A; *jlla* B. ²*A[ulus] G[ellius] 1.11.C 13* written above *qualem* A. ³New paragraph at *Quid* A; not in B.

(folio 73) flammis accendunt, ubi nova nupta hospites omnes excipit, cujus prima nox tot numerat quot Messalina adulteros; sunt alii apud

the entire world to waste?[65] What else is that great "virtue" so celebrated among them with so many panegyrics, what else is it, I ask, but violence and wrong?

lio 72) And that inimical opinion concerning justice has not yet died out completely. Even now among the majority of peoples, praise and true glory [comes from] pillage, deception, guile, rapine, and gaining as much as possible by force of arms; and among the arts of ruling, "justice" is considered supreme, and they believe justice to be such as they represent her to themselves—blind and armed with a sword. "Thieves involved in private larceny," says Cato, "spend their lives in chains and fetters; public thieves in gold and purple."[66]

What [should we think of men's opinions] concerning modesty and chastity? Among the Assyrians it was the custom of women to mingle with men at banquets, their bodies completely naked and exposed to the eyes of all, and they were praised for it, while among other nations women are permitted to go into public [only] fully clothed, or it is against religion for them to reveal their faces, or to be seen by strangers. Among other nations unwed girls are permitted to engage in debauchery; they consider chastity to apply only to married women, and think that women [should] be restrained from their passions only by matrimony. There are others who consecrate the bridal bed by debauchery and ignite their wedding torches with the flames of lust.

lio 73) Among them, the newly married bride receives all the guests; her nuptial night numbers as many adulterers as did Messalina. There

---

[65]*Rapine (ex furto et latrociniis)* recalls Saint Augustine's description of Roman imperialism as simply rapine on a grand scale (*magna latrocinia*: *City of God* IV 4). In the same critical spirit is Hobbes in the dedicatory letter he addresses to William, Count of Devon, conveying a copy of his *De Cive*. Here he speaks of the Roman monster rending the entire world asunder and naming its citizens after the peoples they had plundered, *Opera Latine*, ed. Molesworth, 2:135.

[66]*Attic Nights* XI.18.18.

quos princeps,[1] alii ubi sacerdos sponsae virginitatis spolium pro more obtinet. Garamantes Aethiopes matrimonia privatim ne-
5 sciunt, sed omnibus vulgo in venerem licet, inquit Solinus, quam turpitudinem de iis etiam affirmat P. Mela[,] et[2] talibus sacris propitiaretur deum mater quibus offenderetur matrona[.] ut omittam polygamiam quae his privilegium illis piaculum habetur, quae illic lege jubetur hic morte mulctanda est.
10   De[3] pietate erga parentes, quid putandum est? cum repertae sint totae gentes apud quas[4] adulta progenies parentes occidit, liberi parcis ipsis saeviores, eam adimunt vitam quam adhuc fata largiuntur, ubi non solum statutum est omnibus mori, sed certa mortis praefinitur hora, nec expectanda est sera dies, et tarde marcescentis
15 senii mora, ubi

---

[1]*princeps* Locke's correction for *principes* B; *princeps* A. [2]*et . . . matrona* added by Locke on fol. 72[v]; not in A. [3]New paragraph in A; not in B. [4]*quas* A; *quos* B.

(folio 74) quisque parentis sui carnifex, et inter pietatis officia numeratur parricidium, Νόμος ἐστὶ Σαρδῶος inquit Aelianus τοὺς ἤδη γεγηρακῶτας τῶν πατέρων οἱ παῖδες ῥοπάλοις τύπτοντες ἀνῇρουν, καὶ ἔθαπτον, αἰσχρὸν ἡγούμενοι τὸν λίαν ὑπέργηρον ὄντα ζῆν ἔτι,

are some among whom the ruler, [still] others, [among whom] the priest, receives the prize of a bride's maidenhead by custom. "The Garamantes of Ethiopia recognize no private [institution of] marriage, but," Solinus says, "it is permitted for all to have sexual relations in common,"[67] and P[omponius] Mela confirms this shameful conduct in what he says about them.[68] The kinds of sacrifices by which the mother of the gods was propitiated were such as would offend a married woman.[69] I will not mention polygamy, something which is considered a privilege by some and a sin by others, a practice which is commanded by law in one place and punished by death in another.

Concerning the sense of duty toward parents what are we to think? Entire nations have been found among whom offspring, when they become adults, kill their parents, [and these] children are crueler than the Fates themselves, destroying that life which fate still lavishes; where not only is it laid down that all must die, but a fixed hour for their death has been determined in advance, and no reprieve can be expected, nor any delay in the gradual wasting of old age.

lio 74)   Each is the executioner of his own parent, and parricide is counted among the duties of obligation to one's parents. Aelian says: "There is a custom in Sardinia that the children of fathers who are far advanced in age would kill them by beating them with sticks and bury them, since they thought it disgraceful for someone who had

[67]*De Memorabilibus Mundi* (which Locke had in the edition of Paris, 1503 [LL 2714]), Chapter XXX.2 (p. 130 in Mommsen's edition of *Collectanea Rerum Memorabilium* [1895]).

[68]*De Chorographia*, ed. Frick, 1.8.45, p. 11 (in the Teubner edition of Stuttgart, 1968).

[69]The reference is to the cult of Cybele as it was celebrated in Rome during the Megalensia. This example of a violation of a "universal consent" concerning decency in sexual matters was added by Locke in fol. 73ᵛ. Von Leyden noted the similarity of Locke's language to that of Saint Augustine in *The City of God* II 5. The specific sacrifices that might have offended a Roman matron took place during the Day of Blood, when a bull was castrated in commemoration of Attis and his genitals placed in a ritual vessel.

5 et eodem in loco Berbiccae[1] omnes septuagesimum annum[2]
egressos interficiunt, nec major alios erga liberos suos tenet cura,
cum nuper natos pro libitu exponunt ideoque solum vitam dedisse
videntur ut auferant, sunt qui subolem foemineam[3] tanquam spu-
riam et naturae erratum prorsus negligunt et a finitimis suis in spem
10 prolis suas mercantur uxores,[4] adeo ut quam legem etiam in brutorum animis sanxisse videtur natura, ea se obligari non sentiant
homines, et feritate belluas superent.[5]

   Si qua autem maxime sancta apud omnes videatur lex naturae, ad
cujus observationem instinctu quodam naturae et suo commodo
15 impelli videtur universum humanum genus, ea certe est sui ipsius
praeservatio,[6] quam

---

[1]*Berbiccae* A; *Berbices*(?) B; *Derbices* vL (Locke presumably read *Berbiccae* in his
edition of Aelian). [2]*annum* B; *anum* A. [3]*foemineam* Locke's correction of *foeminiam* B;
foeminiam A. [4]*uxores* omitted after *prolis* but added by Locke after *mercantur* B; *prolis
uxores* A. [5]*superent* A; *superant* B. [6]*praeservatio* A; *preservatio* B.

(folio 75) nonnulli ideo primariam, et fundamentalem legem naturae consti-
tuunt[.] sed ea est consuetudinis et opinionis ⟨non innatae sed adventitiae et⟩[1] a moribus domesticis mutuatae vis, ut homines etiam
in seipsos armet, ut sibi violentas manus inferant, et eodem studio
5 mortem quaerant, quo alii fugiunt; subditi inventi sunt, qui vivum
regem non solum colunt proteguntque, sed sequuntur mortuum,
servi, qui dominos ad umbras comitantur, et ibi praestare obsequium velint, ubi omnes sunt aequales. nec hoc solum audent viri,
animosior pars[2] mortalium, apud Indos enim imbellis et timidus
10 foeminarum sexus audet lethum[3] contemnere et ad demortuos ma-
ritos, per flammas, per mortem properare, conjugales[4] taedas non
nisi rogi flammis extingui patiuntur, et novos potius optant in ipso
sepulchro quaerere thalamos quam viduos pati toros et conjugis

grown too old to continue to live."[70] And in the same passage he says that "the Berbices kill all who have gone beyond their seventieth year."[71] Nor among some others, does there obtain any greater care for children, since they expose their newborn babies as they please and seem to have given life only that they might take it away. And there are peoples who completely neglect a female child as if she were illegitimate or a freak of nature, and they buy their wives from their neighbors in the hope of having [male ?] children by them. And thus, men do not feel themselves bound by that law, which nature seems to have fixed even in the souls of brutes, and they surpass wild beasts in their savagery.

Yet if there exists a law of nature, which might appear to be the most sacred among all men, which the entire human race seems driven to obey by a certain natural instinct and its own interest, this is surely that of self-preservation,

lio 75) which some establish for this reason as the primary and fundamental law of nature. But, such is the power of custom and opinion (which is not innate but derives from some external source) adopted from the conduct of daily life that it arms men even against themselves, and brings them to lay violent hands upon themselves and pursue death with the same eagerness with which others flee from it. Subjects have been found who not only attend and protect their king while he is alive, but who [also] follow him in death; slaves, who accompany their masters among the shades, who would be willing to offer their obedience in a place where all are equal. Nor are males, the more spirited part of the mortal race, the only ones to show such courage. Among the Indians the weak and timid female sex is daring enough to despise extinction and to hasten [to join] their dead husbands through flames, by their own death, and will allow their wedding torches to be extinguished only by the flames of the funeral pyre. They would rather seek a new marriage chamber in the tomb

[70]Aelian, *Varia Historia* IV.1.

[71]Aelian, *Varia Historia* IV.1. Locke's edition of Aelian (Geneva, 1625 [LL 30]) read "Berbices"; modern editors print "Derbices."

desiderium; cujus rei testem se oculatum[5] profitetur Mandelslo in
15 nupero illo Olearii Itinerario, qui (ut narrat ipse)[6] foeminam vidit[7]
juvenem formosam quae

[1]*non . . . et* deleted after *opinionis* B; in A. [2]*pars* B; *par* A. [3]*lethum* Locke's correction
for *legem* B; *lettum* A. [4]*conjugales* A; *Conjugales* B. [5]*oculatum* Locke's correction for
oculatus B; *oculatum* A. [6]No parentheses in A. [7]*vidit* B; *videt* A.

(folio 76) defuncto marito, cum nullis amicorum monitis precibus, vel lachrymis vinci poterat, et in vita retineri, tandem post invitam sex
mensium moram permittente magistratu, ornata tanquam ad nup-
tias ovans[1] et hilari vultu pyram in medio foro extructam ascendit et
5 in mediis flammis laeta expiravit. longum esset singula persequi. nec
mirandum est tam diversas esse hominum de recto et honesto sententias cum in principiis ipsis differant et deus[2] et animarum im-
mortalitas in dubium vocetur, quae licet non sint propositiones
practicae et leges naturae, necessario tamen ad legis naturae exis-
10 tentiam supponi debent[.] nulla enim lex si nullus legislator; aut
frustra si nulla poena. nam[3] aliquos Brasiliae populos et Soldaniae
incolas deum[4] omnino nullum agnoscere aut colere ferunt illi qui
haec loca adire[5] operae pretium duxerunt, quod si nemo tam sensus

itself than endure their empty widow's bed and the longing for their mate. Mandelslo, in the newly published *Voyages of Olearius*,[72] claims that he was an eyewitness to this; he declares, as he relates the event himself, that he saw a young and beautiful woman,

io 76) who, at the death of her husband, when she could be won over by none of the expostulations, entreaties, or tears of her friends and would not be compelled to continue living, finally, with the permission of the officials and after a forced delay of six months, mounted a funeral pyre which had been constructed in the middle of the public square, and, dressed as a bride, with a jubilant heart and joyous expression, expired happily in the midst of the flames. It would be tedious to continue with such examples. Nor is there any reason to be surprised at the diversity of men's opinions concerning what is right and virtuous given the fact that they disagree on even the most fundamental principles, and god and the immortality of the soul are called into doubt. These, although they are not practical propositions or laws of nature, must, nevertheless, be necessarily assumed for the existence of the law of nature, for there can exist no law without a legislator and law will have no force if there is no punishment. For those who have thought it worth their pains to go to these places report that some peoples of Brazil and the inhabitants of the Bay of Soldania worship no god at all.[73] But even if no

---

[72]In Adam Olearius, *The Voyages and Travels of the Ambassadors from the Duke of Holstein, to the Great Duke of Muscovy, and the King of Persia* . . . (London, 1662 [LL 2128]). Mandelslo's account of the *sati* of the young Indian widow comes from bk. I, pp. 40–41.

[73]The "atheism" of the Brazilian Tapinamba is described by Jean de Léry in his *Histoire d'un voyage fait en Bresil* (see n. 54, above). Locke reveals one of the sources for the "atheism" of the Hottentots of Saldanha Bay in South Africa in his *Essay*, ed. Nidditch, I 4.8, p. 87, as "Roe apud Thevenot." In the collection of travels made by Melchisédec Thevenot in his *Relations de Divers voiages curieux* (Paris, 1663), Locke found a brief account of the godlessness of the Hottentots in Sir Thomas Roe's *Memoires* of his voyage to the Great Mogul of Tartary in 1615 (1:2 [LL2889]). But a fuller and more vivid description of this tribe is given by Edward Terry, who was chaplain to Sir Thomas Roe, in his *Voyage to East India* (London, 1655 [LL 2857]), pp. 16–17: "the Sun shines not upon a people in the whole world more barbarous than those which possess it [the Bay]; Beasts in the skin of men rather than men in the skin

omnis, tam rationis et humanitatis expers extiterat[6] unquam, qui
15 numen nullum haberet, quanto quaeso potior est polytheorum sententia, quid Graecorum Latinorum et totius mundi

---

[1]*ovans* A; *orans* B. [2]*deus* A; *Deus* B. [3]*nam* A; *Nam* B. [4]*deum* A; *Deum* B. [5]*adire* Locke's correction for *adiere* B; *adiere* A. [6]*extiterat* Locke's correction for *extiterit* B; *extiterit* A.

(folio 77) Ethnici de diis[1] opinio, qui cum plures deos[2] sibi finxerunt,[3] eosque
inter se pugnantes, uti in bello Trojano, inter se varie affectos,
crudeles fures, adulteros, non mirum videtur si ex deorum[4] talium
voluntate officii sui rationem colligere non poterant, quam illa vitae
5 regulam doceret religio ubi quisque quem, et qualem, velit deum[5]
sibi eligeret et cultum; ubi in hortis crescerent numina, et quotannis
expectare possint deorum[6] messem; ubi[7] bos et Canis divinos meruerunt honores. talem hominum de diis consensum[8] ad mores
recte instituendos nihil omnino profecisse[9] quid miremur? quid hi
10 quaeso, nisi alio nomine athei, aeque enim impossibile est multa aut
esse, aut concipere numina ac nullum, et qui deorum auget numerum, tollit divinitatem. Nec si moratiores gentes, aut sanioris
mentis philosophos[10] appelles, quicquam proficies, cum Judaeis
reliquae omnes gentes Ethnicae sint, et profanae.[11] Graecis barba-
15 rae: Sparta severa illa gens,[12] furtum probet et nefanda Jovis Latialis[13] sacrificia Romana

---

[1]*diis* A; *Diis* B. [2]*deos* A; *Deos* B. [3]*sibi finxerunt* added by Locke in B; not in A. [4]*deorum* A; *Deorum* B. [5]*deum* A; *Deum* B. [6]*deorum* A; *Deorum* B. [7]*ubi* omitted in B. [8]*talem . . . consensum* vL; *talis . . . consensus* A, B. [9]*constat* deleted after *profecisse* A, B. [10]*philosophos* A; *Philosophos* B. [11]*profanae* A; *prophanae* B. [12]*gens* A; *Gens* B. [13]*Latialis* A; *latiatis* B.

one has ever existed so devoid of all sense, reason, and humanity, who believed in no divinity, how much to be preferred, I ask, is the belief of the polytheists? What should one say of the opinion of the Greeks and Romans and

(o 77) the entire Pagan world concerning the gods? These peoples, since they have invented many gods for themselves, and these gods in mutual conflict, as in the Trojan War, and endowed them with a variety of dispositions to one another—cruel, thieving, adulterous[74]—it seems little wonder they could not infer any principle of their duty from the will of gods like these, [or any principle] which that religion could inculcate as a rule of life. For there, each individual could choose for himself the kind of god and worship he liked; where divinities sprouted up in gardens and each year these peoples could expect a divine harvest; where a heifer and a Dog[75] were worthy of divine honors. Why should we be surprised that such an agreement among men concerning the gods was of no help whatsoever in the proper formation of morals? What, I ask, are these peoples except atheists under another name? For it is as impossible for many divinities to be, or to be conceived to be, as none. And who increases the number of the gods, destroys divinity. Nor will you advance your argument by appealing to more civilized nations or philosophers of sounder mind.[76] To the Jews all other nations are Gentiles and unholy; to the Greeks, they are barbarians. Sparta, that austere nation, sanctions theft, and Roman religion the unspeakable sacrifices to Jupiter Latialis.[77]

---

of beasts, as may appear by their ignorance, habit, language, diet, with other things, which make them most brutish. First for God, the great God of Heaven and Earth, whom generally all the people in the world, Heathens, as well as Christians, doe confess, they . . . acknowledge none."

[74]*crudeles, fures, adulteros*. This seems Locke's adaptation of Xenophanes' criticism of the conduct of the Homeric and Hesiodic gods, which Locke would have known from Cicero's version of it in *De Natura Deorum* I 16.42.

[75]Locke obviously has in mind the Egyptian gods Isis/Hathor and the jackal Anubis.

[76]As had Hugo Grotius in the *Prolegomena* to his *De Jure Belli ac Pacis*, p. 17.

[77]Jupiter Latialis was worshiped on Mt. Alban in the Feriae Latinae, or Latin Festival. It was asserted by the Christian enemies of Roman cult (Tertullian *Apologeti-*

(folio 78) religio. quid juvat philosophos[1] adire, cum eorum plus quam ducentas de summo bono sententias recenseat Varro, nec pauciores esse possunt de via quae ad felicitatem[2] deducit opiniones, hoc est de lege naturae: quid[3] et inter philosophos[4] extiterint[5] Diagoras Mile-
5 sius,[6] Theodorus Cyrenaicus,[7] et Protagoras atheismo infames.

Si[8] Christianam religionem professos consulere velis,[9] quid de iis existimandum erit, qui magnum illud humani generis rescindunt vinculum, dum doceant fidem non esse servandam cum haereticis, hoc est cum illis[10] qui Papae dominatum non agnoscunt, et in
10 eandem se tradunt societatem, adeo ut cum civibus forsan servandam fidem putent, erga exteros fraudem et dolum licere. quid[11] Graecorum Romanorumque sapientissimi ne plures referam[12] Socrates et Cato, ad thalamos suos alios admiserunt, amicis accomodarunt uxores, et alienae libidinis facti sunt ministri. ex quibus
15 omnibus liquido constat ex illo qui inter homines est consensu, nequaquam colligi posse legem naturae.

[1]*philosophos* A; *Philosophos* B. [2]*felicitatem* A; *faelicitatem* B. [3]*quid* omitted in B. [4]*philosophos* A; *Philosophos* B. [5]*extiterint* A; *extiterit* B. [6]*Milesius* A, B; *Melius* vL. [7]*Cyrenaicus* A; *Cyrenairus* B. [8]New paragraph in A; perhaps also in B. [9]*velis* Locke's correction for *velim* B; *velim* A. [10]*cum illis* written above *qui* A; *cum illis* struck out after *illis* B. [11]*quid* A; *Quid* B. [12]*ne plures referam* added by Locke in B; in A.

lio 78) What help is there in turning to the philosophers? Varro lists for them more than two hundred opinions concerning the highest good,[78] and there can be no fewer opinions concerning the way that leads to happiness; that is, concerning the law of nature. And what [shall we say] of [the fact that] even among philosophers there arose Diagoras of Miletus,[79] Theodorus of Cyrene, and Protagoras, [all] infamous for their atheism?[80]

If you should care to turn to those who profess to the Christian religion, what judgment should be made of those who sever that great bond of the human race when they teach that faith need not be kept with heretics; that is, those who do not recognize the supremacy of the Pope, and who so closely bind themself into one society that even if they think that faith ought to be kept with [their fellow] citizens, they believe that deceit and treachery are permitted toward those outside [their community].[81] And what of the wisest of the Greeks and Romans, Socrates and Cato, to mention no others— [who] admitted others to their own bed chambers, made available to their friends their wives' favors, and become purveyors to another's lust.[82] From all of these [examples], it is a clear conclusion that the

---

cus 9, and Lactantius *Institutiones Divinae* I 21.3) that human sacrifice was practiced as part of the festival.

[78]As he is cited by Saint Augustine in *The City of God* XIX 1.

[79]Locke slipped here and wrote Diagoras of Miletus for Diagoras of Melos.

[80]In his note on Atheismus in his *Lemmata ethica* of 1659 (Locke MS d.10, p. 3), Locke lists Cicero, *De Natura Deorum* [I 1.2], Diogenes Laertius in his life of Aristippus [his account of Theodorus in *Lives of the Philosophers* II 97], [Plutarch] *De placitis philosophorum* I.7; and Sextus Empiricus, *Outlines of Phyrrhonism* [III 218] as sources for the atheists of antiquity. Locke's three examples of atheistic philosophers are likely to have come from Cicero.

[81]It would seem that Locke has in mind the teaching of the "Papists" and Jesuits that faith need not be kept with heretics, a teaching Robert Sanderson, the first Regius Professor of Divinity at Oxford University, had addressed in his public lectures of 1646, *De juramenti promissorii obligatione praelectiones septem* (London, 1647 [LL 2547]), praelectio IV 8. Sanderson upheld the obligation. For the importance of these lectures and Sanderson's ten lectures *De obligatione Conscientiae* (delivered in 1647, published in London in 1661 [LL 2548]), see n. 38, above, and nn. 84 and 85, below.

[82]Cato of Utica loaned (and must have divorced) his second wife, Marcia, to his friend, the lawyer Hortensius; cf. Plutarch, *Cato Minor* 25. There is no ancient source for the anecdote about Socrates' loan of his wife (either Xanthippe or Myrto), but the source of this malicious inference is to be traced to Socrates' proposal for a community of wives in Plato, *Republic* V 457D; cf. Lucian, *Auction of Lives* 17 and *Symposium* 39.

(folio 79)   2º Dicimus si daretur inter homines unanimis et universalis opinionis alicujus consensus, ille tamen consensus non probaret eam
opinionem esse legem naturae, cum certe ex principiis naturalibus,
non ex fide aliena unicuique deducenda sit lex naturae; et hu-
5 jusmodi consensus de ea re possit esse quae nequaquam sit lex
naturae, ut si apud omnes homines majori in pretio esset aurum
quam plumbum, non inde sequeretur id lege naturae esse sancitum.
si omnes cum Persis humana cadavera canibus voranda exponerent,
aut cum Graecis comburerent[,] non probaret hoc aut illud legem
10 esse naturae et homines obligare[,] cum hujusmodi consensus minime sufficiat ad inducendam obligationem; hujusmodi fateor consensus indicare poterat legem naturae[,] probare non poterat, efficere ut vehementius credam, non ut certius sciam eam esse legem
naturae. certo enim scire non possum utrum haec sit privati cujus-
15 que sententia, fides enim est sed non cognitio. si[1] enim eandem mei
animi reperio esse opinio-

    [1]*si* A; *Si* B.

(folio 80)   nem ante cognitum hujusmodi consensum, consensus illius cognitio
mihi non[1] probat quod ante ex principiis naturalibus cognoscerem.
quod si eam esse animi mei sententiam ante cognitum hujusmodi
hominum consensum non constat, merito etiam dubitare possim, an
5 illa sit et aliorum opinio, cum nulla ratio dari potest cur id omnibus
aliis a natura inesse credam quod mihi deesse sentio, nec sane illi ipsi
homines, qui consentiunt, scire possunt,[2] aliquid bonum esse quia
consentiunt, sed ideo consentiunt quia ex principiis naturalibus,

law of nature can by no means be derived from that agreement which exists among men.

lio 79)   2°, In the second place, we say that even if there were to exist among men a unanimous and universal agreement concerning some opinion or another, this agreement would not prove that opinion to be a law of nature. For surely each individual should deduce the law of nature from natural principles, not from the authority of another. And an agreement of this kind might concern something that could in no way be a law of nature; as [for example], if among all mankind gold were more highly prized than lead, it would not follow from this that this is established by a law of nature. If all men were to join the Persians and expose corpses to be devoured by dogs, or to join the Greeks and burn them, this would not prove that the one [practice] or the other was a law of nature or that it was binding on men, for an agreement of this kind is least capable of inducing [a sense of] obligation. I admit that an agreement of this kind could point to the law of nature, it could not prove it, [it could] bring me to believe in it with greater ardor, [but] not to know with greater certainty that it is a law of nature. Indeed, I cannot know for certain whether this [opinion] is the belief of every private individual; it is [my] faith, not knowledge. For if I discover an opinion to be the same as the opinion within my own mind

lio 80) before such consensus has become known to me, so far as I am concerned, the knowledge of that consensus does not prove what I would already know from natural principles. But, if it is not certain that this is the opinion of my mind before this kind of consensus among men has become known, I could rightly even wonder whether this is the opinion of others too, since no reason can be found why I should believe that there exists in all other men naturally what I feel to be lacking in myself. Nor, further, can those very men who agree among themselves know that something is good because they agree it is, but [rather], they agree because they know

aliquid esse bonum cognoscunt, et cognitio praecedit consensum,
10 nam aliter idem esset simul causa et effectus, et omnium consensus
produceret omnium consensum, quod plane absurdum.

3° De tertio scilicet principiorum consensu non est quod multa
dicam[,] cum principia speculativa ad rem non attinent,

---

[1]*mihi non* A; *non mihi* B. [2]*non* struck out after *scire* B; *scire non* A.

(folio 81) nec res morales ullatenus attingunt[;] de principiis autem practicis
qualis sit hominum consensus, ex[1] supra dictis facile est colligere.

---

[1]*ex* added by Locke in B; in A.

from natural principles that something is good. And [this] knowledge precedes agreement, for otherwise the same thing would be both cause and effect at the same time, and the consent of all [i.e., an effect] would result in the consent of all [i.e., a cause] which is plainly absurd.

3°, There is no reason for me to say much concerning the third kind of consensus, that is, the consensus concerning principles. Speculative principles do not bear on our question,

io 81) nor do they touch on moral matters at all. The nature of men's consensus concerning practical principles can easily be inferred from what has been said above.

(folio 82) **VIII. An Lex naturae homines obligat? Affirmatur[.][1]**

Quum[2] aliqui reperti sunt[3] qui omnem legem naturae ad suam cujusque praeservationem[4] referunt, nec altius[5] illius fundamenta petunt, quam ab amore et instinctu illo, quo unusquisque se amplectitur, sibique quantum potest, ut tutus et incolumnis sit, prospicit;

5 cum quisque se sentit in se conservando, satis sedulum et industrium[,] operae pretium videtur inquirere, quae et quanta sit legis naturae obligatio, cum si sui ipsius[6] cura et conservatio sit omnis hujus legis fons et principium, virtus non tam officium hominis videretur[7] quam commodum, nec homini quid honestum erit nisi

10 quod utile, neque legis hujus observatio tam munus nostrum esset et debitum ad quod natura obligamur, quam privilegium et beneficium, ad quod utilitate ducimur, adeoque sine incommodo forsan non[8] possimus,[9] sine crimine certe possimus eam[10]

---

[1]Title and numeral in Locke's hand in B. *Negatur* deleted after *obligat* B. Title and beginning of text to another question deleted in A: *An Lex naturae sit voluntas divina naturaliter cognoscibilis? Af[firmatur]*. Deleted text in A: *Cum esse legem naturae certum sit nemoque sane mentis unquam dubitaverit.* [2]*Quum . . . fuerit* added on fol. 41[v] in A. [3]*sunt* A, B; *sint* vL. [4]*praeservationem* A; *preservationem* B. [5]*altius* Locke's correction for *alitus* B; *alitus* A. [6]*sui ipsius* A; *sui-ipsius* B. [7]*videretur* Locke's correction for *videtur* B; *videtur* A. [8]*non* Locke's correction for *nos* B; *non* A. [9]*possimus* correction for *possumus* B; *posimus* A; *possumus* vL. [10]*certe possimus eam* A; *certe eam possimus* B; *possumus* vL.

(folio 83) negligere et violare, quandocunque nobis cedere jure nostro libitum fuerit.

Ut[1] vero cognoscatur quomodo et quantum obligat lex naturae, pauca de obligatione praemittenda sunt, quam sic definiunt Juris

5 consulti scilicet[2] quod sit Vinculum[3] juris quo quis astringitur debitum persolvere, ubi per jus intelligunt legem civilem, quae etiam definitio omnimodam obligationem satis commode describit, si per jus legem illam intelligas cujus obligationem definiendam proponis,

io 82) VIII. Is the Law of nature binding on men? It is.[83]

Since some have been found who refer the entire law of nature to
the self-preservation of each individual and seek no deeper foundations for it than self-love and that instinct by which each man cher-
ishes himself, and looks out, so far as he is able, for his own safety
and preservation; [and] inasmuch as everyone feels himself industrious and eager enough in his own preservation, it seems worth our
labor to inquire into the nature and extent of the obligation of the
law of nature. For, if the care and preservation of one's self should
be the fountain and beginning of this entire law, virtue would
appear to be not so much man's duty as his interest, and nothing
would be right for a man were it not useful. And keeping this law
would be not so much a duty and debt to which we are bound by
nature, as a private right and benefit to which we are led by [a sense
of] our own advantage. As a result, whenever it pleases us to yield
our right [to self-preservation], we cannot neglect and break this law
without possible harm [to ourselves],

io 83) but we certainly can without incurring guilt.

To come to a true understanding of how the law of nature is
binding and how great its obligation is, we must first say a few things
about obligation. Legal authorities define obligation so as to make it
the "Bond of law" by which every man is constrained to discharge his
debt, where by "law" they understand civil law.[84] And this definition
is accurate enough as a description of every kind of obligation, if by
law [jus] you understand that [precise] law [legem] whose obligation

---

[83]In MS A Locke has deleted another title: Is the Law of nature the divine will
known by nature? It is.

[84]Juris consulti. This definition of obligation as the bond of conscience goes back to
Justinian, Institutiones III 13, but Locke was familiar with the definition from Robert
Sanderson's first lecture on the obligation of promissory oaths, De juramenti promissorii
obligatione I 11: de Obligatione multa et satis prolixe Juris consulti. Definiunt autem illi
Obligationem quod sit vinculum juris, quo quis astringitur ad solvendum id quod debet ("Legal
authorities [have spoken] of obligation a great deal and with sufficient prolixity. They
define obligation as a 'bond of law', by which each individual is constrained to satisfy
his debt").

adeo ut hic per vinculum juris intelligendum sit vinculum legis
10 naturalis quo quis astringitur persolvere[4] debitum naturale, id scilicet praestare officium quod cuivis ex naturae suae ratione praestandum incumbit, vel poenam admisso[5] crimini debitam subire. ut[6]
vero cognoscamus unde oriatur illud juris vinculum, sciendum est,
neminem nos ad quodvis agendum obligare, vel astringere posse,
15 nisi qui in nos jus, et potestatem habet; et dum imperat quid fieri
velit, quid non, jure tantum utitur suo. adeo ut vinculum illud sit

[1]New paragraph in A; not in B. [2]*scilicet* added by Locke in B; not in A. [3]*Vinculum* A;
vinculum B. [4]*persolvere* B; *per solvere* A. [5]*admisso* B; *adinmisso* (?) A. [6]*ut* A; *Ut* B.

(folio 84) ab illo dominio et imperio, quod superior quivis in nos actionesque
nostras obtinet, et in quantum alteri subiicimur,[1] in tantum obliga-
tioni obnoxii sumus. Vinculum autem illud nos ad debitum persol-
vendum astringit; quod debitum duplex est,
5   1[o2] debitum officii, scilicet quod quis ex edicto superioris potestatis tenetur facere, vel omittere;[3] cum enim voluntas legislatoris nobis
cognita sit, aut ita sufficienter promulgata, ut nisi impedimenti quid
a nobis sit, cognosci potest: ei morem gerere, et per omnia obsequi
tenemur, et hoc est illud quod vocatur debitum officii: conformitas
10 scilicet inter actiones nostras et earum regulam scilicet superioris
potestatis voluntatem. et haec[4] obligatio videtur fluere tum[5] a sapientia legislatoris divina, tum a jure illo quod creator[6] habet in

you propose as something to be defined. And so, here, by [the term] "bond of law" one must understand the bond of the law of nature by which everyone is constrained to discharge a debt of nature, that is, to perform that duty which it is incumbent on each individual as something which must be performed by reason of one's own nature; or, should a crime be confessed to, to submit to the punishment due. To come to a true understanding of the origin of this bond of law it must be known that no one can oblige or constrain us to do anything unless he has right and power over us. And when he commands what he wants done and what not, he relies only on his own right. Thus, this bond

lio 84)   would arise from that authority and power which any superior has over us and our actions. And to the degree we are subject to another, we are liable to an obligation. Now, this bond compels us to acquit ourselves of an obligation. This obligation is twofold:

1°, the obligation which comes from duty, that is, which one is bound to perform or refrain from on the command of a superior power. For once the will of a legislator is known to us, or widely enough proclaimed for it to be known, unless there is some obstacle arising in ourselves, we are bound to conform to it and obey it in all respects. And this is what is called the obligation of our duty:[85] that is, the conformity between our actions and their rule, which is the will of a superior power. And this [kind of] obligation seems to derive at times from the divine wisdom of the legislator, and at times from that right which the creator has over his creation. For every

[85]*illum quod vocatur debitum officii.* Locke is clearly recalling to his Oxford audience the distinction Robert Sanderson made in his *De juramenti promissorii obligatione* I 12 p. 14: *Duplex autem est Debitum. Debitum Officii, quod quis ex sanctione juris tenetur facere; et Debitum Suplicii, quod quis ex sanctione juris tenetur pati, si officium suum neglexerit* (In the English translation of 1655 the distinction is stated as between a "debt, according unto which every man is bound by the precept of law to act" and "debt, according to which every man is bound by the decree of the Law to suffer if he neglect his duty"). Here Locke returns to the two requirements he had established for a law to have its binding force: a law must be the expression of the will of a higher power, and this will must be sufficiently promulgated to those who are bound to it; cf. fol. 60–61 and n. 50, above, and fol. 88.

creaturam suam, in deum enim ultimo resolvitur omnis obligatio,
cujus voluntatis imperio nos morigeros praestare, ideo tenemur,
15 quia cum ab eo accepimus et esse et operari, ab ejus voluntate
utrumque dependet, et eum modum quem ille praescripsit[7] observare debemus, nec minus aequum est

[1]*subiicimur* Locke's correction for *subiicitur* B; *subiicimur* A. [2]New paragraph in A; not in B. [3]*omittere* A; *amittere* B. [4]*haec* vL.; *hac* A, B. [5]*tum* added by Locke in B; not in A. [6]*creator* Locke's correction for *creatum* B; *creator* A. [7]*praescripsit* A; *praescribit* B.

(folio 85) ut id agamus quod omniscienti et summe sapienti visum fuerit.

2° Debitum supplicii, quod oritur ex officii debito non persoluto,
ut illi qui ratione duci et potestati superiori moribus et vitae rectitudine se subjectos fateri[1] nolint, vi et poenis coacti potestati illi se
5 subditos agnoscant, illiusque sentiant vim, cujus sequi[2] nollent voluntatem, et hujus obligationis vis[3] in potestate legislatoris fundari
videtur, ut quos monita movere non possunt,[4] cogat potentia. nec
vero omnis obligatio videtur consistere et ultimo terminari in potentia illa, quae delinquentes coercere possit et punire nocentes, sed
10 potius in potestate et dominio illo quod[5] in alium aliquis habet, sive
jure naturae et creationis, cum[6] ei merito omnia subiiciuntur, a quo
et primo facta sunt et perpetuo conservantur, vel jure donationis,
cum deus,[7] cujus omnia sunt, partem imperii sui in aliquem trans-
tulit, et jus imperandi tribuit, ut primogenitis et monarchis; vel jure
15 pacti, cum quis volens alteri se emancipavit; et se alterius voluntati
subjecit; omnis enim obligatio conscientiam alligat et animo ipsi
vinculum iniicit,

[1]*fateri* correction for *solere* B; *fateri* A. [2]*sequi* A; *si qui* B. [3]*hujus obligationis vis* Locke's correction for *haec obligatio vi* B; *haec obligatio vi* A. [4]*possunt* A, B; *possint* vL. [5]*quod* our correction for *quem* A, B. [6]*cum* Locke's correction for *cui* A, B. [7]*deus* A; *Deus* B.

(folio 86) adeo ut non poenae metus, sed recti ratio nos obligat, et conscientia
de moribus fert sententiam, et admisso crimine nos merito poenae

[kind of] obligation can ultimately be referred back to god, to the command of whose will we must show ourselves obedient. We are obligated because we have received both our being and proper function from him, on whose will both depend, and we ought to observe the limit he has prescribed. Nor is it any less proper that we should do

(lio 85) what has been decided by him who is all-knowing and supremely wise.

2°, the debt of punishment, which arises from an obligation of a duty which has not been discharged and [requires] that those who in their conduct and the rectitude of their lives are unwilling to be led by reason and refuse to acknowledge themselves subject to a superior power are compelled to recognize that they are subject to this power by force and punishments, and to feel the force of him whose will they would refuse to obey. And the force of this obligation seems to be founded on the power of the legislator to make superior force compel those whom warnings cannot move. In truth, all obligation does not seem to consist in, and finally to be limited by, that power which can coerce those who fail to pay their debts and can punish the guilty, but rather in the power and that authority which someone holds over another; either by right of nature and creation, since all things are rightly subject to that by which they have both first been created and continue to be preserved; or by the right of donation, as when god, to whom all things belong, has transferred some part of his authority to another and granted the right of ruling, as [he has] in the case of firstborn sons and monarchs; or by the right of a compact, as when someone has willingly delivered himself over to another and made himself subject to another's will. Every [form of] obligation binds [our] conscience and lays a bond upon the mind itself,

(lio 86) and thus it is not fear of punishment that binds us but our determination of what is right; and our conscience passes its verdict on our

obnoxios esse judicat; verum enim illud poetae, se judice. nemo
nocens absolvitur;[1] quod plane aliter esset si solum poenae[2] metus
5 obligationem induceret, quod quis in se facile sentiret: et aliam
obsequii sui rationem perciperet, cum piratae captivus serviret, aliam cum[3] principi obediret subditus: aliudque esset apud se neglecti
erga[4] regem obsequii judicium[,] aliud cum pyratae aut praedonis
mandata sciens transgrederetur; cum hic permittente conscientia
10 jure usus suo saluti tantum consulerit; illic condemnante conscientia
jus alterius violaret.

    Deinde[5] de obligatione observandum est alia obligare effective,
alia solum terminative. effective[6] id obligat quod est prima causa
omnis obligationis, et a qua fluit formalis illius ratio, et id est volun-
15 tas superioris; ideo enim obligamur ad aliquid quia is sub cujus
ditione sumus, id velit. terminative[7] id obligat quod praescribit
modum et mensuram obligationis, et officii nostri;

---

[1]*absolvitur* B; *obsolvitur* A. [2]*solum poenae* A; *poenae solum* B. [3]*aliam cum* added by
Locke in B; not in A; *et principi* A. [4]*erga* correction for *apud* B; *erga* A. [5]*Deinde* B; *deinde*
A (perhaps no new paragraph intended). [6]*effective* A; *Effective* B. [7]*terminative* A;
Terminative B.

conduct, and, if a crime is confessed to, rightly judges that we are liable to punishment. For the saying of the poet is true: "No one who is guilty is acquitted when he himself is judge."[86] Clearly, this would not be the case if only fear of punishment were to induce [a sense of] obligation, something anyone could easily perceive in himself. And he would perceive one principle of his obligation, when, as a captive, he were enslaved to a pirate, another, when, as a subject, he had to show obedience to a prince. And his own judgment on neglecting the obedience [he owes] to a king would be one thing, but something quite different should he knowingly transgress the commands of a pirate or brigand. In the one case, with the permission of his own conscience and relying on his own right, he has thought only of his own safety, but in the other he would have violated the right of another and his conscience would have condemned him for it.

Concerning obligation, it must next be observed that some things are binding "effectively," others only "terminatively."[87] That which is the first cause of all obligation, and from which its formal definition flows, binds "effectively," and this is the will of a superior. Indeed, we are bound to something, because he, under whose power we are, would will it. That which prescribes the mode and measure of our obligation and duty binds "terminatively."

---

[86]*se judice nemo nocens absolvitur*. The phrase comes from Juvenal, *Satire* XIII 2–3: "Whatever crime is committed as a bad example is galling to its author; this is his first punishment, that, when he stands before himself as judge, no one guilty of a crime is acquitted."

[87]*alia obligare effective, alia solum terminative*. Again, the distinction comes from Sanderson. In his lectures *De obligatione Conscientiae*, lecture V 8: *Sciendum . . . Legis hunc effectum, vim sc. obligativam, fundari in Voluntate et Potestate legislatoris: ita ut proprie loquendo, non tam Lex ipsa, quam Voluntas et Potestas Legislatoris, obliget effective; causando scil. vel inducendo obligationem per modum Causae efficientis. Dici tamen potest et solet Lex obligare terminative, sc. ut terminus obligationis, et per modum Causae exemplaris: quia est id ad quod obligatur quis, qui ex ejus praescriptione operetur: sicut artifex, in operando dirigitur ab exemplari sibi proposito* ("It should be understood that the effect of this law is founded upon the will and power of its legislator. Thus, to put the matter in its proper terms, it is not so much the law that binds 'effectively' as does the will and the power of the legislator, by being its cause, that is, and bringing it about in the manner of an efficient cause. Even so, the law can be said and often is said to bind 'terminatively,' that is, as the terms of the obligation and in the manner of a formal cause; because it is that to which each man is bound, who operates following its prescription, just as the artisan in his work is directed by the pattern that has been set before him").The terms *effective* and *terminative* are, of course, derived from the Aristotelian and then scholastic distinction between an efficient and a formal cause.

(folio 87) quod nihil aliud est quam declaratio istius voluntatis, quam alio
nomine legem vocamus. a Deo[1] enim optimo maximo obligamur
quia vult, hujus vero voluntatis obligationem et obsequii nostri rationem terminat declaratio, quia ad aliud non obligamur nisi quod
5 legislator aliquo modo notum fecerit et promulgavit se velle.

Obligant insuper aliqua per se, et vi sua, aliqua per aliud, et
virtute aliena. 1⁰ per se et vi sua, et sic solum obligat voluntas divina
sive[2] lumine naturae cognoscibilis et tunc est de qua disputamus lex
naturae; vel per viros ϑεοπνεύστους vel alio modo revelata, et tunc
10 est lex divina positiva.[3] 2⁰ per aliud, vel[4] virtute mutuatitia obligat
voluntas superioris cujusvis alterius, sive regis sit, sive parentis, cui
ex voluntate divina subiicimur; totum illud imperium quod in alios
obtinent,[5] et jus leges ferendi,[6] et ad obsequium obligandi a solo deo
mutuantur legislatores reliqui,[7] quibus ideo tenemur obedire quia
15 deus[8] sic vellet sic jubet, adeo ut illis obtemperando deo etiam
paremus, his ita positis dicimus,

[1]*a Deo* Locke's correction for *adeo* B; *a deo* A. [2]*sive* A; *sine* B. [3]*positiva* A; *posituia* B.
[4]*vel* A; *et* B. [5]*superiores* deleted above *obtinent* B; not in A. [6]*leges ferendi* vL.; *legis ferendi*
(*ferendi* correction for *ferendo*) B; *leges ferendo* A. *superiores reliqui* added then deleted
by Locke above *ferendi* B; not in A. [7]*legislatores reliqui* added by Locke in B; not in A.
[8]*deus* A; *Deus* B.

(folio 88) Quod lex naturae obligat omnes homines primo et per se, et virtute
sua. quod sequentibus argumentis confirmare conabimur.

1⁰[1] Quia haec lex omnia habet quae ad obligationem alicujus legis
requiruntur. Deus[2] enim legis hujus author hanc voluit esse morum
5 et vitae nostrae regulam, et sufficienter promulgavit, ut quisvis si
studium si industriam adhibere, mentemque ad illius cognitionem
advertere[3] velit scire possit, adeo ut cum nihil aliud ad inducendam
obligationem requiratur praeter dominium et justam imperantis
potestatem, et patefactam illius voluntatem, nemo dubitare potest
10 legem naturae homines obligare.

1⁰ Cum deus[4] super omnia summus sit, tantumque in nos jus

olio 87) This is nothing other than the declaration of that will, which by another name we call law. For we are bound by God, who is best and greatest, because he wills; in effect, the declaration of his will determines the principle of [our] obligation and our obedience, because we are only bound to what a legislator has in some manner made known and published as his will.

Beyond this, some things are binding of themselves, and by their own force; others by something else, and by virtue of something else. 1º, The will of god is binding of itself and by its own force, and only in this manner, whether it is knowable by the light of nature, and is thus the law of nature which is the object of our disputation, or whether [it is] revealed by men "inspired of god" or some other means, and is thus a positive divine law. 2º, The will of any other superior is binding by something other than itself or by virtue of a derivative power, whether [it is the will] of a king or a parent, to whom we are subject by divine will. All other legislators derive all the authority they hold over others from god alone, both the right of making laws and binding [men] to obey them. For this reason we are bound to obey them because such would be god's will and such is his command, and consequently, by obeying these we are also obedient to god. Now that these [distinctions] have been established in this manner, we say:

olio 88) that the law of nature is binding on all men, before any other law, both of itself, and by its own force. This we shall attempt to establish by the following arguments:

1º, Because this law meets all the requirements [necessary] for the obligation of any law; for God, the author of this law, willed it to be the rule of our conduct and life, and he published it sufficiently that anyone could know it, if he were willing to devote the time and energy, and turn his mind to its understanding. As a result, since nothing more is required for bringing obedience about than the authority and the just power of the ruler and [the fact of] his will having been made clear, no one can doubt that the law of nature is binding upon men.

2º, Since god is superior to all things, [and] he holds as much right

habet et imperium, quantum in nosmet ipsos[5] habere non possimus, cumque corpus, animam, vitam, quicquid sumus, quicquid habemus, quicquid etiam esse possumus[,] ei soli unice debemus, par est,

15 ut ad praescriptum voluntatis illius vivamus, deus nos ex nihilo fecit et in nihilum si libet iterum redac-

[1]New paragraph in A; not in B. Numeral added by Locke (?) in margin of B to indicate break. [2]*Deus* A, B. [3]*advertere* Locke's correction for *applicare* B; *applicare* A. [4]*deus* A; *Deus* B. [5]*nos met ipsos* A; *nosmetipsos* B.

(folio 89) turus[.] ei igitur summo jure et summa necessitate subiicimur. 2º lex[1] haec est hujus omnipotentis legislatoris voluntas nobis ex lumine et principiis naturae innotescens, cujus cognitio neminem latere potest nisi qui caecitatem tenebrasque amat, et ut officium

5 suum effugiat exuit naturam[.]

2º Si lex naturae homines non obligat, obligare etiam non potest lex divina positiva,[2] quod nemo dixerit; fundamentum enim obligationis utrobique eadem est, scilicet voluntas supremi numinis: differunt solum promulgandi ratione et diverso cognitionis nostrae

10 modo, hanc enim lumine naturae et ex principiis naturalibus certo scimus, illam fide apprehendimus.

3º Si lex naturae homines non obligat, nec lex quaevis humana positiva eos obligare potest, cum magistratus civilis leges, vim suam omnem, ex hujus legis obligatione mutuentur, certe quoad maxi-

15 mam mortalium partem; ad quos cum revelationis divinae certa cognitio non pervenerit, nullam aliam divinam et virtute sua obligantem legem habent praeter naturalem, adeo ut inter eos

[1]*lex* A; *Lex* B. [2]*positiva* B; *possitiva* A.

(folio 90) legem naturae si tollas, omnem inter homines civitatem, imperium, ordinem et societatem simul evertis: non enim ideo ex metu regi obtemperandum est, quia potentior cogere potest, hoc enim esset tyrannorum, latronum et pyratarum imperium stabilire, sed ex con-

and authority over us as we cannot hold over ourselves, since we owe
to him and to him alone our body, soul, life, whatever we are,
whatever we possess, and also whatever we can be, it is right that we
live [obedient] to the prescription of his will. God has created us out
of nothing and, if it is his pleasure, he will return us to nothing
again.

lio 89) We are, therefore, subject to him by supreme right and absolute
necessity.

3°, This law is the will of this all-powerful legislator which becomes known to us by the light and principles of nature. Knowledge
of it can be hidden to no one except to the lover of blindness and
darkness, who, to escape his duty, would cast off his nature.

4°, If the law of nature is not binding on men, god's divine,
positive law cannot be binding, [and] this no one will claim. In the
case of either [law], the foundation of obligation is the same, that is,
the will of the supreme divine power [numen]. These laws differ only
in the manner of their being promulgated and the distinct modes of
our coming to know them. We have certain knowledge of the law of
nature, by the light of nature and from natural principles; divine law
we apprehend by faith.

5°, If the law of nature is not binding on men, neither can any
human positive law bind them, since the laws of the civil magistrate
derive all their force from the binding power of this law. This is
surely true so far as concerns the greatest part of mankind, to whom
the certain knowledge of divine revelation has not penetrated. They
have no other law but natural [law], which is divine, and binding by
virtue of itself; consequently,

lio 90) if you would abolish the law of nature, you overturn at one blow all
government among men, [all] authority, rank, and society. Nor
must we obey a king out of fear, because he is more powerful and
can compel us. For this would be to establish the power of tyrants,
thieves, and pirates; but [we must] out of conscience, because he

5 scientia, quia jure in nos imperium obtinet, jubente scilicet lege[1]
naturae ut obtemperemus regi principibus[2] et legislatori vel quo-
cunque demum nomine superiorem voces: adeo ut legis civilis obligatio ex lege naturae pendeat, nec tantum ad obsequium mag-
istratui praestandum[3] potestate illius cogimur quantum jure natu-
10 rae obligamur.

[IX].   An Lex naturae obliget bruta? Negatur[.][4]

[1]*lege* B; *lega* A. [2]*ut obtemperemus regi principibus* A; *ut obtemperari principibus* B.
[3]*praestandum* correction for *praestantum* B; *praestantum* A. [4]Title in Locke's hand; no
numeral in B; not in A.

obtains his rule over us by right, that is, at the command of the law of nature, that we obey a king, princes, and a legislator, or whatever name you would give a superior. Thus, the obligation of civil law depends on the law of nature, nor are we compelled so much to show obedience to a magistrate by virtue of his power as we are bound by the law [*jus*] of nature.

IX. Is the Law of nature binding on brutes?
    It is not.

(folio 91) [X]. An obligatio legis[1] naturae sit perpetua et Universalis?
Affirmatur[.][2]

Varias et multiplices esse hominum de lege[3] naturae et officii sui
ratione opiniones,[4] unica forsan res est, de qua idem sentiunt omnes
mortales, quod etiam si tacerent linguae, satis loquerentur mores,
tam in diversum abeuntes; cum passim reperiantur, non solum
5   pauci et privatae sortis homines, sed totae gentes, in quibus nullum
legis sensum, nullam morum rectitudinem observare licet. alii
etiam[5] sunt, et plurimi populi, qui aliqua saltem legis naturae praecepta, sine criminis conscientia negligunt, quibus non solum in
more, sed et laude positum[6] est, ea patrare, et probare scelera, quae
10   aliis recte sentientibus, et secundum naturam viventibus maxime
sunt detestanda. hinc furta apud hos licita et laudata; nec rapaces
latronum manus ullis conscientiae vinculis a vi et injuria coercentur,
apud alios nullus[7] stupri

---

[1]*legis* B; *Legis* A. [2]Title in Locke's hand; no numeral B. [3]*lege* A; *Lege* B. [4]*opiniones*
added by Locke in B; added then deleted in A. [5]*etiam* Locke's correction for *autem* B;
alii autem A; *Alii* B. [6]*positum* Locke's correction for *postium* B; *postium* A. [7]*nullus* A;
nullys B.

(folio 92) pudor, hic nulla deorum[1] templa aut altaria, illic humano sanguine
conspersa;[2] quod cum ita sit, dubitari merito possit, an totum genus
humanum, vagum et incertum, Institutis diversissimis assuetum,
motibusque plane contrariis actum, obliget lex naturae; cum vix
5   credi possit, tam obscura esse naturae dictata, ut universas lateant
gentes; nonnullos nasci homines tam mente, quam oculis captos,
quibus duce opus est, quique quo eundum sit nesciunt, facile conceditur, universos autem populos caecos natos quis dixerit? aut id

(lio 91)   [X]. Is the obligation of the law of nature
             perpetual and Universal? It is.

That men have various and manifold opinions concerning the law
of nature and the basis of their duty is perhaps the only thing about
which all mortals have the same opinion; [a truth] which, even if
their tongues were still, their conduct would express clearly enough
as they diverge in so many different directions. Not only are a few to
be discovered here and there, not only men of private condition but
even entire nations, among whom there can be observed no sense of
law, no rectitude of conduct; there are other peoples too—and there
are a great many of these—who without any conscience of wrong
pay no heed to at least some of the precepts of the law of nature; for
whom it is not only customary but praiseworthy to commit and
sanction crimes which are proper objects of the greatest detestation
to other peoples who think soundly and who live according to
nature. And so, theft is permitted among some peoples and praised;
and the grasping hands of robbers are not restrained from violence
and crime by any fetters of conscience. Among others there exists no
shame in debauchery;

(lio 92)   in one place there exist no temples or altars to the gods, in others
these are spattered with human blood. Since this is the case, one can
rightly doubt that the law of nature is binding upon the human race
as a whole, unstable and variable [as it is], accustomed to the most
different kinds of Institutions, driven by motions which are clearly
contrary, although it is hardly credible that the dictates of nature are
so obscure that they are hidden from entire nations. It can be readily
granted that some men are born defective of mind, as well as of
sight, who need some guide, who do not know in what direction to
move. [But] who will claim that entire peoples are born blind, or that

esse secundum naturam, quod totae gentes et hominum multitudo
10 prorsus ignorat; lumenque pectoribus humanis inditum, aut a tenebris omnino non differre,[3] aut ignis fatui instar incerta luce in
errores seducere, hoc esset naturae convicium facere, cujus dum
indulgentiam praedicamus, saevissimam experiremur[4] tyrannidem;
quae enim[5] unquam tanta fuit vel Sicula[6] crudelitas, ut eam[7] sub-
15 ditos

---

[1]*deorum* A; *Deorum* B. [2]*conspersa* correction for *dispersa* B; *conspersa* A. [3]*differre* B;
differe A. [4]*experiremur* Locke's correction for *experimur* B; *experimur* A. [5]*enim* added by
Locke in B; not in A. [6]*Sicula* A; *sicula* B. [7]*eam* Locke's correction for *cum* B; *eam* A.

(folio 93) observare vellet legem, quam interim occultaret, ei morem gerere
voluntati quam scire non poterant; Draconis[1] leges sanguine scriptas legimus, sed et scriptae fuerunt, ut sciri possint: tam crudelis
certe esse non potest omnium mater natura, ut ei[2] legi mortales
5 parere velit, quam non docuit, non sufficienter promulgavit, unde
concludendum videtur, aut legem naturae alicubi nullam esse, aut
ea aliquos saltem populos non teneri, adeoque obligationem legis
naturae non esse universalem.

His nequicquam obstantibus, asserimus Legis naturae obligatio-
10 nem perpetuam esse et universalem.

Dari hujus legis[3] obligationem jamjam probavimus, ista vero obligatio quanta sit, venit nunc discutienda,[4] dicimus igitur, legis naturae obligationem, esse primo perpetuam, hoc est, nullum esse tempus in quo liceret homini hujus legis praecepta violare, nullum hic
15 datur interregnum, nulla Saturnalia, aut libertatis sive licentiae in
hoc imperio intervalla[.][5] aeterna sunt hujus legis vincula, et humano generi coaeva, simul nascuntur

---

[1]*Draconis* A; *Dracenis* B. [2]*ei . . . promulgavit* added by Locke on fol. 92ᵛ in B; in A.
[3]*legis* A; *Legis* B. [4]*discutienda* Locke's correction for *discutiendum* B; *discutienda* A.
[5]*intervalla* added by Locke in B; deleted in A.

something which entire races and the multitude of mankind are completely unaware of is "according to nature" and that a light is placed in the men's hearts either not to differ in the least from darkness or, like the *ignis fatuus*, to lead them into error by its uncertain light? [To claim] this would be to insult nature: while we proclaim her kindness, we would be suffering her most cruel tyranny. What cruelty, even that of Sicily,[88] was so great that it would will its subjects to observe a law which it would at the same time conceal from them and to show themselves obedient to a will that they could not know?

lio 93) We read that the laws of Draco were written in blood,[89] but they were *written*, so that they could be known. Surely, nature, the mother of all, cannot be so cruel that she would want mortals to obey a law which she has not taught, which she has not adequately promulgated. From these considerations it seems necessary to conclude that either there is no law of nature anywhere or that some peoples are not bound by this law and thus that the obligation of the law of nature is not universal.

Against these objections, which are not decisive, we assert that the obligation of the Law of nature is perpetual and universal. We have already established the obligation of this law; we must now proceed to a discussion of the extent of this obligation. We say, therefore, that the obligation of the law of nature is, first, perpetual, that is, that there is no time in which a man would be permitted to violate the precepts of this law; here there exists no interregnum, no holidays or Mardi Gras, nor any periods of liberty or licence under this rule.[90] The bonds of this law are eternal and coeval with the human race; they are born with it and they die with it.

[88]*Sicula crudelitas*. The most readily accessible account of the cruelty of Phalaris, tyrant of Acragas in Sicily, was that of Cicero, in his *Verrines* IV 33.73. Here he describes how Phalaris tortured his enemies by thrusting them into a bronze bull and kindling a fire under it.

[89]*Draconis leges sanguine scriptas legimus*. This was the description of Demades, an Athenian politician of the late fourth century; cf. Plutarch *Life of Solon* 17.2.

[90]*nullum hic datur interregnum, nulla Saturnalia*. Here Locke is speaking in his pagan voice; cf. Translator's Introduction, sec. 3.

(folio 94) et simul intereunt, non autem ita sumi debet perpetua haec obligatio, quasi homines tenerentur, semper praestare omnia, quae lex
naturae jubet, hoc plane impossibile esset, cum diversis simul ac-
tionibus non sufficit unus homo: nec magis pluribus simul adesse
5 potest[1] officiis, quam corpus pluribus locis.[2] sed obligationem naturae ita perpetuam esse dicimus, ut nullum sit tempus, aut esse
potest, in quo lex naturae homines, aut hominem quemvis, quicquam agere jubet, in quo ad praestandum obsequium non tenetur,
adeo ut obligatio sit perpetua, actus vero non requiritur perpetuus,
10 nunquam mutatur legis obligatio, quamvis saepe mutentur et tem-
pora et circumstantiae actionum quibus circumscribitur obsequium
nostrum; cessare aliquando possumus ab agendo, secundum legem,
agere vero contra legem non possumus: in hoc vitae itinere, quies
aliquando conceditur, error nunquam. verum de legis naturae obli-
15 gatione haec observanda sunt,

[1]*adesse potest* A; *potest adesse* B. [2]*locis* Locke's correction for *legis* B; *locis* A.

(folio 95)   1° Aliqua esse, quae omnino prohibentur, et ad haec obligamur,
ad semper uti loqui amant Scholastici, hoc est, nullum esse temporis
momentum in quo hujusmodi aliquid sine crimine admittere licet,
uti furtum homicidium et id genus alia, adeoque aliquem fortunis
5 suis per vim aut fraudem evertere, perpetuum habet in se crimen,
nec quisquam sine reatu, se alieno sanguine polluere potest, ab his et
hujusmodi aliis perpetuo abstinere tenemur.

2° Alia sunt, quorum habitus, a nobis lege naturae requiruntur,
qualia sunt reverentia et timor numinis, pietas erga parentes, amor
10 vicini, et id genus alia, ad haec[1] etiam obligamur ad semper, nec
quodvis datur momentum temporis, in quo hos licet exuere mentis
habitus, aut aliter quam lex naturae praescribit esse erga res illas
affectos.[2]

lio 94) But this obligation should not be taken to mean that men are always bound to obey everything the law of nature commands. This would be clearly impossible, for one man alone is not capable of a number of different actions at the same time. One man can no more be involved in many actions at the same time than can a body stand in many places [at once]. But we say that the obligation of nature is perpetual in the sense that there is and can be no time in which, [if] the law of nature commands men, or any given individual, to do something, he is not bound to show himself obedient [to it]. For this reason its obligation is perpetual, although perpetual action is not a necessary condition of this law. The obligation of this law never changes, although the times and circumstances of the actions by which our obedience is defined might change. On occasion, we can cease acting in conformity with this law, but we cannot act against the law. On the journey of this life a pause is sometimes granted, straying never.

Now these observations concerning the obligation of the law of nature must be made:

lio 95)   1°, There exist some things which are absolutely prohibited, and we are obliged to [avoid] these "for forever" [ad semper], as the Schoolmen like to say. That is, there exists no moment in time when it is lawful to allow anything such as stealing, murder, and other things of this kind without [committing] a crime. And, thus, to deprive a person of his wealth and property by force or by fraud is an action which constitutes of itself a perpetual offense; nor can anyone pollute himself with another's blood without incurring guilt. We are forever bound to refrain from these actions and others of this kind.

2°, There are other matters in which we are required by the law of nature to have certain dispositions such as reverence for and fear of the divinity, a sense of duty toward one's parents, the love of one's neighbor, and other feelings of this kind. To these we are bound forever. Nor is there any moment in which it is lawful to divest ourselves of these dispositions of mind or for our attitudes and feelings to be other than what the law of nature prescribes toward these things.

3° Alia sunt, quorum externi actus jubentur, verbi gratia cultus
15 numinis externus, afflicti vicini consolatio, laborantis sublevatio,
esurientis cibatio, quibus[3] non obligamur ad semper, sed certo
solum

[1]*haec* A; *hac* B. [2]*affectos* A; *affectas* B. [3]*in* deleted before *quibus* B; in A.

(folio 96) tempore et modo, non enim quemlibet hominem, aut quovis tempore tecto excipere,[1] et cibo reficere tenemur, sed tunc solum
quando miseri calamitas elyemosynam[2] a nobis postulat, et res
nostra familiaris charitati subministrat.
5   4° Alia denique sunt in quibus substantia actionis non jubetur, sed
solum circumstantiae, verbi gratia in hominem inter se consuetudine et communi vita, de vicino suo sermonem habere et alienis
rebus se immiscere[3] quis tenetur? nemo sane, aut loqui, aut tacere
aliquis potest sine crimine; quod si forte alterius mentionem quis
10 facere[4] velit, jubet sane lex naturae, ut candide, ut amice loquatur,
eaque dicat, quae alterius famam, aut·existimationem laedere non
possunt, in his materia actionis indifferens est, circumstantiae deter-
minatae. In his non obligamur absolute, sed tantum ex hypothesi, et
in nostra situm est potestate, nostraeque prudentiae permissum, an
15 aliquas hujusmodi actiones praestare velimus, in quibus obligamur
⟨et nobis facessere negotium⟩.[5] In his omnibus uti patet obligatio
legis aeque perpetua est,

[1]*excipere* added by Locke in B; *exceipe* (?) A. [2]*elyemosynam* A; *eleyemosynam* B. [3]*immiscere* added by Locke in B; in A. [4]*facere* Locke's correction for *faceret* B; *faceret* A. [5]*et . . .
negotium* deleted after *obligamur* B; in A.

3°, There are other matters which demand some overt actions; for example, the public worship of divinity, the comforting of a neighbor in time of affliction, the relief of someone in trouble, giving food to the hungry. To these we are not bound forever but only at a certain time and in a certain manner.

ᵒlio 96) We are not bound to give shelter to all and sundry at each and every moment or to restore them with food, but only when the desperate condition of an unfortunate demands alms of us and our private resources supply the means to our charity.

4°, Finally, there are other matters in which the substance of an action is not prescribed but only its circumstances. For example, in the association of men among themselves and in their common life, who is obliged to gossip about his neighbor and meddle in another's affairs? No one, surely. Anybody can speak or remain silent without offense. But, should someone choose to speak of another, the law of nature does indeed command that he speak candidly and in a friendly manner and that what he says should not injure the good name or repute of another. In these cases the matter of the action is indifferent, the circumstances determined. In these things we are not obliged absolutely, but only "hypothetically,"[91] and it rests within our power and is left to our prudence [to determine whether] we want to undertake the kinds of actions which involve us in obliga-

[91]*In his non obligamur absolute sed tantum ex hypothesi.* That is, the law of nature is mute on whether we should speak as Locke prescribes. Locke's use of the terms "absolute" and "hypothetical" reflects the distinction made by Samuel Pufendorf in his *Elementa Jurisprudentiae* (The Hague, 1660 [LL a 2404], which I cite in the revised edition of 1672 [LL 2405]), I Definition XVI 16. p. 183: *Deinde inter praecepta iuris naturae alia sunt Absoluta, quae quosvis homines in quovis statu obligant; alia Hypothetica, quae certum aliquem statum aut actum ab hominum arbitrio dependentem supponit, seu quae versantur circa ea quae voluntatem hominis consequantur* ("Then among the precepts of the law of nature: some are absolute. These are binding upon any men of any station. Others are hypothetical. These posit some certain status or action, which depends upon the will of the individual, [or] which concern the kinds of actions that are the results of an individual's will"). Pufendorf illustrates the hypothetical precept of the law of nature by noting that the law of nature obliges no one to sell, but the individual who chooses to sell a commodity cannot do so at an unreasonable price or to the harm of the buyer.

(folio 97) officii nostri munera non aeque perpetua: in duobus prioribus semper obligamur ad actualem obedientiam, in duobus posterioribus
obligamur etiam semper ad ea praestanda, quae solum per intervalla et successive, habita ratione loci, temporis, et circumstantia-
5 rum, agere debemus; adeo ut cessat aliquando actio, obligatio num-
quam.

Deinde legis[1] naturae obligationem universalem esse dicimus,
non quod quaelibet lex naturae quemlibet obligat hominem, hoc
enim fieri non possit, cum plurima legis hujus praecepta, diversas
10 hominum inter se relationes respiciunt, et in iis fundantur: multa
sunt principum privilegia, plebi haud concessa, multa subditorum
officia, qua subditi sunt, quae in regem convenire non possunt;
imperatoris est gregariis, suas destinare stationes, et militum tenere;
nec deceret parentem, liberos suos officiose et humiliter salutare; de
15 quibus sic breviter statuendum est, praecepta illa legis naturae[2] quae
absoluta sunt, in quibus continentur furta, stupra, calumniae, et
altera ex parte religio[,]

[1]*Legis* A, B; *Deinde* inserted before *Legis* A (hence capitalization of *Legis*). [2]*naturae* B;
natura A.

(folio 98) caritas, fides, etc.[,] haec inquam et hujus modi alia, omnes qui[1]
ubique sunt homines aeque obligant, tam reges quam subditos, cum
plebe patres, parentes simul et liberos, nec minus barbaros quam
Graecos; nec quivis populus aut homo tam ab omni humanitate
5 remotus est, tam efferus, tam exlex, qui hisce legis vinculis non
tenetur; quae vero naturae decreta diversas respiciunt hominum
sortes, et inter se relationes; non aliter homines obligant, quam
prout munera, sive privata, sive publica, exigunt: aliud regis of-

tion. In all these cases, as is obvious, the obligation of the law is equally perpetual,

lio 97) [but] the specific charges of our duty are not perpetual in the same way. Under the first two [headings] we are bound to an actual obedience, under the last two we are also bound always to undertake actions which we ought to perform, [but] only from time to time and in succession, taking account of their place, time, and circumstances. Consequently, [our] action can sometimes cease, [our] obligation never.

Next, we say that the obligation of the law of nature is universal, not that any given law of nature binds any man whomsoever. This, indeed, could not happen since most of the precepts of this law regard different relations of men among themselves and in these they have their foundation. Many are the privileges of princes which are hardly granted to commoners; many are the duties of subjects, by virtue of the fact that they are subjects, which cannot be fitting for a king. It is the part of a commander to assign to his troops their proper positions and that of his soldiers to keep them. And it would not be fitting for a parent to greet his children with ceremony and humility. Concerning these matters we must briefly settle the question as follows: those precepts of the law of nature which are absolute—included among which are [prohibitions against] theft, debauchery, calumny, and, on the other hand, [the injunction to] religion,

lio 98) charity, faith, etc.—these I say and other [precepts] of this kind, are equally binding on all men wherever men exist, kings as well as subjects, senators together with the commoners, parents and children together, barbarians no less than Greeks. Nor is there any people or any man whatsoever so removed from humanity, so savage, so beyond the pale of law, who is not held by these bonds of law. And the decrees of nature which concern the different conditions of men and their relations among themselves are binding on men only to the extent that their functions, either private or public, demand.

ficium, aliud subditi; unusquisque subditus tenetur parere principi;
10 sed unusquisque homo non tenetur esse subditus; quidam enim[2]
nascuntur reges; nutrire et educere liberos, patris officium est,
nemo autem cogitur esse pater: adeo ut obligatio legis naturae
eadem est ubique; vitae solum conditio varia: idemque plane est
officium subditi apud Garamantas et Indos; ac apud Athenienses
15 aut Romanos: His ita positis dicimus legis naturae obligationem, et
per omnia saecula et per universum terrarum orbem vim

[1]*qui* vL; *quae* A, B. [2]*enim* added by Locke in B; in A.

(folio 99) suam illibatam et inconcussam obtinere[.]
   1° Quia si omnes homines non obligat, ratio est, vel quia alicui
parti generis humani, aut omnino lata[1] non sit, aut iterum abrogata;
sed neutrum horum dici potest.
5   2° Quia dici[2] non potest, aliquos homines ita liberos natos esse, ut
huic quidem legi minime subiiciantur, non enim privatum hoc aut
positivum jus, pro temporum occasione et praesenti commodo natum, sed fixa et aeterna morum regula, quam dictat ipsa ratio,
adeoque humanae naturae principiis infixum haeret; et mutetur
10 prius oportet humana natura, quam lex haec, aut mutari possit, aut
abrogari; convenientia enim est inter utramque, quodque jam con-
venit naturae rationali quatenus rationalis est, in aeternum con-
veniat est necesse: eademque ratio easdem dictabit ubique morum
regulas: quandoquidem[3] igitur omnes homines sint natura rationa-
15 les, et convenientia sit inter hanc legem, et naturam rationalem;
quae convenientia lumine naturae cognoscibilis est, necesse est
omnes rationali natura praeditos, i.e. omnes ubique

[1]*lata* A; *laeta* B. [2]*dici* Locke's correction for *credi* B; *credi* correction for *dici* A.
[3]*quandoquidem* A; *Quandoquidem* B.

(folio   homines hac lege teneri, adeo ut si aliquos saltem homines obliget
100)   lex naturalis, eodem plane jure et omnes obliget[1] necesse sit,[2] cum

The function of a king is one thing, that of a subject another. Each and every subject is bound to obey [his] prince, but each individual human is not, indeed, compelled to be a subject. Some are born kings. The nurture and education of children is the duty of a father, but no man is obliged to be a father. As a result, the obligation of the law of nature is the same everywhere, only the condition of life varies. Clearly, the duty of a subject is the same among the Garamantes and the Indians as it is among the Athenians or the Romans. Now that these [distinctions] have been laid down in this manner, we say that the obligation of the law of nature holds its force undiminished and unshaken throughout all ages and over the entire globe:

lio 99)   1°, Because, if it is not binding on all men, the reason is either that it has not been enacted for some part of the human race at all, or that it was repealed. But neither of these can be affirmed.

2°, Because it cannot be affirmed that some men have been born in a state of such freedom that they are hardly subject even to this particular law. For this is not a private or positive enactment [*jus*] which has arisen to meet a particular circumstance and a present advantage, but a fixed and eternal rule of conduct, dictated by reason itself, and for this reason something fixed and inherent in human nature. And it would be necessary for human nature to change before this law could either change or be abrogated. For there exists a harmony between the two of these, and what now conforms to a rational nature, insofar as it is rational, must necessarily conform eternally. And this same reason will dictate the same rules of conduct everywhere. Inasmuch, therefore, as all men are rational by nature and there exists a harmony between this law and a rational nature—a harmony knowable by the light of nature—it is necessary that all men endowed with a rational nature—that is, all men everywhere—

(folio   are bound by this law, so that if the law of nature should be binding
100)   on at least some men, by this same title it must clearly be binding on

par sit apud omnes homines ratio obligationis, idem cognoscendi
modus, eademque natura, non enim ex fluxa et mutabili voluntate
5 pendet haec lex, sed ex aeterno rerum ordine, mihi enim videntur
quidam immutabiles esse rerum status, et quaedam officia ex necessitate orta, quae aliter esse non possunt; non quod natura (vel ut
rectius[3] dicam) deus, non potuit aliter fecisse hominem; sed cum ita
factus sit, ratione et aliis suis facultatibus instructus, ad hanc vitae
10 conditionem natus, sequuntur necessario ex nativa ipsius constitutione aliqua illius, et certa officia, quae aliter esse non possunt; mihi[4]
enim videtur tam[5] necessario sequi ex natura hominis, si homo sit,
quod tenetur amare, et venerari deum,[6] et alia etiam praestare
naturae rationali convenientia, hoc est observare

[1]*obliget* Locke's correction of *obligat* B; *obligat* A. [2]*sit* Locke's correction for *est* B; *est*
A. [3]*rectius* Locke's correction for *rebus* B; *rectius* A. [4]*mihi enim* Locke's correction for
adeo enim mihi B; *adeo enim mihi* A. [5]*tam* added by Locke in B; not in A. [6]*deum* A; *Deum*
B.

(folio legem naturae, quam sequitur ex natura trianguli, si triangulus sit,
101) quod tres illius anguli sunt, aequales duobus rectis, quamvis plurimi
forsan sunt homines, adeo ignavi,[1] adeo socordes, qui dum animum
non advertant, utramque hanc[2] ignorant veritatem tam perspi-
5 cuam, tam certam, ut nihil magis, adeo ut legem hanc homines ad
unum omnes obligare, dubitare nemo possit; unde etiam constat
  3° jus[3] hoc naturale nunquam abrogatum iri, cum homines legem
hanc obrogare[4] non possint,[5] ei enim subiiciuntur, subditorum autem non est pro libitu suo, leges refigere; nec certe deus[6] velit, cum
10 enim ex infinita et aeterna sua sapientia, ita fecit hominem, ut haec
illius officia[7] ex ipsa hominis natura necessario sequerentur, haud
certe mutabit factum, et novam producet hominum progeniem,
quibus alia sit lex et morum regula, quandoquidem cum humana
natura, quae jam est, lex[8] naturae stat simul caditque. potuit[9] deus
15 homines ita creasse ut oculis carerent nec iis opus esset, dummodo
vero oculis utantur[10] eosque aperire velint et sol luceat, necesse est
cognoscant noctis et diei vicissitudines[,] colorum percipiant dif-
ferentias, et inter curvum et rectum quid intersit oculis videre[.]

all as well. The basis of this obligation is equal among all men, the mode of their coming to know it the same, their nature the same, for this law depends not on a will which is fluid and changeable, but on the eternal order of things. In my opinion, some states of things seem to be immutable, and some duties, which cannot be otherwise, seem to have arisen out of necessity; not that nature (or, to speak more correctly) god could not have created man other than he is, but, since he has been created as he is, provided with reason and his other faculties, there follow from the constitution of man at birth some definite duties he must perform, which cannot be other than what they are. For it seems to me to follow as necessarily from the nature of man, if he be a man, that he is bound to love and reverence god, and to perform other duties which are in conformity with a rational nature—that is to observe

(folio 101) the law of nature—as it follows from the nature of a triangle, if it be a triangle, that its three angles are equal to two right angles, even though there possibly exist very many men so indolent, so dense, who, since they pay no attention, are ignorant of both these truths which are so clear, so certain, that nothing can be more [obvious]. So it is that no one can doubt that this law is binding upon all men. Whence it is also certain that

3°, this natural law [*jus*] will never be abrogated, since men cannot alter this law [*legem*]. They are subject to it and it is not for subjects to refashion laws at their own pleasure. Nor surely would god will this, since out of his infinite and eternal wisdom he created man such that these his duties would necessarily follow from his very nature. And surely he will hardly change man, once he has been created, and bring forth a new generation of men who would have another law and another rule of conduct, inasmuch as the law of nature stands and falls together with human nature as it now exists. God could have created men such that they had no eyes and no need of them; but provided they make use of the eyes they have and are willing to open them and, provided the sun shines, they must of necessity come to know the alternation of day and night, perceive the differences among colors, and see with [these] eyes the difference between the straight and curved.

Alia argumenta ad probandum universalem legis naturae obligationem deduci poterant

[1]*ignavi* A, B; *ignari* vL. [2]*hanc* added by Locke in B; not in A. [3]*jus* A; *Jus* B. [4]*obrogare*
Locke's correction for *obligare* B; *abrogare* A. [5]*possint* Locke's correction for *possunt* B;
possunt A. [6]*deus* A; *Deus* B. [7]*officia* vL; *officio* A, B. [8]*et* deleted before *lex* B; in A.
[9]*potuit . . . videre* added by Locke on fol. 100ᵛ in B; not in A. [10]*utantur* vL; *utuntur* B.

(folio
102)
a posteriori,[1] ab incommodis scilicet quae sequerentur si supponeretur alicubi cessare hanc obligationem, nulla enim esset religio, nulla
inter homines societas, nulla fides et id genus innumera, quae vel
leviter attigisse satis est.

5   Restat[2] jam ut dubiis nonnullis hac de re breviter occurramus.

1° enim[3] sic probari potest, legis naturae obligationem non esse
perpetuam et universalem, haec[4] scilicet omnibus consentientibus
lex est naturae, ut[5] suum cuique tribuatur, vel nemo quod alienum
est abripiat et sibi habeat; hujus legis obligatio jubente deo[6] cessare
10   potest, ut ab Hebraeis, dum Aegypto decederent et invaderent Palestinam[7] factum legimus.

Ad hoc respondemus, negando minorem, nam si deus[8] juberet
aliquem mutuo acceptum non restituere, non cessaret legis naturae
obligatio, sed rei ipsius dominum, non violatur lex, sed mutatur
15   dominus,[9] prior enim dominus cum possessione rei amittit simul et
jus ad rem; Bona enim fortunae nunquam ita nostra sunt, ut dei[10]
esse desinant, ille supremus rerum omnium dominus, cuilibet pro
arbitrio suo sine injuria, de[11] suo

[1]*posteriori* vL; *posteriore* A, B. [2]New paragraph at *Restat* in A; probably also in B.
[3]*enim* A; *Enim* B. [4]*haec* vL; *hac* A, B. [5]*ut* added by Locke in B; not in A. [6]*deo* A; *Deo* B.
[7]*Palestinam* B; *Palaestinam* A. [8]*deus* A; *Deus* B. [9]*dominus* A; *Dominus* B. [10]*dei* A; *Dei* B.
[11]*de* A; *De* B.

(folio
103)
donare potest.

2° Si ad idem obsequium parentibus praestandum aliquando tenemur, aliquando non tenemur, ergo perpetua non est legis naturae

Other arguments could be deduced to prove the universal obligation of the law of nature

(folio a posteriori—that is, from the disadvantages which would follow
102) were it supposed that this obligation would not be in force at some
place or other. For [then] there would exist no religion, no society
among men, no faith, and countless other disadvantages of this kind
that it is enough to have touched on them only lightly.

It remains briefly to meet some doubts concerning this matter:

1°, That the obligation of the law of nature is not perpetual and
universal can be proven in following manner: by the agreement of
all, this is a law of nature—that to each should be given what belongs
to him or that no one should seize what belongs to another and keep
it for himself. But the obligation of this law can be suspended by the
command of god, as we read was done in the case of the Hebrews
when they came out of Egypt and entered Palestine.[92]

To this we reply by denying the minor premise.[93] For were god to
command a person not to return a thing he has received as a loan,
the obligation of the law of nature would not cease, but [rather] the
ownership of the thing itself. The law is not broken, but the owner
changes, for along with his possession of the thing the former owner
loses his right to the thing. For the goods of fortune are never our
possessions in such a way that they cease to belong to god. He is the
supreme master over all things; he can grant a gift from his own
possession to whomever he pleases without injury, according to his
own judgment.

(folio 2°, If we are bound to offer to our parents the same obedience at
103) one time and not at another, the obligation of the law of nature is not

[92] In their exodus out of Egypt, the Israelites were commanded by God to carry with
them the gold and clothing of the Egyptians; Exodus 3:22, 11:2, and 12:35–36.
[93] *negando minorem*. The explicit form of the syllogism would be: (1) Every man has
the right to his own property (major premise). (2) But God suspended the right of the
Egyptians to their own property in the exodus of the people of Israel out of Egypt
(minor premise). Therefore, the binding force of the law of nature is not perpetual.

obligatio, sed aliud jubente principe, non tenemur obsequi parenti-
5 bus, Ergo[1] respondemus quod tenemur observare mandata paren-
tum, in licitis tantum, quae obligatio nunquam tollitur, si enim aliud
imperet rex,[2] parentis jussa fiunt illicita verbi gratia domi manere et
rei familiaris curam gerere, cum rex ad militiam evocat, adeo ut non
cesset omnino legis naturae obligatio[,] sed mutatur rei ipsius nat-
10 ura.

3° Si quis dubitet an universalis sit obligatio, quia tam variae sint
de officio suo inter homines sententiae, tam diversi mores, sciendum
est, istum mortalium, et in vita et in opinionibus dissensum non esse,
quia alia ac alia est lex naturae apud diversas gentes, sed quia aut
15 diuturna consuetudine et domesticis exemplis seducti, aut passioni-
bus in transversum acti, tradunt se in aliorum mores, et dum sibi
rationis

[1]*Ergo* capitalized by Locke in B; *ergo* A. [2]*rex* Locke's correction for *lex* B; *rex* A.

(folio   suae usum non permittunt, sed appetitui parent, brutorum more
104)   gregem sequuntur[.] aeque enim erroribus obnoxius est qui aperire
nolit[1] oculos, ac qui caecus nascitur, etsi forsan via impedita non sit,
et oculorum acies satis sit acuta.
5   De infantibus et fatuis non est quod laboremus, etsi enim omnes
obliget lex quibus datur, non tamen eos obligat quibus non datur,
nec datur iis a quibus cognosci non potest.

[1]*nolit* correction for *nollit* B; *nollit* A.

therefore perpetual, for, when a prince gives us a different command, we are not bound to obey our parents. We respond, therefore, that we are bound to observe the orders of parents, but only in matters which are lawful. This obligation is never removed, for if a king should give a command to the contrary, the commands of a parent become unlawful: for example, to remain at home and attend to the affairs of the household when the king summons to military service. Thus, the obligation of the law of nature would not cease in the least, but the nature of the case itself changes.

3°, Should a person come to doubt whether the obligation of the law of nature is universal because the opinions of men concerning their duty are so varied, their morals so conflicting, he should know that this disagreement of mortals, both in [the conduct of] their lives and in their opinions, does not exist because the law of nature changes from nation to nation but [rather] because [men are] either seduced by long established habits or the examples [they discover] at home, or are driven athwart [reason] by their passions, and surrender themselves to the morals of others, and, as long as they do not permit themselves to rely on their own reason,

(folio 104) but yield to their appetites, they follow the herd in the manner of brute beasts. Indeed, he who is unwilling to open his eyes is as prone to error as he who is born blind, even if by chance his road were free of obstacles and his power of vision sufficiently acute.

There is no need to belabor the question of babes and fools, for even if the law of nature were binding on all to whom it is given, yet it is not on those to whom it is not given, and it is not given to those by whom it cannot be known.

(folio [XI]. An privata cujusque utilitas sit fundamentum
105)   legis naturae?[1] Negatur[.]

    Aliqui sunt, qui legis naturae oppugnationem aggressi, illud sibi
assumpserunt argumentum, jura scilicet[2] homines utilitate sibi
sanxisse[3] varia pro moribus, et apud eosdem pro temporibus saepe
mutata: jus autem naturale esse nullum, omnes enim et homines et
5 animantes[4] ad utilitates suas natura ducente ferri, proinde, aut nullam esse legem naturae, aut si sit aliqua, summam esse stultitiam,
quoniam sibi nocet alienis[5] commodis consulens, haec et hujusmodi[6] alia in Academia sua disputavit olim Carneades, cujus acerrimum[7] ingenium, et eloquentiae vis nihil intactum, nihil paene[8]
10 inconcussum praetermisit, nec defuerunt ab illa

[1]Title in Locke's hand, no numeral in B; question mark after *naturae* omitted in B.
[2]*scilicet* added by Locke in B; not in A. [3]*sanxisse* vL; *saxisse* A, B. [4]*et* deleted after
animantes A, B. [5]*alienis* Locke's correction for *aliens* B; *aliens* A. [6]*hujusmodi* A, B;
ejusmodi vL. [7]*acerrimum* B; *acerimum* A. [8]*paene* B; *pene* A.

(folio 105) **[XI]. Does the private interest of each individual constitute the foundation of the law of nature? It does not.**

There are some who[94] in their assault against the defenses of the law of nature have taken up this argument: that men have established laws for their own advantage—laws which vary to conform to their morals and which are often changed among these same people to suit their age. There is, however, no natural law [*jus*] for all; both humans and animals are moved to their own advantage at nature's guidance. Moreover, [these adversaries claim] that either there exists no law of nature, or, were such a law to exist, it would constitute the height of folly, since a person who takes into consideration what is of benefit to others does injury to himself. These arguments and others like them were once urged in his Academy by Carneades,[95] whose extremely acute intelligence and whose powerful eloquence left nothing intact, virtually nothing unshaken. Nor from that age onward have there been lacking those

---

[94]*Aliqui sunt qui*. The source of this argument is ultimately Carneades. His argument was reported in Cicero's *De Republica* III 12.21, but our only surviving source for this report is Lactantius *Divinae Institutiones* V 16.3. Locke's source for the language he attributes to "some" is the nearly verbatim citation in the *Prolegomena* to Hugo Grotius's *De Jure Belli ac Pacis*, p. ii. Both Grotius and Locke omit the word *scilicet* after *sanxisset*, and Locke omits *alias* before *animantes*.

[95]Carneades (214/13–129/28 B.C.) was the founder of the "New" Academy. We have only reports of him, but his dialectical acuity and oratorical powers were much admired in antiquity, especially by Cicero, cf. *Academica* I 12.16; *De Oratore* II 38.161 and III 18.68; *De Finibus* III 12.41; Plutarch, *Cato the Younger* 22; and Diogenes Laertius IV 63. Locke's characterization of his assaults on received opinions (and his term *oppugnationem*) echoes the judgment of Cicero in *De Oratore* II 38.161: *Carneadi vero vis incredibilis illa dicendi et varietas perquam esset optanda nobis, qui nullam umquam in illis suis disputationibus rem defendit, quam non probarit, nullam oppugnavit, quam non everterit* ("Now the incredible power and diversity of Carneades' oratory is something we should especially imitate. In his well-known debates he defended no position he did not establish and assaulted none he did not overthrow"). In his valedictory address as moral censor in 1664, Locke chose very similar language to describe the debates with his students in Christ Church out of which his questions concerning the law of nature arose: *Legem illam de qua omnis dimicatio saepius amissam frustra quaesiveram, nisi quam lingua Vestra mihi extorsit eandem restitueret vita; adeo ut dubitari possit utrum disputationes Vestrae legem naturae acrius oppugnarent an mores defenderint* ("I would have sought that law, over which was all our frequent strife, in vain and often lost it, had not your lives restored a law your tongues had wrested from me. And one can ask whether your conduct defended or your debates assaulted this law with greater keenness"), fol. 133, *John Locke: Essays*, ed. von Leyden, pp. 236–39.

(folio
106)

usque aetate, qui summo studio ad hanc sententiam accesserunt,
quibus cum defuerunt virtutes, et eae animi dotes quarum ope ad
honores et divitias sibi munirent[1] aditum, inique cum humano generi actum querebantur, et res publicas non sine injuria geri conten-
5 derunt, dum communibus et nativis commodis, et in commune bonum natis prohiberentur, adeoque excutienda esse imperiorum
juga, libertatem naturalem asserendam clamarunt, et jus omne et
aequum non aliena lege sed propria cujusque[2] utilitate esse aestimandum: huic vero tam iniquae opinioni, senior mortalium pars,
10 cui aliquis inerat humanitatis sensus, aliqua societatis cura, semper
obstitit: verum ut paulo accuratius[3] rem definiamus, praemittenda
est aliqua terminorum explicatio, quid nempe per

[1]*munirent* inserted by Locke in B; in A. [2]*cujusque* B; *cuiusque* A. [3]*ut paulo accuratius* A;
ut acuratius B.

(folio
107)

fundamentum legis naturae velimus et quid deinde per privatam
cujusque utilitatem[.]
        1º Per fundamentum legis naturae id volumus cui innituntur, et
cui tanquam fundamento superstruuntur[1] alia omnia, et minus pa-
5 tentia illius legis praecepta, et ab eo aliquo modo deduci possunt,
adeoque vim suam omnem, et obligationem ex eo obtinent quod
cum ea, tanquam primaria et fundamentali lege conveniunt, quae
omnium aliarum legum inde pendentium regula est et mensura.
        2º Cum dicimus privatam cujusque utilitatem non esse funda-
10 mentum legis naturae, non ita accipi volumus, quasi opposita essent
inter se jus commune hominum et utilitas cujusque privata, ma-

(folio who have flocked to this doctrine with the greatest enthusiasm.
106) These, since they were lacking in the virtues and those endowments
of mind by the help of which they could pave for themselves the way
to honors and wealth, complained that the human race had been
treated unfairly and contended that states were governed not without injustice, since they were deprived of advantages which are
common and natural and which come into being for the good of all.
For this reason they clamored that the yoke of [all] authority should
be shaken off, and natural liberty vindicated, and that all right [*jus*]
and all justice [*aequum*] should be determined not by another's law
[*lege*], but by the interest of each individual. But the saner part of
mankind, which possessed some sense of humanity and some concern for society, has always opposed this opinion and its great iniquity.

Now, to define this matter with somewhat greater precision, we
must first explain some terms: what we mean by the foundation of
natural law

(folio and then what we mean by the private interest of each individual.
107)   1°, By the foundation of natural law we understand that which
supports and upon which are erected, as upon a foundation, all the
other precepts of this law, even the less obvious, and that from which
[these precepts] can be deduced in some manner. As a consequence,
these derive their entire force and their binding power from this
[foundation] because they are in agreement with this primary and,
as it were, fundamental law, which is the rule and measure of all the
other laws which depend upon it.

2°, When we claim that the private interest of each individual is
not the foundation of the law of nature we do not want to be
understood to claim that the common right [*jus*] of men and the
private interest[96] of each individual are things opposed to one an-

---

[96]*Jus commune hominum et utilitas cujusque privata.* That Locke means "right" by *jus*
and not "the common rules of human equity" (von Leyden) is clear from the language of his second treatise in *Two Treatises*, ed. Laslett, sec. 51, p. 344: "And thus it is
very easie to conceive without any difficulty, *how Labour could at first begin a title of
Property* in the common things of Nature, and how the spending of it on our uses

ximum enim munimentum rei cujusque privatae lex est naturae,
sine cujus observatione, rem suam possidere suisque commodis in-
servire nemini licet, adeoque cuivis humanum genus, hominumque
mores

[1]superstruuntur Locke's correction for *inaedificantur* B; *inaedificantur* A.

(folio   recte secum perpendenti, certum erit, nihil aeque communi cujus-
108)   que utilitati conducere, nihil aeque res hominum tutas et securas
custodire, ac observatio legis naturae, verum negamus id cuique
licere, quod ipse pro re nata judicet sibi commodum fore, frustra
5   enim statuis privatam cujusque utilitatem esse aequi et recti regulam, nisi privato cuique permittis ut pro se ipse judicet, ut quid sibi
sit utile ipse aestimet, nemo enim alterius commodi aequus et justus
esse potest aestimator, et illum illudis solum[1] specie utilitatis, cui id
licitum asseris quod utile est, in alterius vero potestate[2] situm velis,
10   ut statuat quid sit utile quid non; adeo ut status quaestionis hic
demum sit. An quod privatus quisque pro re nata judicet sibi rebusque suis utile fore, id esse secundum legem naturae, eoque nomine
sibi non solum licitum esse, sed et necessarium? nec quicquam in
natura

[1]*solum* struck out after *illum*, then added by Locke after *illudis* B; *illum solum* A.
[2]*potestate* Locke's correction for *potestatem* B; *potestate* A.

(folio   obligare nisi quatenus aliquam immediate[1] prae se ferat utilitatem?
109)   quod negamus.
     1º Quia id non potest esse fundamentum legis naturae sive pri-
maria lex, ex qua obligatio aliarum ejusdem naturae legum minus
5   universalium non pendet. sed ex hoc fundamento non pendet ali-

other, for the law of nature is the greatest defense of the private property of the individual. Were it not observed, no one could possess his own property or labor for his own benefit. Thus, to whoever considers and weighs properly the human race and men's customs

(folio 108) it will appear certain that nothing is as conducive to the common advantage of the individual, nothing so protective of the safety and security of men's possessions, as the observance of the law of nature. But we deny that each individual is free to judge by himself what would be of advantage to himself [simply] as the occasion arises. Indeed, unless you leave each private individual to judge for himself so that he calculates himself what is useful to himself, you gain nothing by establishing the interest of each individual as the rule of what is right and proper. For no one can be a fair and just assessor of what is good for another, and under the guise of self-interest, you simply deceive the person for whom you claim the freedom to do what is useful. In truth, you would want the decision of what is useful and what is not to reside in the power of another. So the state of [our] question now comes to this: whether what each private individual judges to be useful to himself and to his own affairs as the occasion arises conforms to the law of nature and, by this title, it is not only lawful for him but even necessary. And that nothing in nature is binding

(folio 109) except insofar as it is something which carries with it some immediate advantage. This we deny.

1º, Because the foundation of the law of nature or [any] primary law cannot be something upon which the binding force of other less universal laws of the same kind does not depend. But the obligation

---

bounded it. So that there could be no reason of quarrelling about the Title, nor any doubt about the largeness, of the Possession it gave. Right and conveniency went together; for as a Man had a Right to all he could employ his Labour upon, so he had no temptation to labour for more than he could make use of."

arum legum obligatio, si enim percurrere velis omnia vitae humanae officia, nullum invenies ex sola utilitate natum, quodque
obligat ex hoc solum, quod commodum sit: cum multae sint et
maximae virtutes, quae in eo solum consistunt, ut cum dispendio
10 nostro aliis prosimus, hujusmodi virtutibus ad astra olim evecti et in
deorum numerum ascripti sunt heroes, qui caelum congestis et
undique conquisitis pecuniis non emerunt, sed labore, sed periculis,
sed liberalitate; non privatis studuerunt commodis, sed utilitati pub-
licae, et totius humani generis; alii laboribus, alii lucubrationibus,
15 alii morte immortalitatem meruerunt, nemo ignavia aut avaritia

[1]*immediate* inserted by Locke in B; not in A.

(folio aut magnus aut probus factus est; quod si Primaria[1] esset lex natu-
110) rae ut sibi quisque rebusque[2] suis privatis consuleret, magna illa
virtutum exempla literarum monumentis consecrata oblivioni
danda essent, ut interiret prorsus tantae insaniae tantae nequitiae
5 memoria. Ii enim ipsi quos jam pro summis optimisque viris mi-
ramur, non solum stulti, sed et nefarii, ac sceleratissimi essent habendi, qui tanto cum studio, se suasque res contempserunt, ut majori solum pretio mercarentur turpitudinem, ut rem suam simul
abiicerent et innocentiam, et in eo sibi laborandum putarent, ut
10 damna simul crescerent, et crimina; si utilitatem recti regulam esse
volumus, tui, Alcides, labores crucem potius meruerunt quam apo-
theosim; et naturae ipsi magis quam monstris bellum indixisti, Curtii qui patriae causa in patentem insiluit voraginem, et ne suis Roma
minis sepeliretur vivus terram[3] subivit, non

[1]*Primaria* A; *primaria* B. [2]*rebusque* Locke's correction for *plusque* B; *rebusque* A.
[3]*terram* Locke's correction for *terras* B; *terras* A.

of other laws does not rest upon this foundation. Indeed, if you were to survey all the duties of human life, you would find none that has its origin in interest alone and which is binding only by virtue of the fact that it might be of advantage. For there are many virtues, and the greatest virtues, which consist only in our helping others at our own expense. By virtues of this kind heroes were once elevated to the stars and included in the roll of the gods. They did not purchase [their place in] heaven by virtue of monies piled up and acquired from all sources, but by toil, by dangers, by generosity. They did not pursue their own private gain, but the public interest and that of the entire human race. Some proved themselves worthy of immortality by their labors, others by their studies, others by their death. No one has become great or worthy through indolence or avarice.

(folio 110) But if the Primary law of nature directed each to take thought of himself and his own private affairs, those great examples of virtue which have been consecrated in the monuments of literature should be relegated to oblivion that the memory of such madness and vice should perish utterly. For those very men whom we now admire as the greatest and the best, would have to be considered not only foolish, but vicious, and the greatest of criminals. These are men who by such endeavors held themselves and their own fortunes in contempt only in order to purchase their disgrace at a higher price, to cast away their own fortunes along with innocence, and to come to believe that the only end of their labors was to increase their crimes with their losses. If we want self-interest to be the rule of rectitude— your labors, Hercules, deserved a gallows rather than a place in heaven, and you declared war on nature herself rather than on monsters. And the virtue of Curtius,[97] who for the sake of his country lept into a yawning abyss, and, to prevent Rome from being

[97]*Curtii.* Marcus Curtius, whose sacrifice of his life became a part of the legend of Roman archaic *virtus*. According to Livy *Ab urbe condita* VII 6.5 and Valerius Maximus *Memorabilia* V 6.2 (the chapter on devotion to one's country), a huge chasm opened in the area of the Roman forum (the so-called lacus Curtius); in response to an oracle that Rome should sacrifice her best to fill the portentious chasm, Marcus mounted his horse and plunged into it; thereafter, the chasm filled up.

(folio
111)

tam virtus fuit, quam insania; vitae simul valedixit et innocentiae, eodemque tempore intravit sepulchrum, et meruit mortem. benignissima certe merito dicenda est omnium mater natura, cum officia nostra non solum necessaria esse vellet sed jucunda, et ditia, nec
5 ullas esse virtutes nisi fructuosas; optime cum humano genere actum est, ut tantum crescat virtus quantum ipsa pecunia crescit; quorsum igitur laudamus Fabritii inopiam? et verborum splendore nefarias ejus ornamus sordes? qui fortunam suam et virtutem vendere mallet quam patriam; qui rempublicam stulte sibi anteposuit,
10 et seipso habuit cariorem?[1] Quanto rectius magnus Catilinae animus, qui naturae praeceptis optime imbutus, suum mundi capiti praetulit, nec timuit hostile ipsius Romae muris aratrum imprimere, dummodo sibi inde sperare liceret messem. Audiat forsan Cicero

[1]*cariorem* A; *chariorem* B.

buried by her own internal threats, entered the earth when still alive, was not so much virtue as insanity.[98]

(folio 111) He bade farewell to his life and at the same time to his innocence, and at the moment he entered his grave he deserved death. Without doubt, nature, the mother of all things, should rightly be called most kind since she willed our duties to be not only necessary but pleasant and profitable, and only those things to be virtues which are fruitful. The human race has been treated in the best possible manner so that as virtue increases, so does wealth itself. Why then do we praise the poverty of Fabricius[99] and invest with the splendor of our words his low and filthy vice—the kind of man who preferred to sell his fortune and virtue rather than his fatherland, and who foolishly preferred his republic to himself and held it as something of more value than himself? By contrast, the great spirit of Catiline showed more rectitude when he, imbued in the best fashion with the precepts of nature, preferred his own [interest] to the head of the world, nor feared driving his hostile plow[100] into the walls of Rome herself, provided he could expect from this some harvest for himself. Cicero perhaps can be styled "father of his country,"[101]

[98]For the confusion of language in the moral universe of Carneades, see Locke's anticipations of his argument in Question I, fol. 20.

[99]*Fabritii inopiam*. Locke had in mind Gaius Fabricius Luscinus's legendary refusal to accept a gift, despite his extreme poverty, from Pyrrhus, king of Epirus, after the Roman defeat at Asculum in 278 B.C.; cf. Plutarch's account of the episode in his *Life of Pyrrhus* 20. Fabricius's poverty is often evoked as an example of old Roman ways; cf. Valerius Maximus *Memorabilia* IV 4.3 and 10 and Cicero *De Officiis* III 22.86 (LL 714–717), where Locke could have found his contrast between *virtus* and *utilitas* stated explicitly.

[100]*hostile ipsius Romae muris aratrum imprimere*. Locke borrows his phrase from Horace *Odes* I 16.20–21 (*imprimeretque muris / hostile aratrum exercitus insolens*). Just as a furrow marked the site for the walls of a Roman city, a plow obliterated the traces of these walls when the city was destroyed. The practice is described by Modestinus in *Digest* VII 4.21.

[101]*Cicero pater patriae*. Cicero often reminds his audiences of the title awarded to him by the senate of Rome for suppressing the Catilinarian conspiracy in 63 B.C.; *In Pisonem* 6; *Pro Sestio* 121; *Phillipic* II 12; *Ad Atticum* IX 10.3; cf. Plutarch's *Cicero* 23.6.

(folio 112) pater patriae, hic certe Genuinus naturae filius, et imperium orbis dum Romam invasit magis meruit; quam Tullius qui defendit: pudet sane hanc infamiam naturae inurere, et tantam turpitudinem illius institutis imputare, cumque nihil tam sanctum sit, quod aliquando non violaverit avaritia, officii rationem in lucro ponere et recti regulam utilitatem statuere, quid aliud esset quam omni nequitiae fenestram aperire?

2⁰ Ea non potest esse lex naturae primaria, cujus violatio necessaria est, sed si utilitas cujusque privata sit fundamentum istius legis, eversum iri necesse est, cum omnium simul utilitati consulere impossibile sit.[1] unica enim est et eadem semper universae stirpis humanae haereditas, nec pro nascentium numero augetur. ad[2] hominum commoditates et usus certam rerum ubertatem natura largita est, et ea quae gignuntur, certo modo et numero donata sunt consulto, non fortuito nata, nec cum hominum necessitate aut avaritia crescunt[.] nobiscum[3] non nascitur vestitus, nec homines more testudinum cognata habent, et secum una crescentia domicilia

---

[1]*sit* Locke's correction for *est* B; *est* A. [2]*ad . . . crescunt* added by Locke on fol. 111ᵛ in B; not in A. [3]*nobiscum* A; *Nobiscum* B.

(folio 113) circumgerunt. quoties inter homines crescit aut cupido, aut necessitas habendi, non protenduntur illico mundi limites, victus, vestitus, ornamenta, divitiae, et caetera omnia hujus vitae bona in communi posita sunt, et dum sibi rapit quantum quisque potest, quantum suo addit acervo, tantum alieno detrahit, nec[1] cuivis licet nisi per alterius damna ditescere. Regeret hic fortasse aliquis, quod cum dicimus utilitatem cujusque esse legis naturae fundamentum, id non ita intelligi debere,[2] quasi quisque teneretur faelix esse et beatus, et rebus omnibus abunde affluere, sed unus quisque homo quantum in se est obligatur sibi consulere, adeoque recti mensuram esse utilitatem propriam, in eaque fundari omnia

---

[1]*nec* A; *neque* B. [2]*debere* Locke's correction for *debet* B; *debere* A.

(folio
112)
[but] surely this [Catiline] was a True Born son of nature and, since he invaded Rome, he was more deserving of empire over the world than Tully who defended it. In truth, it is repugnant to brand nature with such disgrace and to impute such a degree of viciousness to her institutions. And, since there exists nothing so sacred that at one time or another avarice has not violated it, what would placing the basis of [one's] duty upon profit and establishing interest as a rule of rectitude amount to but throwing the window open to all kinds of vice?

2º, That law whose violation is necessary cannot be the primary law of nature. But, if the interest of each individual is the foundation of this law, it must necessarily be overthrown since it would be impossible to take into account the interest of all at one and the same time. The human race has only one patrimony and this is always the same and it is not increased in proportion to the number of births. Nature has been generous with a fixed abundance of things for the benefit and use of men. And her products are deliberately distributed in a fixed manner and number, [and are] not produced at random, nor do they increase with the need or avarice of men. We are not born with clothing and men do not have homes and shelters furnished them at birth, and which grow as they do

(folio
113)
and which they carry about with them as do tortoises. And, whenever either the desire or the need for possessions increases among men, the limits of the world are not automatically extended. Food, clothing, adornments, riches, and all other such goods of this life are placed in common. And whenever one man seizes for himself as much as he can, he takes away from another as much as he piles up for himself. Nor is it possible for anyone to grow wealthy except through someone else's loss. At this point someone would possibly correct [us by saying] that, when we claim that the interest of each individual is the foundation of the law of nature, this should not be interpreted to mean that everyone should be obliged to be happy and blessed and to have an abundance of all [kinds of] goods, but that each and every man, as much as it is in his power, is bound to take account of his own interest, and for this reason the rule of

(folio 114) vitae officia. quo posito sequitur 1º,[1] quod ad id obligantur homines quod fieri non potest, tenetur enim quisque sibi rerum utilium parare et possidere quam maximam copiam, quod dum fit necesse est ut alteri relinquatur quam minima, cum certum sit quod nihil
5 emolumenti tibi accrescit, quod alteri non aufertur; quod plane contrarium est, si alia ponamus[2] virtutum fundamenta, virtutes enim ipsae inter se non pugnant, nec homines committunt, accendunt se mutuo foventque; mea justitia alterius non tollit aequitatem; nec principis munificentia officit subditorum liberalitati, sanctitas
10 patris non corrumpit liberos, nec Catonis temperantia efficere potest[3] ut minus severus sit Cicero, inter se non pugnant

[1]1º B; *primo* A. [2]*ponamus* Locke's correction for *faciamus* B; *faciamus* A. [3]*potest* added by Locke in B; not in A.

(folio 115) vitae officia, nec homines invicem armant; quod ex hoc 2º supposito[1] necessario sequitur, et homines (uti loquuntur) lege naturae in statu belli sunt. tollitur omnis societas et societatis vinculum fides, quae enim promissorum implendorum ratio, quae societatis custo-
5 dia, qui hominum convictus, cum id omne aequum justumque sit, quod utile? quid enim aliud esse poterit[2] hominum inter se con-

rectitude is one's proper interest, and all of the duties of life have their foundation in this interest.

(folio 114) On this supposition, it follows first that men are bound to something which cannot come about. For each individual is bound to secure and to possess the greatest possible supply of things useful to him. And, so long as this is the case, it is necessary that as little as possible is left for another, since it is certain that no gain accrues to you which is not taken away from another—which clearly involves a contradiction, were we to lay down any foundations for virtue other [than the law of nature]. For the virtues themselves are not in conflict with one another nor do they compel men [to conflict], they kindle and mutually foster one another. Justice on my part does not destroy the fairness of another, nor does the munificence of a prince stand in the way of the generosity of his subjects; a father's sanctity does not corrupt his children, nor can the austerity of Cato result in making Cicero less severe. The duties of life do not conflict with one another,

(folio 115) nor do they arm men against one another. This [state] would necessarily follow on our second assumption, and men under the law of nature are, as they say, in a state of war.[102] All society and trust, the bond of society, are destroyed. What reason [would there be] for keeping promises, what force for the preservation of society, what life and association among men, when all justice and equity is [only] what is useful. What will the commerce of men among themselves be

---

[102]*sequitur ut homines (uti loquuntur) lege naturae in statu belli sunt.* Locke clearly has Hobbes in mind, although he uses the plural; cf. n. 59, above. Locke's own dissenting view of the difference between the state of nature and a natural state of war is expressed in sec. 19 of the second treatise, *Two Treatises,* ed. Laslett, p. 321, where he refers to "some men" confounding them: "Men living together according to reason without a common Superior on Earth, with Authority to judge between them, is *properly the State of Nature.* But force, or a declared design of force upon the Person of another, where there is no common Superior on Earth to appeal to for relief, *is the State of War.*"

suetudo, quam fraus,[3] vis[,] odium[,] rapina, caedes, et id genus
alia:[4] cum cuilibet homini non solum liceret sed necesse esset id
quovis modo ab alio abripere, quod ille pariter tenetur defendere,
10 unde

3º oritur[5] argumentum, nempe id non potest esse fundamentum
legis naturae. quo posito,[6] omnis justitia, amicitia, liberalitas,

---

[1]*supposito* B; *supposio* A. [2]*poterit* Locke's correction for *poterat* B; *poterat* A. [3]*vis*
deleted before *fraus*; reinserted by Locke after *fraus* B; *vis, fraus* A. [4]*et id genus alia*
added by Locke; *etc.* deleted B; *et caetera* A. [5]*oritur* A; *Oritur* B. [6]*tollitur* deleted after
posito B; in A.

(folio   e vita tollitur, quae enim justitia ubi nulla proprietas aut dominium,
116)   aut quae proprietas? ubi cuivis licet non solum id possidere quod
suum est, sed id suum cujusque est, quod possidet, quod utile est:
verum hic breviter observare licet, hujus sententiae propugnatores
5   petere morum principia et vitae regulam, potius ex appetitu et
inclinatione hominum naturali, quam ex legis obligatione, quasi id
moraliter optimum esset, quod plures appetunt, unde etiam hoc
insuper sequitur, aut legis naturae nullam esse obligationem, quod
nemo dixerit, tum enim lex non est; aut eam esse vitae humanae
10   conditionem, ut non liceret homini cedere jure suo, aut alteri bene-
facere sine certa spe lucri. si enim rectitudo alicujus actionis nascatur
ex utilitate, et,

(folio   homines obligantur[1] ad eam rectitudinem; nescio quo pacto, liceret
117)   cuiquam, aliquid amico largire, donare, impendere, vel quovis alio

but fraud, violence, enmity, rapine, bloodshed and other things of this kind, in a state when it would not only be permitted but necessary for any individual to wrest from another by any means what he is equally bound to defend. Whence,

3°, The argument arises: that this cannot be the foundation of the law of nature. On this supposition, all justice, friendship, generosity is removed from life.

(folio 116) For what justice [can there be] where there is no property or private ownership,[103] or what property where each is allowed, not only to possess what belongs to him but the property of each individual is what he possesses, what is useful to him? But here it is permissible to make a brief observation: the champions of this doctrine seek the principles of morals and the rule of life from the natural appetites and inclinations of men rather than the obligation of the law, as if what is morally best is the object most men strive for. From this the additional consequence follows: either the law of nature has no binding power—which no one will say, for then it is not a law—or the condition of human life is such that it would not be lawful for a man to yield anything of his own right or to benefit another without the certain expectation of profit. For, if the rightness of any action were to arise out of its advantage,

(folio 117) and men were bound to this [kind of] rectitude, I do not know how it would be permitted for anyone to be generous to a friend, to give a

[103]*Quae enim justitia ubi nulla proprietas aut dominium?* Cf. Locke's *Essay*, ed. Nidditch, IV 3.18 p. 549: "*Where there is no Property there is no Injustice*, is a Proposition as certain as any Demonstration in Euclid: . . . the *Idea* of *Property*, being a right to anything; and the *Idea* to which the name *Injustice* is given, being the Invasion or Violation of that right." The same axiom of ethical thought is stated again in *Some Thoughts concerning Education*, sec. 110 in *The Educational Writings of John Locke*, ed. James L. Axtell (Cambridge: Cambridge University Press, 1968), p. 214: "Children cannot well comprehend what *Injustice* is till they understand property, and how particular Persons come by it"; cf. Hobbes, *Leviathan* I 15: "Where there is no Own, that is Property, there is no Injustice."

modo gratis beneficium conferre, sine legis hujus violatione, quod
quam absonum sit, quam a ratione, et humana natura, et vita ho-
5 nesta alienum aliorum judicio permitto.

Verum[2] obiici potest, si[3] ex observatione legis naturae et ex omni
vitae officio semper sequatur commodum, nec quicquam agere possumus secundum legem naturae, quod magnam post se non trahat
vel immediate vel mediate utilitatem[.] ergo fundamentum legis
10 naturae est cujusque utilitas, sed minor patet; ex hujus enim legis
observatione nascitur pax, concordia, amicitia, impunitas,[4] se-

[1]*nascantur* deleted before *obligantur* B; not in A. [2]New paragraph at *Verum* in A; not
in B. [3]*si* B; *Si* A. [4]*impunitas* added by Locke in B; not in A.

(folio curitas, rerum nostrarum possessio, et ut omnia uno verbo complec-
118) tar felicitas.[1]

Ad[2] haec sic respondemus. Utilitas non est fundamentum legis,
aut ratio obligationis, sed obsequii consequentia, aliud enim est si
5 actio per se aliquod afferat emolumentum, aliud si ea ratione prosit,
quod conformis sit legi, qua lege abrogata[3] nullum in ea esset omnino commodum, verbi grati[a][4] promissis stare, licet sit incommodum:[5] distinguendum enim est, inter actionem ipsam, et obedientiam, actio enim ipsa incommoda esse potest, exempli causa
10 depositi restitutio quae rem nostram minuit, obedientia utilis quatenus poenam sceleri debitam averruncat,[6] quae poena debita non
esset, adeoque non fugienda,

[1]*felicitas* B; *faelicitas* A. [2]New paragraph in A; perhaps also in B. [3]*abrogata* Locke's
correction for *amota* B; *amota* A. [4]*grati* A, B. [5]*incommodum* B; *inccomodum* A. [6]*averruncat*
A; *averruneat* B.

(folio si recti regula, praesens esset commodum, adeo ut actionis rectitudo
119) non pendet ex utilitate, sed utilitas consequitur ex rectitudine.

Sic Cogitavit[1]

J. Locke

5 1664

[1]*Sic Cogitavit* . . . and date in Locke's hand in B; not in A.

gift, spend money, or to confer a benefit in any other manner without payment in return and not violate this law. I leave others to judge how absurd this is, how foreign to reason, to human nature, and to an honorable life.

But the objection can be made that, if, upon the observation of the law of nature and every duty of life, there always follows some benefit, and we can do nothing in following the law of nature which does not bring with it some great advantage either directly or indirectly, the foundation of the law of nature is therefore the interest of each individual. But the minor premise is obvious; for from the keeping of this law peace arises, concord, friendship, freedom from [fear of unjust] punishments, security, the possession of our own property, and, to

(folio 118) embrace all these in a single word, happiness.

To these [objections] we make this response: interest is not a foundation of law or a basis of obligation, but the consequence of obedience. It is one thing if an action entails some benefit by itself, another if it should be advantageous by reason of the fact that it is in conformity to the law; but were this law repealed, there would be no benefit whatsoever in acting [in this way]. To give an example: to abide by one's promises might be granted disadvantageous. Now, one must distinguish between an action taken by itself and obedience; for the action itself can be disadvantageous, as for example, the return of a deposit which diminishes our wealth. Obedience is useful to the extent that it averts punishment which must be paid for a crime. This punishment would not have to be paid and, thus, would not be something to avoid,

(folio 119) if the criterion of recititude were present advantage. So the rightness of an action does not depend on interest, but interest follows from rectitude.

So thought

1664 J. Locke

Bibliography

Works of Locke

The Correspondence of John Locke. Edited by E. S. de Beer. 8 vols. Oxford: Clarendon Press, 1976–.

John Locke: An Essay concerning Human Understanding. Edited by Peter H. Nidditch. Oxford: Clarendon Press, 1975.

John Locke: Epistola de Tolerantia. A Letter on Toleration. Edited by Raymond Klibansky, translated by J. W. Gough. Oxford: Clarendon Press, 1968.

John Locke: Essays on the Law of Nature. The Latin Text with a Translation and Notes, together with Transcripts of Locke's Shorthand Journal for 1676. Edited by W. von Leyden. Oxford: Clarendon Press, 1954.

John Locke: Two Tracts on Government. Edited by Philip Abrams. Cambridge: Cambridge University Press, 1967.

John Locke: Two Treatises of Government. Edited by Peter Laslett. Cambridge: Cambridge University Press, 1960.

Some Thoughts concerning Education, in *The Educational Writings of John Locke*. Edited by James L. Axtell. Cambridge: Cambridge University Press, 1968.

The Works of John Locke in ten volumes. 10th ed. London, 1801.

The Works of John Locke. 10 vols. London, 1823. Reprint. Aalen, Darmstadt: Scientia Verlag, 1963.

Works of Others

Allen, J. W. *A History of Political Thought in the Sixteenth Century*. London: Methuen, 1928.

Aquinas, Saint Thomas. *St. Thomae Aquinatis D. A. in X libros Ethicorum*

Aristotelis ad Nicomachum Expositio. Edited by P. Fr. Raymundi and M. Spiazzi, O.P. Turin, 1964.

————. *Summa Theologiae.* Volume 28, *Law and Political Theory.* Edited and translated by Thomas Gilby, O.P. Cambridge: Blackfriars, 1966.

Averroes. *Aristotelis Stagiritae libri Moralem totam Philosophiam complectentes, cum Averrois Cordubensis in Moralia Nicomachia Expositione.* Venice, 1574.

Bold, Samuel. *Some Considerations on the Principal Objections and Arguments . . . against Mr. Locke's Essay of Humane Understanding.* London: A. and J. Churchill, 1699.

Bramhall, John. *A Defence of True Liberty.* London, 1655.

Browne, Sir Thomas. *Pseudodoxia Epidemica.* Edited by Robin Robbins. Oxford: Clarendon Press, 1981.

Cicero. *On the Commonwealth.* Translated by George Holland Sabine and Stanley Barney Smith. Columbus, Ohio: The State University Press, 1929.

Clarendon, Edward Hyde. *A Brief View and Survey of the dangerous and pernicious Errors to Church and State in Mr. Hobbes' Book, entitled Leviathan.* London, 1676.

Cranston, Maurice. *John Locke: A Biography.* London: Longmans, Green, 1957.

Culverwell [Culverwel], Nathanael. *An Elegant and Learned Discourse of the Light of Nature.* London, 1652; edited by Robert A. Greene and Hugh MacCallum: Toronto: University of Toronto Press, 1971.

Cumberland, Richard. *De Legibus Naturae Disquisitio Philosophica.* London, 1672.

Descartes, René. *Discourse on Method, and Meditations.* Translated by Laurence J. Lafleur. New York: Library of the Liberal Arts, 1960.

————. *Oeuvres de Descartes.* Edited by Charles Adam and Paul Tannery. 13 vols. Paris, 1891–1912; new ed.: Paris, 1971.

Edwards, John. *A Breif Vindication of the Fundamental Articles of the Christian Faith.* London, 1697.

Grotius, Hugo. *De Jure Belli ac Pacis.* Paris, 1625.

Harrison, John, and Laslett, Peter. *The Library of John Locke.* 2nd ed. Oxford: Clarendon Press, 1971.

Hobbes, Thomas. *Leviathan.* London, 1651.

————. *Thomae Hobbes Malmesburiensis Opera Philosophica quae latine scripsit.* Edited by William Molesworth. London, 1839–1845. Reprint. Aalen, Darmstadt: Verlag Scientia, 1961.

Hooker, Richard. *Of the Laws of Ecclesiastical Polity.* London, 1593. Included as vol. 1 of his *Works.* Edited by John Keble and revised by R. W. Church and F. Paget. 3 vols. Oxford: Clarendon Press, 1888.

King, Lord Peter. *The Life and Letters of John Locke, With Extracts from his Correspondence, Journals, and Common-place Books.* London, 1884. Reprint. New York: Garland, 1984.

Léry, Jean de. *Histoire d'un voyage fait en Bresil.* La Rochelle, 1578; edited by Jean-Claude Morisot: Geneva: Librarie Droz, 1975.

Macaulay, Thomas. *History of England.* 5 vols. New York: Harper and Brothers, 1856.

Mallet, Charles Edward. *A History of the University of Oxford.* 2 vols. New York: Longmans, Green, 1924.

Mintz, Samuel I. *The Hunting of Leviathan.* Cambridge: Cambridge University Press, 1962.

More, Henry. *Opera Omnia.* Edited by Serge Hutin. Hildesheim: Georg Olms, 1966.

Nidditch, P. H. "The Forthcoming Critical Edition of Locke's Works: A Report by the General Editor." *Locke Newsletter* 5 (1974): 9–17.

Olearius, Adam. *The Voyages and Travels of the Ambassadors from the Duke of Holstein, to the Great Duke of Muscovy, and the King of Persia, Begun in the year MDCXXXIII and finished in MDCXXXIX . . . whereto are added the Travels of John Albert Mandelslo from Persia, into the East Indies . . . Faithfully rendered into English by John Davies, of Kidwelly.* London, 1662.

Parker, Samuel. *A Demonstration of the Divine Authority of the Law of Nature and of the Christian Religion.* London, 1681.

Pieper, Josef. *Guide to Thomas Aquinas.* New York: New American Library, 1964.

Pufendorf, Samuel. *Elementa Jurisprudentiae.* The Hague, 1660.

———. *Elementorum Jurisprudentiae Universalis Libri II.* Cambridge, 1672. Reprinted in *The Classics of International Law*, no. 15. Edited by James Brown Scott. Oxford: Clarendon Press, 1931.

Sanderson, Robert. *De juramenti promissorii obligatione praelectiones septem.* London, 1647.

———. *De obligatione Conscientiae.* London, 1661.

———. *Several Cases of Conscience Discussed. . . .* London: Tho. Leach, 1660.

Spinoza, Benedict de. *Opera.* Edited by Carl Gebhardt. 4 vols. Heidelberg: Carl Winter, 1972.

Suarez, Francisco. *Tractatus de Legibus ac Deo Legislatore.* Antwerp, 1613.

Terry, Edward. *A Voyage to East India.* London, 1655.

Thevenot, Melchisédec. *Relations de Divers Voiages curieux.* Paris, 1663.

Tyrrell, James. *A Breif Disquisition of the Law of Nature. According to the principles and Method laid down in the Reverend Dr. Cumberland's (now Bishop of Petersboroughs) Latin Treatise on that subject, as also His confutations of Mr.*

Hobb's Principles put into another Method. With the Right Reverend Author's Approbation. London, 1692.

Wood, Anthony. *The Life and Times of Anthony Wood.* Edited by Andrew Clark. 5 vols. Oxford: Oxford Historical Society, 1891–1892.

Yolton, John W. *John Locke: Problems and Perspectives.* Cambridge: Cambridge University Press, 1969.

Index

257

Library of Congress Cataloging-in-Publication Data

Locke, John, 1632–1704.
  [Selections. English. 1990]
  Questions concerning the law of nature / John Locke ; with an introduction, text, and translation by Robert Horwitz, Jenny Strauss Clay, and Diskin Clay.
      p.   cm.
  English and Latin.
  "A total of three manuscripts of Locke's reflections concerning the law of nature were penned over a period of some sixteen or more years between 1664 (or earlier) and 1681–1682"—P.
  Includes bibliographical references.
  ISBN 0-8014-2348-1 (alk. paper)
  1. Locke, John, 1632–1704—Contributions in natural law. 2. Natural law.
I. Horwitz, Robert H. II. Clay, Jenny Strauss. III. Clay, Diskin. IV. Title.
K457.L6A2   1990
340'.112—dc20   89-46178

CPSIA information can be obtained at www.ICGtesting.com
Printed in the USA
BVOW04s1230200114

342326BV00003B/9/P